The School Promoters

Education and Social Class in Mid-Nineteenth Century Upper Canada

Alison Prentice

M&S

Canadian Cataloguing in Publication Data

Prentice, Alison, 1934 –
   The school promoters

(The Canadian social history series)
Includes bibliographical references and index.
ISBN 0-7710-7181-7

1. Education – Ontario – History.   2. Educational sociology – Ontario – History.   I. Title.   II. Series.

IA418.06P74 1977   370′.9713   C77-008261-0

Front cover photo: Public Archives, Ontario

Printed and bound in Canada
by Webcom Limited

McClelland & Stewart Inc.
The Canadian Publishers
481 University Avenue
Toronto, Ontario   M5G 2E9

Contents

The Canadian Social History Series/5

Acknowledgements/7

Notes on Sources/9

Abbreviations/12

Introduction: The Public School Movement
in Upper Canada and Ontario/13

1 Human and Child Nature:
  The Search for Perfection/25

2 Upper Canada at Mid-Century:
  The Necessity of Progress/45

3 Education and the Creation of
  a Respectable Class/66

4 Occupations in Transition:
  The Danger of Downward Mobility/88

5 The Integration and Invigoration of
  the Labouring Classes and the Poor/119

6 Class and the Schools/138

7 Nature, Order and National Education:
  The Government as Parent/170

Index/187

The Canadian Social History Series

Social history is about people. This series is concerned with broadening the understanding of Canadian history, widening it from a story of past politics to a portrayal of the context in which Canadians have lived and interreacted with one another.

The series takes the broadest possible view of the subject matter of social history. It is concerned not only to encompass as much of the sweep of Canadian history as possible, but also to exploit the whole range of scholarship in this country. That means that it is interested in the social history of our native peoples, in immigration and acculturation, in the development of social institutions such as the family, classes, and voluntary organizations, in ideas and attitudes in their social context, in the social dimension of occupations and industries, in community formation and urban growth, in social movements such as the temperance crusade, the movement for prison reform, and that for the liberation of women, in sports and leisure activities. Social history is the history of the full range of human life, and this series will attempt to represent that range.

Canadian social history is still in its infancy. In few of the areas mentioned above has scholarship developed to the point at which a monograph covering any one of them for the whole time-span could be written. This series, therefore, proposes to take advantage of the work being done on specialized areas and fairly brief chronological periods. Without being narrow, the volumes will present in-depth studies of major themes, rather than sweeping generalities over the whole of Canadian history. Obviously it is hoped that, eventually, the series will build to a comprehensive social history of Canada; in the meantime, the individual volumes will be exemplary of both the subject matter and the approaches of that social history.

Our aim is a series which will be of use both to general readers and to students of history. All of those interested in the development of this country will find excitement in these studies of the major themes of social history. At the same time, these are works of original scholarship, opening up new areas of Canadian history for students and academics. So, the books contain the documentation necessary to guide students to the key sources, but are not so weighed down with scholarly paraphernalia as to lose their clarity and readability. Canadians, whether or not they are scholars, are growing ever more concerned to discover their real history. We hope this series will contribute to that discovery.

S. F. Wise
Michael S. Cross

Acknowledgements

As with all histories, the sources of this book are in part personal. For much of my life I have been a student and for a good part of it I have also been both a parent and a teacher. As a teacher, I was most clearly confronted with the question of class and education by a plain speaking principal, who stated that discipline was no problem in his school because the teachers there made more money than the parents of the pupils. As a parent I have been involved with schools from the outside. Periodic frustration with schools or school systems that seemed insensitive to individual or family concerns taught me much about the potential for conflict in the politics of education. Finally, like all students no doubt from the beginning of time, I have been amazed at the contradictory and perverse things that are occasionally said and done in the name of education. Yet it has to be said that in all three roles – as parent, student and teacher – I have also encountered at various times and in many different places, sympathetic educational environments and great teachers. Among those teachers whose guidance has made an enormous difference to me, I would particularly like to thank Katharine Lamont, Michael Katz and Maurice Careless, whose kindness and interest in my work over the years has been vital to whatever success it has had. To my fellow students and other historians who have encouraged my work, my thanks also, especially to Natalie Davis and Susan Houston, and to Harvey Graff, Ned Hagerman and Keith McLeod, whose good cheer and unflagging enthusiasm for my efforts have helped to kindle my own. In addition, I wish to express my appreciation to Atkinson College, York University for a timely research grant and to colleagues at both York and the Ontario Institute for Studies in Education who, in ways too numerous to mention, have encouraged research in the history of education. They have done so in the belief that to understand our educational past is at least to hope to act more intelligently and

7

humanely in the present, a belief which I share and which was the basic reason for writing this book. Thanks also to Syd Wise, Michael Cross and John Roberts, whose interest in Canadian social history made its publication possible and whose editorial skills contributed in large measure to whatever merit the book may have. Lastly, special thanks to the secretaries, students and colleagues, to the members of my family and friends who have tolerated an absent-minded historian in their midst and, fortunately for me, continue to do so.

Alison Prentice

Note on Sources

The Education Papers, or Record Group 2, of the Ontario Archives were the basic manuscript source for this study. Consisting of the official records of those provincial agencies that were made responsible for schools from the founding of the first Upper Canadian Board of Education in 1824, the papers are a goldmine of information and official opinion on schools, their promoters, teachers and clients in the mid-nineteenth century. One of the most valuable parts of the collection is the correspondence of the provincial Department of Public Instruction. The incoming correspondence, preserved in Series C-6-C and consisting of over three hundred boxes of letters dating from 1841 to 1876, necessarily contains much that is routine. But it also includes hundreds of fascinating letters of inquiry, complaint or comment on an immense variety of topics related to education, from correspondents in all corners of the province. Copies of outgoing letters up to 1860 and drafts of outgoing correspondence for the period after 1860 are held in Series C 1 and C 2. These contain the Department's answers to questions and complaints, as well as the official letters from Ryerson and his deputies to officers of the government, local officials, newspaper editors and the like, on local and provincial school matters. Series B of the Education Papers, which includes the minutes of the second Board of Education, of the Council of Public Instruction which replaced it in 1850, and a letterbook of related correspondence, is also valuable, chiefly for the light these papers shed on the growth and inner management of the provincial Education Department and Normal School. In addition, the minutes record the school regulations, curricula and textbooks approved or authorized by the central administration. Although each of the other series contain items of interest, they cannot be listed here. For a useful guide, the reader is referred to Roy Reynold's survey of the incoming departmental correspondence for the year 1865, *Analysis of Record Group 2, Ontario Archives Series C-6-C 1865* (Ontario Institute for Studies in Education, Department of History and Philosophy, Education Records Series No. 4). The introduction, pp. 1-9, consists of a brief survey of the whole record group.

Of the printed sources available to the student of mid-nineteenth century Ontario education, the best known perhaps is the twenty-eight volume *Documentary History of Education in Upper Canada,* edited by J. George Hodgins. After a long career in the Education Department as Deputy Superintendent, then Deputy Minister, Hodgins took on the job of Department "historiographer" and it was in this capacity that he devoted his remaining years to recording the development of Ontario's educational institutions. The resulting *Documentary History,* which was only the largest of several series published by Hodgins, reproduces all of the major laws affecting schools, colleges and universities in Ontario, as well as a huge selection of relevant petitions, speeches, recorded debates, letters, reports and reminiscences for the period from 1791 to 1876. Because the editor found relatively few documents for the years prior to 1844, the collection focuses almost exclusively on the Ryerson period. It is also, as might be expected, heavily biased in favour of Ryerson and the general course that educational reform took during his superintendency. Criticism and controversy are not altogether excluded, but with the exception of some well documented debates on higher education, the opposition to the Chief Superintendent of Schools and to the political stance and social attitudes that he represented finds little space in Hodgins' work.

Other major sources for the study of mid-nineteenth century educational history are the *Annual Reports of the Chief Superintendent of Schools* (variously titled), the superintendent's special reports, and the *Journal of Education for Upper Canada.* The reports as well as the *Journal* were mid-century innovations and, as government critics loudly complained, both were also major vehicles of Education Department propaganda. The *Annual Reports* consist of an introductory summary of the state of the schools by Ryerson, followed by the statistical tables compiled by the Department and a long appendix containing excerpts from the reports of local school authorities to the Chief Superintendent. Many of the *Annual Reports* also include additional appendices reproducing circulars, school regulations, examinations and other items that the Department wished to publicize. The special reports focus on institutions and ideas that Ryerson was promoting, like the normal school or special training for the deaf, or on issues like the separate school question. It is true that quite a lot of the material from the annual and special reports found its way into the *Journal of Education* and that, in addition, a great many journal articles were reprinted from American, European or other Canadian sources. Yet important Ryerson speeches and editorials not reproduced elsewhere may also be found in it, as well as original pieces by other British North Americans on education and related subjects. While no material of "a controversial nature" was accepted by the editors (who were Hodgins and Ryerson) many of the social and educational issues of the day are reflected in the pages of the *Journal* in spite of this apparent restriction.

A more revealing vehicle of educational debate in the period, however, was the public letter. The numerous collections of official and unofficial correspondence which were published in pamphlet form, as participants in various public debates sought wider support for their views, are therefore essential sources for mid-nineteenth century educational history. Equally valuable are the numerous pamphlets reproducing speeches, public lectures and sermons on topics related to education and the schools. Finally, there are the textbooks which were published during the period, slim but important documents that sometimes reveal as much about the values and concerns of their authors as about curricula and teaching methods in the schools. It is textbooks such as *The Youth's Guard Against Crime* by Israel Lewis (Kingston, 1844), or pamphlets like Adam Townley's *Seven Letters on the Non-Religious Common School System of Canada and the United States* (Toronto, 1853) or Walter Eales' *Lectures on the Benefits to be Derived from Mechanics' Institutes* (Toronto, 1851) that reveal how far formal education in the mid-nineteenth century continued to extend beyond the immediate orbit of the nascent public school system or of Egerton Ryerson and his deputies in the provincial Department of Public Instruction.

In this vein, it is perhaps not unreasonable to mention here some sources for nineteenth century educational history that were not consulted in depth for this study, but which clearly have much to offer student of the period. These fall into five major categories: diaries and family papers; newspapers; school, academy, college and university records, including attendance registers and trustee board minutes; the records of other educational institutions, such as reformatories and orphanages; and quantitative sources like the manuscript census.* It is through the imaginative use of such local literary and quantitative records, in combination with the official and provincial educational literature, that future students will be able to deepen our understanding of the complex changes in child rearing and schooling that took place in the mid-nineteenth century.

* For examples of the use of such sources, consult the works of Ian Davey, Harvey Graff, Susan Houston and Michael Katz, cited in the footnotes. Useful guides to some of the basic literature may be found in the Educational Records Series published by the Department of History and Philosophy of the Ontario Institute for Studies in Education. This series includes, in addition to the analysis of Record Group 2, C-6-C 1865 cited above, guides to relevant pamphlets, printed government documents and references to education in private papers in the Ontario Archives, as well as to a variety of other local and provincial records of interest to students of educational history.

Abbreviations

Annual Report	*Annual Report of the Normal, Model, Grammar and Common Schools in Upper Canada, by the Chief Superintendent of Schools.* (Titles vary, depending on the year.)
DHE	*Documentary History of Education in Upper Canada.*
JEUC	*Journal of Education for Upper Canada.*
RG 2, PAO	**Record Group 2 (Education Records), Provincial Archives of Ontario.**

The Public School Movement in Upper Canada and Ontario

I heard one of the most able men say he had managed to get along and he did not know, but his children could do so too. However, since some of his poorer neighbours' children have the blessing of Free Schools, they have been able to show him that learning qualifies even children to fill a useful position in society, so that now he is anxious to have his children educated.

The School Superintendent,
Kernebee, Frontenac County, 1866[1]

The history of education, like all history, is full of myths. In Canada, as elsewhere, it has had its share of heroes and villains, of triumphs and tragedies. And no subject in this history has been more distorted by myth – or neglect – than the emergence, during the middle of the nineteenth century in Upper Canada and Ontario, of the public school system.

A reason for this, perhaps, is that the nineteenth century school movement has tended to interest professional educators more than it has interested professional historians.[2] More important, however, is the fact that few historians, professional or otherwise, have questioned the basic premises which appeared to motivate the expansion of schooling. Schools and school systems were generally taken for granted, as requiring little or no explanation of their origin, or justification for their continuing existence. A final reason for the relative obscurity of the nineteenth century school movement has been the tendency of historians to focus on its chief heroes – or villains. In the case of Upper Canada and Ontario, this led researchers to concentrate on the personality and achievements of the Reverend Egerton Ryerson, who as superintendent of the province's schools from 1844 to 1876, was one of the most vocal and effective of Canada's educational missionaries. Certainly it has been difficult to detach the creation of the Ontario school system, one which was as seminal for Canada as certain eastern state systems were for the American republic, from this one man, who thought of himself as its founder and regarded it as his great life's work. But the tendency to focus on Ryerson, and on some of the more notorious religious and political controversies in which he was involved, has until recently led to the relative neglect both of other debates arising out of the public school movement and of other Upper Canadian educators whose role in this history is less well known.[3]

Even when dealing with the history of public schools directly, the tendency has been to take what might be called an "evolutionary" approach to the subject, to emphasize the creation of educational institutions where before there were few or none, the development of new educational methods and of free schooling, or the elevation of teaching to the status of a profession.[4] While perfectly legitimate within the limitations of these purposes, such an approach to nineteenth century educational history in Ontario has nevertheless left many gaps in our knowledge. In addition, it has sometimes obscured our understanding of the events in question. This is because it was based on the assumption that the creations of Ryerson and his contemporaries, if not the inevitable outcome of divine necessity, at least supplied a notable and obvious lack in Upper Canadian social policy. The role of educational innovators therefore emerged in typical accounts of the period as generally progressive, even democratic in tendency, and as reflecting broad popular need, if not demand, while the opponents of educational reform were typed as necessarily men of a narrow or reactionary cast of mind.

As a result, although many of the forces brought to bear on the educational developments of the period from the 1840s to the 1870s have been examined, especially in their religious or political context, few historians have gone very deeply into the question of causes. When they have discussed causes the tendency to view mid-century school reform rather vaguely as a necessary response to the evils of illiteracy and mass ignorance has, until very recently, prevailed. As a result, the myth of a school movement largely motivated by democratic and humanitarian impulses has been allowed to persist almost unquestioned.[5]

Almost equally obscured by myth-making or neglect has been the even more basic question of what mid-nineteenth century school reformers really wanted or achieved. What was the real substance of the profound changes in education which Ryerson, many of his contemporaries and most subsequent historians have regarded as so self-evidently necessary or desirable? Certainly an enormous amount of school legislation was passed just before and during the Ryerson era. There were the landmark laws of 1841, 1846, 1850 and 1871, which provided for a provincial school system and for free and ultimately compulsory elementary schooling, as well as a host of lesser laws and regulations affecting Upper Canadian education. The question that is central to this book is a very general one: what did the educational innovations embodied in these laws and regulations really mean to the men who promoted them, and to their clients, adversaries and heirs? More specifically, what were the economic and social implications of educational reform in mid-nineteenth century Ontario?

To answer these questions, one must go back, first of all, to what existed before the 1840s, to ask, however briefly, how Ontario children were educated in the early nineteenth century. Here too, mythology has until recently prevailed and the historian would like to have a great deal more information than is currently available.[6] Nevertheless, certain general observations can be made.

Prior to the Ryerson era in Upper Canada and, indeed, nearly everywhere else in the western world in the early nineteenth century, education was characteristically "voluntary" and informal. The usual and perhaps the fundamental educational institutions were the household, workshop and field, since the vast majority of children learned most of what they needed to know from their parents, or from adults in other families to whom they were bound as servants or apprentices. Where churches and commercial activity existed or penetrated in Upper Canada, important supplements to this informal education were sermons, Sunday schools and camp meetings, as well as the gatherings that inevitably took place in houses and shops, villages and towns. Quite a few Upper Canadian children were educated more formally, some by family tutors, others in small schools which men and women ran as private ventures, most often in their own rooms or houses. There also existed, in the larger towns, a few relatively large monitorial schools, run by religious societies for the instruction of the children of the poor. Finally, in 1807, the Upper Canadian legislature had voted funds for district grammar schools, and legislation in 1816 had provided for government-aided local common schools as well, although these were much less generously supported.

Variety in the settings of formal education was matched by an entirely voluntarist approach to its existence. In most schools, children of all ages gathered in small groups under one teacher for a few months or years, to learn the three R's and a little religion and morals, at a season when they were able to walk to school and their labour was not required at home. The schools, teachers and times of attendance were generally of their parents' or guardians' own choosing. Some of the more ambitious boys stayed in school long enough to study geography, surveying or the classics; a few even went off to college or university in the United States, Great Britain, or, perhaps, continental Europe. But these were few in number. The vast majority of Upper Canadians seem to have been satisfied with a minimal schooling for their children — at home, at a neighbour's, or at the local common school where these existed. Uniformity, if there was any, consisted in the typical brevity of the formal educational experience and in the unchanging nature of the traditional curriculum. Since fees had to be paid regardless of whether the school was partially government supported or entirely a private venture, there was really no clear distinction in the early nineteenth century between private and public education, or if there was one, it was very different from the distinction that later emerged.[7] Most of the families that sent children to school, therefore, expected to pay something for this schooling. It is of singular interest that this mixture of the public and the private, and of the casual and the formal in the education of Upper Canadian children, seems to have produced a basic literacy for the majority of people in the province.[8]

Clearly not all were satisfied with this state of affairs, however. The mid-nineteenth century saw immense change. In the political sphere, Upper Canada united with Lower Canada to form the Province of Canada in 1841 and, then, with Confederation in 1867, became the Province of Ontario. And as if to accompany these fundamental political transformations, educational practices and institutions within its boundaries had also begun to be profoundly altered.

To begin with, much of the voluntarism that had been characteristic of early nineteenth century schooling gradually disappeared. Enabling legislation dating from 1847 and 1850 at first encouraged municipalities to supplement provincial grants by property taxes, in order to make the common schools free; by the School Act of 1871, the provision of free common schools by each municipality became mandatory. By the same law, all Ontario children between the ages of seven and twelve were for the first time compelled to attend some school for at least four months of any given school year. These developments not only made compulsory in principle what had formerly been seen as entirely voluntary, but also signalled a changing relationship between the school and the state. By 1871, the common school had become a public institution in the modern sense of the term, an institution not only paid for out of public funds, but with publicly defined goals. Indeed, its new role was reflected in the fact that henceforth it was to be officially known as the public rather than the common school.

Secondly, the common or elementary public school had become part of what was increasingly seen as a highly articulated *system* of schools. A growing demand for something "higher" than the common school as well as the expansion of the grammar schools gradually led to the perception of a need for a secondary school that would build on an edifice of consecutively organized, graded elementary instruction completed in the common school. Here too, changing concepts were reflected in changed names. By the 1871 School Act, the new secondary institutions that had evolved from central common schools and grammar schools were to be known as high schools and collegiate institutes. Local responsibility for these schools amounted to the requirement that a sum, equal to at least one-half of the provincial grant for any given school, be raised from local taxes and contributed to its support.

Perhaps even more pervasive in their immediate impact than either the decline of voluntarism or the development of graded public and secondary schools, were the accumulated results of a quarter of a century of centralization in Ontario education. This trend began with the School Act of 1841, which created the office of Superintendent of Common Schools for the united Province of Canada. The powers of the office were exercised by an assistant superintendent for each province, who in turn was aided in Upper Canada, after 1843, by locally appointed school superintendents who managed the provincial grant on the local level, certified the teachers and inspected the schools of their respective regions or communities. At the same time, the School Law of 1843 re-established the traditional elected trustees for the management of the internal affairs of each school section, which the 1841 act had temporarily eliminated. The trustees hired the teacher, managed whatever property the school might have or acquire and exercised control for the time being over what might properly be called the content of the educational experience.

From these beginnings, further legislation and regulation gradually wove a pattern of tightening controls, so that by the 1870s a great deal had been taken out of the hands of parents, lay super-intendents and even of purely local authorities when it came to the schooling of their children. Thus the School Act of 1846, by which the Upper Canadian assistant superintendent became known as the Chief Superintendent of Common Schools for the province, also created a provincial normal school, which would train teachers and gradually set uniform standards for certifying teachers throughout the province. The act also provided for a provincial Board of Education (after 1850 known as the Council of Public Instruction) with regulatory powers over the normal, common and separate schools* of Upper Canada. Both the council and the normal school were in fact very much under the thumb of the chief superintendent, who in the 1850s also extended his authority to include the regulation of the grammar schools of the province, through the Council of Public Instruction and two provincially-appointed grammar school inspectors. Finally, in 1871, a professional and provincially controlled inspectorate for public and separate schools took over many of the responsibilities of the more locally controlled lay superintendency which had existed since 1843.

What were the effects of these developments? It would be wrong to exaggerate the immediate impact of centralization, but Ontario schooling in the 1870s had taken on a new character in many ways. The choice of courses of study, school books, school rules and prayers, which prior to the Ryerson era had been left to the discretion of parents and local school section authorities, was by 1871 clearly in the hands of central bodies – either provincial or municipal – as were the complex rules and regulations which increasingly governed the qualifications, hiring and behaviour of teachers and other previously unheard of functionaries within the growing public school systems. Equally lost to parental or purely local control in many cases were the regulation of school attendance, school financing and a host of other items related to the founding and organization of schools. On the provincial level, a chief superintendent of education, soon to be translated into a minister of education, presided over all publicly financed elementary and secondary schooling as well as the training of

---

* Separate schools began with the School Law of 1841, which provided that they were to be permitted whenever a number of the inhabitants of any township or parish differed in religious adherence from the majority and wished to have them, thereby becoming eligible for a share of the provincial grant provided to common schools. Their development parallelled that of the common schools during the Ryerson period, and was the subject of much controversy.

teachers in Ontario. On the local level, central boards of education were in the process of creating systems of their own in the province's counties and cities. In the face of competition from these growing public systems, the small household and private venture schools of the early nineteenth century virtually disappeared.

But the most spectacular change of all, perhaps, was the jump in sheer numbers, as great increases occurred not only in the proportion of Upper Canadian children enrolled in schools, but also in the average length of time that their schools were kept open and in the number of pupils in single schools or classrooms. From Table 1 it can be seen that, in 1876, there were two-and-a-half times as many school-age children as there had been in 1846, but the number of pupils registered as attending the common schools had more than quadrupled. There had apparently been one teacher for every thirty-five pupils in 1846; thirty years later the ratio of registered pupils to teachers was seventy-five to one. Schools, which had doubled in number during the three decades in question, stayed open in 1876 for 11½ months compared to 8½ in 1846. They had almost tripled, moreover, the number of students they individually accommodated.[9]

TABLE 1
Changes in Upper Canadian Schooling Patterns 1846 - 1876

	1846	1876
School Age Children (5-16 years of age)	204,580	502,250
Children registered in the common schools	101,912	465,243
	or 49.8%	or 92.6%
Common School Teachers	2,925	6,185
Common Schools in Operation	2,589	4,875
Pupil-Teacher Ratio	34.8	75.2
Pupil-School Ratio	39.4	95.4
Average number of months schools open	8½	11½

From the *Annual Report of the Normal, Model, High and Public Schools of Ontario* (1876) Table Q, pp. 78-80. The percentages are approximate, and overstate the case slightly, since some pupils were under 5 or over 16 years of age. The figures for 1876 refer to what by then were known as the "public" or elementary schools.

One could argue that many of the qualitative changes in education during this mid-century period – the transition from the informal and largely voluntary, to formal, institutional and compulsory education under the aegis of the state – occurred largely as a result of numbers. It would certainly appear that, as more and more children attended common schools, whole new methods and organizational concepts seemed essential, at least to those who were most closely involved in educational reform. But the basic question remains: why were more and more children encouraged, and finally compelled, to go to school?

The answer to this question is, as might be expected, an extremely complex one, and perhaps can never be more than approximate. One must rely on literary evidence that is often contradictory – the ever-changing opinions of the most articulate among the school promoters, and, as in the case of the father whose opinion is cited at the beginning of this chapter, the very occasional parent. If the written records accurately reveal the true state of educators' intentions, the general answer is that increasing numbers of children were sent to school for longer and longer periods of time because of perceived or anticipated changes both in the nature of the environment, and in the nature and needs of children. Which is more important is hard to say. Increasingly, many school promoters saw the community as a dangerous or unsuitable environment for the child. At the same time, the child was viewed as especially susceptible to dangerous influences, and therefore in need of the school, conceived of as a protective environment. In addition, the schools and the increasing numbers of children who went to them clearly became causal factors in themselves. One gains the impression that because there were schools and more and more children went to them, on a regular basis, people gradually became convinced that all children ought to go regularly to school.

Of course, there was never a perfect consensus on the subject. A few articulate Upper Canadians were outspokenly opposed to mass education; these people, however, tended to be dismissed by school promoters as blatant reactionaries. Then there were others who agreed with the general need for more widespread formal education, but went around, like the advocates of separate schools, promoting fervent debates about what kind of children ought to go to which kind of school, to the great distress of those who claimed that they favoured unitary school systems for all children.

In these debates and discussions, the views of Egerton Ryerson and his chief supporters tended to dominate. For one thing they had at their disposal the growing resources of the Education Department, resources which they used to great effect. Ryerson himself was especially visible. His public career spanned this crucial period of Ontario development, beginning in 1826 when he first crossed swords with the earlier Upper Canadian proponent of formal schooling, but under established church auspices, the

Reverend Dr. John Strachan, and ending only when he retired from the chief superintendency in 1876. He was involved in public debate throughout the period, first as a preacher and then as editor of the Methodist *Christian Guardian,* as chief promoter and then first principal of Victoria College, and finally, from 1844, as Assistant and then Chief Superintendent of Schools for Upper Canada. As superintendent, he published voluminously not only through the official organ that he created for the purpose, the ubiquitous *Journal of Education for Upper Canada,* but in a variety of papers and formats. In addition, during the years of his superintendency, Ryerson maintained his connection with higher education by serving on the governing boards of and joining in public debate about Victoria College and the University of Toronto. Finally, even at the end of his career, Ryerson continued to write. Along with several histories and an autobiography based on journals kept from his youth, he produced between 1871 and his death in 1882 three small but revealing textbooks, outlining for school children and their families what he thought they ought to believe about man and his obligations in society, and about education. His output was enormous, his opinions were strongly held and pungently expressed. It is thus inevitable that much of the material for this book should be drawn from Ryerson's extensive published works.

But Ryerson cannot engage us exclusively. His plans for Canadian education were supported or opposed, elaborated upon or altered, by countless others – teachers, parents, trustees, local superintendents, interested gentlemen, preachers, priests and politicians – many of whom took the trouble to express in a few words, or analyse and examine in great depth, their feelings and opinions about the educational needs of Upper Canada and Canadians.

The study that follows, therefore, is an attempt to go beyond the ideas of one man to the prevailing ideology of the times, to understand the hopes and fears of the educational reformers of Upper Canada and of some of their opponents during the Ryerson era. It is, secondly, an attempt to understand what actually happened to school children and their teachers during the period. In order to uncover contemporary perceptions of the need for mass schooling, the study first examines the ideas entertained by Upper Canadian school promoters on such fundamentals as human and child nature and the nature of their own society. Secondly, an attempt is made to assess educators' attitudes to the complex question of class. How did the school promoters perceive the social structure of their times, and how did this affect their views on education? Finally the last two chapters examine the organization of schools and the place of teachers within school systems, and try to reach some conclusions about the period as a whole. What was the reality as opposed to the ideology of educational reform, as it actually affected school children and their instructors during the Ryerson era? The last chapter in this section seeks to understand the answers to this question in terms of the role on the one hand of nature, and on the other of the state, in education. It is to be hoped that an understanding of the ideas of Upper Canadian educators about nature and the state, about class, society and human nature, will deepen our knowledge not only of nineteenth century Ontario, but also of the purposes and structure of the school systems which were one of the major legacies of their times to ours.

Two problems of definition or identification emerge in this study. The first is to identify the people whose ideas are being dicussed. Here I have chosen to be as broad as possible. While the focus remains of necessity on key educational innovators like Egerton Ryerson or the well known grammar school inspector of the 1860's, George Paxton Young, the real subjects of this book are all those who promoted the expansion or the improvement of schooling in mid-nineteenth century Upper Canada. Expansion and improvement, while not always compatible with each other, were nevertheless goals shared by the majority of those who took an interest in education. From college principals like the Reverend Samuel Nelles of Victoria or Daniel Wilson of University College, to the most obscure of the local school superintendents, what they had in common was that they were promoters of schools.

Secondly, the question of class emerges. How is the word defined in the context of this book? The answer is, I hope, historically. In searching for attitudes to class, I have attempted to let the school promoters speak for themselves. It is their gradual formulation of a definition of class that this study seeks to explain.

NOTES

[1]*Annual Report by the Chief Superintendent of Schools for Upper Canada for the Year 1866,* Appendix A, pp. 18-19. (Hereafter cited as *Annual Report* for the given year. For other abbreviations, see abbreviations section at beginning of book.)

[2]The Ontario schoolmen most responsible for the writing of much of the province's educational history were J. George Hodgins, J. Harold Putman, J. G. Althouse and Charles E. Phillips, whose works are

described in footnotes 3 and 4 below. In the United States, the congratulatory approach to educational history of school promoter Ellwood Patterson Cubberley set the pattern until Bernard Bailyn and Lawrence A. Cremin called for a more critical reworking of it in the wider context of American social and intellectual history. See Bailyn, *Education in the Forming of American Society* (New York, 1960) and Cremin, *The Wonderful World of Ellwood Patterson Cubberley; an Essay on the Historiography of American Education* (New York, 1965).

³The tendency to dwell on Ryerson started with John George Hodgins, who followed a long career as Ryerson's chief protegé in the Education Office with a second career as official historiographer of the Ontario Department of Education. Ryerson's writings and acts predominate in Hodgins' *Documentary History of Education in Upper Canada, from the Passing of the Constitutional Act of 1791 to the Close of Dr. Ryerson's Administration of the Education Department in 1876* (Toronto, 1894-1910) 28 vols. (Hereafter cited as DHE.) Hodgins was also responsible for the editing and posthumous publication of Ryerson's autobiography, *The Story of My Life, by Egerton Ryerson* (Toronto, 1883) and edited *The Ryerson Memorial Volume; Prepared on the Occasion of the Unveiling of the Ryerson Statue in the Grounds of the Education Department on the Queen's Birthday, 1889* (Toronto, 1889). J. Harold Putman's study of nineteenth century education focuses on the Chief Superintendent of Schools, as is evident from his title, *Egerton Ryerson and Education in Upper Canada* (Toronto, 1912). These authors and Ryerson's several biographers, as one might expect, have tended to eulogize the man as well as to exaggerate his role in the development of educational institutions in Ontario. See Nathanael Burwash, *Egerton Ryerson,* in the Makers of Canada series, (Toronto, 1903); C. B. Sissons, *Egerton Ryerson: His Life and Letters* (Toronto, 1937-1947) 2 vols.; and Clara Thomas, *Ryerson of Upper Canada* (Toronto, 1969). The most scholarly of the biographies is Sissons' work, which places Ryerson the schoolman in the context of Upper Canadian religious and political history. See also Sissons, ed., *My Dearest Sophie: Letters from Egerton Ryerson to his Daughter* (Toronto, 1955). For scholarly studies dealing with some of the traditional themes of Upper Canadian educational history, see John S. Moir, *Church and State in Canada West: Three Studies in the Relation of Denominationalism and Nationalism, 1841-1867* (Toronto, 1959); Franklin A. Walker, *Catholic Education and Politics in Upper Canada, a Study of the Documentation relative to the Origins of Catholic Elementary Schools in the Ontario System* (Toronto, 1955).

⁴See, for example, J. G. Althouse, *The Ontario Teacher: a Historical Account of Progress, 1800-1910* (D. Paed. diss. University of Toronto, 1929; Ontario Teachers' Federation, 1967) and Charles E. Phillips, *The Development of Education in Canada* (Toronto, 1957). The same tendencies are to be found in the works of Hodgins and Putman cited above.

⁵J. D. Wilson, R. M. Stamp and L. P. Audet, eds., *Canadian Education: A History* (Scarborough, Ont., 1970) is a recent and very useful text on the history of Canadian education, but one which does not entirely avoid the traditional biases. Brief studies of a more radically revisionist nature may be found in Michael B. Katz and Paul H. Mattingly, eds.,

Education and Social Change: Themes from Ontario's Past (New York, 1975). Much current writing in Canadian educational history has been influenced by the work of Bernard Bailyn and Lawrence A. Cremin, cited above, and, more recently, by the work of Michael B. Katz, which focuses on nineteenth century educational change. See his *The Irony of Early School Reform: Educational Innovation in Mid-Nineteenth Century Massachusetts* (Cambridge, Mass., 1968), and other studies by Katz cited below.

[6]The brief survey of nineteenth century Upper Canadian education and school law which follows relies on the accounts of Putman, Althouse, Phillips and Wilson, in the works cited above, and on Hodgins' *Documentary History* which reproduces most of the important laws in full. For the early history of schooling in Upper Canada, see also George W. Spragge, "Elementary Education in Upper Canada, 1820-1840," *Ontario History*, XLIII, (July, 1951). More recent studies of the pre-Ryerson and early Ryerson periods which are especially useful are Susan E. Houston, "Politics, Schools and Social Change in Upper Canada," and R. D. Gidney, "Elementary Education in Upper Canada: A Reassessment," in *Education and Social Change*, pp. 3-56.

[7]For discussions of changing definitions of private and public education in this period, see *ibid.*, p. 21, and Carl F. Kaestle, *Evolution of an Urban School System: New York, 1750-1850* (Cambridge, Mass., 1973), pp. 16-18.

[8]Harvey J. Graff, "Literacy and Social Structure in the Nineteenth Century City" (Ph.D. diss., University of Toronto, 1975). Based on evidence from nineteenth century Ontario, this thesis is an important contribution to the history of literacy. See also Graff, "Towards a Meaning of Literacy; Literacy and Social Structure in Hamilton, Ontario, 1861," in *Education and Social Change*, pp. 246-70.

[9]Some of these figures may well be exaggerated. The numbers in the statistical tables of the chief superintendent's annual reports do not always perfectly agree with the numbers in local published accounts or in manuscript sources. Secondly, since provincial grants were tied to enrolment and average attendance figures, there was reason for local authorities to exaggerate them. Nevertheless, the published provincial tables are probably sufficiently accurate to give an idea of general trends. They also reveal what Education Department officials thought, or wished other Canadians to think, was going on. Detailed analysis of school enrolment and attendance patterns may be found in Michael B. Katz, "Who Went to School?" and Ian E. Davey, "School Reform and School Attendance: The Hamilton Central School, 1853-1861," in *Education and Social Change*, pp. 271-314, and Ian E. Davey, "Trends in Female School Attendance in Mid-Nineteenth Century Ontario," *Social History/histoire sociale*, VIII (November, 1975), 238-54. The latter reveals the extent to which increased pupil enrolment in the mid-century years may be accounted for by the growing numbers of girls attending school. See also Davey's excellent "Educational Reform and the Working Class: School Attendance in Hamilton, Ontario, 1851-1891" (Ph.D. diss., University of Toronto, 1975).

Chapter 1

Human and Child Nature: The Search for Perfection

> If the human soul without education be compared to marble in the quarry, and education to the art of statuary, then with us the statue is merely cut out and rough chipped to the rude semblance of a man, instead of being chiselled and polished to a glorious type of the human face and figure, radiant with life and intelligence like the "statue that enchants the world."
>
> *The Monthly Review,*
> Toronto, 1841[1]

Mid-nineteenth century school promoters often seem to have been by turn both pessimists and optimists. One wonders, in fact, whether the phenomenon of mass schooling would have occurred at all without the extreme ambivalence towards human affairs which appears to have been characteristic of most of them. They liked little of what they saw in the world around them: men seemed infinitely corruptible and society infinitely depraved. At the same time, no generation ever had greater faith in man's potential for improvement, or in the possibility of a perfect society at some unspecified date in the future. It was despair in the face of existing human weakness, coupled with a growing belief in the ultimate perfectibility of human nature, that provided one of the essential dynamics of mid-nineteenth century educational reform. The "world of men," as Egerton Ryerson called it, seemed evil, chaotic. The movement to send all children to school was, above all, a movement to bring sanctity and order to human affairs.

These attitudes had two sources. As men of their time and place, Upper Canadian school promoters were deeply affected by the social and political dislocations that rocked their world.

They were not immune from the stresses that accompanied the rebellions of 1837/38, the social and political clashes and economic developments of the mid-century years, and their analysis of Upper Canadian society and of the hopes and fears of their times is our primary concern in this book. Yet a related and equally important source of their thought was the heritage of evangelical Christianity, infused as it increasingly was with the attempt to understand the nature of man and life in scientific terms. What was man? How could his potential for improvement be understood and controlled? The evangelical belief that, despite the persistence of sin in the world all people were capable of being saved, was fundamental to the crusade for educational reform. Salvation, at the same time, was increasingly portrayed in secular terms, as at least in part as much a matter of happiness in this world as of peace in the next.

That the good life could perhaps be extended to all people within a given society and even to the entire world was a possibility that came to obsess nineteenth century reformers. Social ills like crime and immorality, which had once been looked upon as inevitable proof of Original Sin, or at least of the presence of sin within a particular society, were increasingly seen as having environmental causes outside and sometimes beyond the control of the individuals concerned. Reformers tended to argue that if these causes could be removed, crime and immorality themselves would also disappear.[2] Applied to children, this view gave birth to the general notion that, given the right environment or the right education, the young were almost infinitely perfectible.

The wholesale attempt to transplant societies from the Old World to the New must have invited an especially questioning look at human nature and potential and at the relationship of men and women to their environment. The difficulties encountered were often a source of profound pessimism. Was the human spirit capable of conquering raw nature in Upper Canada? Could a truly Christian civilization survive in the wilderness? If the answers to such questions were often negative in the extreme, they seem sometimes to have been an excuse for an equally exaggerated optimism. In 1848, a memorial from the District of Colborne to the united Canadian legislature responded to the proposed Upper Canadian normal school by hailing the educational improvement that was bound to result from the training of teachers. What was in store for the province, according to the memorial, was no less than a "mighty intellectual and moral reformation" of its people. Clearly the future would be happy, if the present was not.[3] In 1865, the Toronto

Board of Education was still looking to the future; its great goal was to make future generations better than the existing one.[4] The recurring theme was that human beings could be, and indeed would have to be, improved.

If man were to be improved, it became increasingly obvious that educators and other improvers needed to understand something about him. What were the "secret fountains of action" which motivated men and how could educators hope to harness them?[5] John Strachan, who was Upper Canada's chief promoter of formal education during the first third of the nineteenth century, attempted to answer this question in a pamphlet on the management of grammar schools which he published in 1829. In this exceptionally detailed and concrete description of the methods that he had employed in his own school, Strachan revealed his belief that education was, or ought to be, a science. Considerable knowledge of human nature, he argued, was required of the successful teacher, and this was not acquired in a day.[6] To Egerton Ryerson in 1842, a scientific analysis of human nature was essential to any plan for human progress and it followed, therefore, that human education ought to become a science. But a decade later when much of his major school legislation was already on the books, Ryerson still believed that very little had been accomplished so far in the field. Indeed, in no area had more experiments been made, with so little progress "towards the definiteness and dignity of a science," than in that of public education.[7]

Perhaps Ryerson intended the emphasis to be on the word "public" which he was probably still using in the same sense that Strachan had used it to describe schools in 1829 – that is to designate the education of relatively large numbers of children outside the family home.[8] Certainly the motivating or training of individual children or children at home had been analysed by western philosophers to a far greater extent than that of children in large groups or schools. One thinks immediately of the lengthy treatises on the subject by Locke or Rousseau. Indeed, it was no doubt the spread of formal schooling outside the family household that to a large extent inspired the concern to develop further a science of education or child behaviour, just as the grouping of men in institutions like prisons, asylums or factories must have given considerable impetus to studies in adult psychology and behaviour.

There were critics in mid-nineteenth century Upper Canada, as in other places and times, who doubted whether concrete results would ever come from "laborious investigations of the human mind." But most educators seemed to accept the opinion that man's nature was governed by laws which really could be investigated and understood, and which would certainly affect schooling. In 1861, the *Journal of Education for Upper Canada* reported that a Schoolmasters' Social Science Association had been formed in the province to study the laws of "human well-being" insofar as they affected "the teaching and training of the young," and at least one aspiring school inspector named Charles Clarkson accompanied the thesis on school organization and discipline which he submitted to the Education Department in 1871 with a letter expressing the hope that it was abreast of what he called "the educative science" of the day.[9]

Despite all pretensions to a science of education, however, most educators continued to base both their pessimism about man and their hopes for his improvement on the traditional three-faculty view of human nature. According to Ryerson in 1847, for example, all men were endowed with physical, intellectual and moral faculties or powers. A school superintendent from South Burgess argued in 1854 that man was an entity having a body, reason and a moral sense. No matter how the idea was expressed, however, all seemed to agree on one essential point: that the physical part of human nature was opposed to all the rest. Man was at war with himself. If his higher nature won, he was on the verge of the sublime; if not, he approached an abyss. As one Upper Canadian promoter of Mechanics' Institutes put it, the "extremes of majesty and meanness" met in the nature of man. His feet were rooted in the slime, but his mind was capable of travelling beyond physical care to the heavens above.[10]

Yet whatever the innate capabilities of the mind, it was the belief of most school men that they were rarely developed. The dominant faculty, they generally argued, and the one most likely to be victorious in any conflict between reason and passion or moral principle and physical indulgence was what one mid-century American educator labelled "self-love."[11]

Egerton Ryerson certainly took this position. Clearly disturbed by the thought of overpowering physical need of any kind, Ryerson predicted that if the moral and intellectual faculties were not consciously developed in a man, he would be left a "mere material being – a mere mass of bones and sinews, and bodily appetites and passions." Ryerson saw life as a war, with the intellect and the heart ranged against the body. Sometimes he argued that the heart was more important than the mind and that the moral feelings ought to be cultivated rather than the intellect. Certainly he believed this to be essential when intellectual development was already weak, as he claimed was often the case among North American Indians and among the labouring classes. Both, he argued, were "controlled by their *feelings* – as almost the only rule of action – in proportion to the absence or partial character of their intellectual development." Ryerson argued that the same was true of adolescents, a point which was to become vital to his and other people's defence of denominational colleges. The "religious and moral feelings," they claimed, were dominant at the age when youth went to college; hence the necessity of strong religious influences at this critical period of life.[12]

On other occasions, Ryerson stressed the intellectual side of man's nature. The mind, he argued in the 1870s, was that which man had "in common with the angels and with God." Perhaps indeed conscience and mind were one entity, as the chief superintendent was able to admit at this time, when the three-faculty view of human nature was perhaps beginning to go out of fashion. It did not matter. The fundamental point was still the same: the rest was "earth."[13]

The whole argument for improving man through education was in fact deeply rooted in an overwhelming fear of man's physical nature. "A sensual man is a mere animal. Sensuality is the greatest enemy to human progress," declared the *Journal of Education* in April, 1860. The *Journal* was paraphrasing a Ryerson speech to the parents and pupils of the John Street School, a common school in Toronto. The nature of the audience was not without significance. Common school children above all had to be warned against the encroaching demands of the body, lest they should mistake them for life. The good life meant progress and improvement. Sensuality was not life. Sensuality was "the grave of all social progress."[14]

When their purposes required it, educators sometimes abandoned such dualism and recognized the essential unity of the human being and the fact that no element in a person's makeup could be ignored. John Strachan took this position when, in 1853, as the Anglican Bishop of Toronto, he defended church-run schools, explaining that moral education was too often left out in those run by the state. Noting that "the Body and Soul must be united" to make the perfect man, he concluded that a sound education had to include both divine and secular knowledge.[15] Ryerson had occasion to state a similar view when arguing on behalf of denominational colleges. Man's physical, intellectual and moral natures could not really be separated, he stated in 1847: it was in the harmonious development of all

29

aspects of his being that perfection consisted.[16] As with Strachan, however, the purpose of the argument was to show that the moral side of his nature was neglected to man's ultimate peril. The physical or secular side needed, if anything, to be suppressed.

The inseparable relationship of mind to body was also recognized when it came to the learning process. Daniel Wilson, who, as Professor of History and Literature at University College was another local authority on educational matters during the Ryerson era, made this point in a talk which he gave to the Upper Canadian Teachers' Association in 1865. Education, Wilson said on this occasion, proceeded through "every gateway of knowledge which the senses supply."[17] Ryerson believed that the senses were so many "inlets of knowledge" and that the more of them that were called into play in the teaching of the child, the more effective the process.[18] Most educators also argued that the training of the body was essential to the full development of the mind. But the emphasis was clearly always on training, or on the senses as gateways to "higher" knowledge. Appreciation of the physical facts of human existence rarely if ever went further.

Indeed, to Egerton Ryerson, starvation of the mind was more criminal than starvation of the body. While political economy, science and education were important, they were meaningless if strictly secular, for society's first duty was to man's higher nature:

> I have often revolved in my mind . . . the theories of those political economists, who maintain that the essential well-being of man consists in health of body, sufficiency of food, and personal liberty, – and who propose to remedy the existing ills of society and bring about the universal reign of millennial happiness, by altered forms of government, improved balances of power, other distributions of property, new constitutions and laws of the latest invention, from the exhaustless manufactory of human ingenuity and speculation. I have also endeavoured to examine the dogmas of those professed philosophers, who, independent of any Divine Agency, and leaving Christianity altogether out of the question, are about to create all things new by the magic power of science and education. In both of these plausible and too widely-spread theories, there appears to me to be this radical defect, an irrational as well as anti-scriptural omission: Man, as a *moral* being, is entirely overlooked.[19]

Yet man's moral sense was always embattled. It was the Methodist view, Ryerson's opinion, and one shared by many contemporary reformers, that man was "very far gone from original righteousness, and of his own nature inclined to evil." There was no guarantee that a man's conscience would lead him away from the paths of sin, for moral law was not innate. It could only be introduced to the mind by Christian revelation, and thus by Christian education.[20]

Attitudes to human nature had their counterpart in developing theories about the nature of childhood. Was the infant innocent or guilty? Most nineteenth century educators leaned towards the Lockean view that a child was born without knowledge of either good or evil. How then did the child learn? The question was of particular interest to Henry Esson, the Calvinist educator who, following a period as a schoolmaster in Montreal, was Professor of Mental and Moral Philosophy at Toronto's Presbyterian Knox College, between 1844 and 1853. Shortly before he died, Esson published an essay which dealt in part with the problem of early childhood development, and which argued that the mind of the new-born child consisted of a sort of "innate alphabet" which observed the world and from which all things grew. The alphabet, however, seems to have provided only undirected potential; anything could be learned. Esson concluded therefore that the early years of childhood were vital, that there was no part of human education "more important or more universally influential" than that which occurred during the first three or four years of life. "The impressions of childhood, how ineffaceable are they!" effused an Upper Canadian newspaper in the 1840s, reiterating the same theme. "How, amid the confusion and dissipation of later life, do they still abide . . . like burning coals, smothered, but not extinguished, amid the rubbish that afterwards they consume!"[21]

Belief in the susceptibility of the child was reflected in the incredible powers for good or for evil that were frequently attributed to teachers. According to the Colborne Memorial of 1848, for example, schoolmasters made an impression on their charges which could never be erased. It was foolhardy not to take the question seriously, the memorial argued. Whatever opinions might be entertained to the contrary, teachers were essentially all-powerful over their pupils. They were the "dictators of their sentiments and manners, the Guardians of their Virtues, and in a high degree the masters of their future destinies in this world and the next." When he spoke to the Upper Canadian Teachers' Association in 1865, Daniel Wilson attempted to make his audience aware of the teacher's enormous powers. The young mind was a pure tablet, he told them, on which teachers wrote what they willed. Theirs were no idle words, but "impulses pregnant with good or evil, far-reaching and comprehensive as time itself." As Ryerson had noted in his annual report for 1864, the human being was a creature of imitation. Who therefore could calculate the amount of evil an unprincipled teacher might do?[22]

One is tempted to conclude from statements like these that nineteenth century educators saw the child as fundamentally innocent, that the great danger was their corruption by evil influences outside themselves. But, like their attitudes to mankind as a whole, educators' feelings about children were not really that simple. It was not that children were completely innocent, although this word was much used, but that they were almost infinitely malleable. Such malleability was a dangerous, almost evil condition in itself. Daniel Wilson compared the young mind to "a calm pellucid stream," but it was one which reflected the shadow as well as the sunshine. It therefore became the teacher to guard "that pure mirror" from all the storms of passion and impurities that might disturb or cloud it. Ryerson's approach was similar. "The helplessness and innocence of infancy look up to us for its future destinies. Will we give it bread or scorpions?" he asked. Children were clay, to be moulded into "vessels of honour or dishonour – to be made the ornament or disgrace, the benefactors or the plagues, the blessings or curse of their race." It was education that made the difference. An uneducated child would grow up into "a mere animal" with tastes and sympathies "as degraded and pernicious as they might be exalted and useful."[23]

The dualism is once again unmistakable, and implies that like the adult it imitated, the child was potentially far from pure. Indeed the basic tendency of the child was to remain "an animal" if education did not intervene. A prize essay reprinted in the *Journal of Education for Upper Canada* of March, 1848, managed to talk about the innocence of childhood one minute and the need to repress its wild passions the next,[24] and is typical both of the confusion surrounding the subject and of attitudes that were increasingly prevalent on both sides of the Atlantic. As the French historian, Philippe Ariès, has pointed out in his history of the family, the principle of infant "innocence," which had been developing since the seventeenth century, really led to two sorts of behaviour towards childhood: an attempt to protect it against "pollution by life," in particular against the sexuality that was less and less tolerated even in adults; and an effort to strengthen it by the development of reason and character.[25] In North America, as in Europe, these attitudes seem to have triumphed in the nineteenth century. And also, as in Europe, it was the educators who promoted them. In Upper Canada, the *Journal of Education* printed article after article about the sanctity and specialness of childhood and its awesome influence upon the future of man.[26]

If a major purpose of education was the suppression of animal passions, it is not surprising that the theme of restraint was constant in these nineteenth century writings, and that education was often virtually equated with restraint. As Ryerson once put it, school lessons were of little value unless accompanied by "lessons of order." "A man cannot teach as he pleases, if he cannot enforce his lessons," he pointed out to a correspondent in 1847.[27] Sometimes educators referred to theories which suggested a course opposite to one of imposed restraints. The thesis on school organization and discipline submitted to the Education Department in 1871 by Charles Clarkson, for instance, made much of the natural order of child development, arguing that nature called forth first the senses, then the imagination and finally the powers of reason. The belief in natural development, which implied that the teacher look to the child rather than the reverse, was also promoted by the Knox College philosopher, Henry Esson, and by the Upper Canadian Grammar School inspector, G. R. Cockburn, who in a report to the government on the grammar school in 1859, argued that "real knowledge and a healthy mental bearing" could be communicated in half the time, if only teachers were more aware of the "laws" of human growth. Too often the principle was lost sight of, Cockburn claimed, and the human mind treated by the schoolmaster "as an inert mass to be crushed into shape in his iron mould."[28] As Ryerson had pointed out in his first long report on elementary instruction in 1846, educators no longer believed that children could be treated like machines. True education was far from a mechanical process. To Samuel Nelles, a respected teacher and the Principal of Victoria College from 1850 to 1887, the main point to be emphasized was the fact that all children should not be treated the same. "It is impossible to run children like bullets all in one mould," he told a meeting of the Ontario Teachers' Association in 1869, "and it would be no addition to the charm of life could it be done."[29]

But in spite of such efforts to take into account the diverse needs of children as a group or as individuals, the major impulse seems always in the end to have been to emphasize the need for restraint. The problem was that children were increasingly seen to be different from adults. Not only was their innocence in need of protection, but, as various educators pointed out, they were noted for their special need of activity, or for their inability to reason and to arrive at conclusions. They were too active, too unreasoning, in fact; an essential characteristic seemed increasingly to be their inability to reach certain standards that were more and more sought among grown-ups; hence the frequent use of the word "child" or its derivatives to suggest inadequacy.[30]

For many educators, the weakness and incapacity of the young was the main reason for insisting on schools. It was not safe to leave children to their own devices. Henry Esson was among those who tried very hard to soften the potential conflict between the child and the demands of Victorian respectability and reason. He argued that early childhood development was a process of nature, but that, after all, nature could be improved upon. It did not "disdainfully reject or exclude the co-operation of human agency." In fact it might receive "important aid from human art, and from man, acting as her minister, as an usher in her great school."[31]

The majority of Upper Canadian educators, however, made much more of the need for strict adult control over children. "School organization and discipline" were not the prescribed topics for the theses of aspiring school inspectors in 1871 by accident. Discipline and organization were increasingly the major concerns of men who clearly rejected the more extreme versions of child-oriented or natural education espoused by nineteenth century European philosophers like Pestalozzi. The faculty view of human nature always seemed to imply the necessity of control. The desirable faculties could not be left to develop by themselves; it was believed that they needed exercise and training.[32] And questions of discipline and organization assumed increasing importance too, as the schools became larger and larger, and the children, as a result of being brought together for longer and longer periods of time, seemed more and more unmanageable.

Ryerson and his contemporaries were able to see that education in its broadest sense meant something more than supervision by adults or restraint and the repression of animal passions – that in reality all children were pupils and the whole world their teacher. "As every child is being educated by all that he sees and hears and learns, so is every adult person an educator by all that he does and says, and counsels." Most educators also agreed, as Daniel Wilson pointed out in 1865, that the education of children was something that went on all the time. But the reality was inadequate to the day. Ideal education was what most school promoters wanted, and ideal education in their view was a conscious process, comparable to the tilling of the land and the sowing of seed. If it did not take place, weeds and thistles would inevitably grow. "Inner motives" were insufficient, as Charles Clarkson pointed out in his thesis. Children needed to be governed.[33] Hence the school was seen less often as an environment for the natural development of the child, and much more frequently as a place where properly selected adults attempted to control this development. The maintenance of adult authority was clearly a primary goal.

There was not always total agreement on how to achieve the necessary control. Most educators, however, seemed to accept the fact that in the final analysis the teacher could only rely on two motives in school children, the urge to compete for rewards and the desire to avoid penalties. The majority continued to feel that corporal punishment was a necessity both in the home and at school and although there were local superintendents who expressed doubts about the wisdom of giving prizes to school children, and whose views would have found sympathy among increasing numbers of American and European educators at this time, there was little official support for such beliefs in Upper Canada. Few superintendents, in any case, dared to express openly their opposition to Ryerson's official policy, during the last decade or so of his superintendency, which was to encourage a system of rewards through provincial subsidies to schools that purchased prizes from the Education Office.[34] There was also little public debate on corporal punishment, although the matter was certainly raised in Education Office correspondence and in Ryerson's annual report to the government in 1864. What opposition there was to prizes, the chief superintendent attempted to crush by appealing to divine law. It was the order of Providence that the diligent should be rewarded while others were sent away empty; only the envious and the negligent, "misguided" parents and "stationary" teachers would oppose the system of rewards in schools or its promotion by the Education Office. Divine law also justified the use of corporal punishment:

> In the arrangements of Providence, law, penalty meets us wherever we go. No wisdom or moral force in rulers or administrations was ever sufficient of itself to sustain an orderly government. Nations, States, armies, navies, need compulsion, as well as advice and persuasion ... If this is true of men, it is especially true of children, who are only men of smaller growth, and more unformed and undisciplined.[35]

All men needed to be restrained, but children more so.

Ryerson's perception of children as small men who differed from adults mainly in needing greater restraint suggests a view of childhood less idealized than that of contemporaries who insisted that children were very different from, and especially a great

35

deal more innocent than adults. We have already seen that even those who used the term "innocent" often really meant "weak." Ariès has argued that emphasis on the innocence and specialness of childhood was an educated upper class, then a middle class phenomenon, one which filtered down only gradually to the working classes in France, and was also accepted more slowly in England than in continental Europe.[36] Was Ryerson, then, reflecting the British and predominantly humble class origins of Upper Canadians in taking the traditional view that children were, after all, only small men? John Strachan once referred to the child as "the most interesting of all objects," an opinion which Ariès relates to the earliest stirrings of the new innocent view of childhood. A child became an object to be played with, but still not to be taken too seriously because so many of them died.[37] Of course, Strachan did take older children seriously, but also complained very early in his career that in Upper Canada, children did not remain such for very long, because even well-to-do parents expected them to get through their schooling quickly in order to enter the working world.[38] The demands of a new world environment may have thus complemented British and lower class conservatism to produce a society where children could be seen as "men of smaller growth" or even as objects – weak perhaps, but not all that special – for longer than elsewhere in the western world. The phenomenon was also noticed in the United States, where foreign travellers found American children less disciplined than their European contemporaries – more precocious and adult, like the boisterous, undisciplined children and adults of an earlier time in Europe.[39]

Whatever their outlook compared to other people, it is quite certain that the whole question of childhood – its nature and definition – was in a state of considerable flux for nineteenth century Upper Canadians. Many questions besides school discipline were greatly complicated by the perplexing problem of distinguishing the child from the adult. When exactly could the child be considered responsible? That the proper age for instructing children in adult religious or moral duties was being debated is suggested by criticisms of such enquiry, and the argument that adult responsibility started early. The child old enough to distinguish between right and wrong was also old enough to sin, or to commit a crime.[40]

Israel Lewis, the author of an Upper Canadian manual on the law for children and their families that was published in Kingston in 1844, outlined the distinctions of age as they were then understood in the courts. Because "infancy" was equivalent to lunacy or idiocy in British law, Lewis pointed out, infants were not considered responsible for their acts. Children who fell into this category varied in age according to the issue at hand: for civil matters, all those under twenty-one; for breaches of the peace, those under fifteen; for felony, only those under seven years of age were considered infants. Lewis informed his readers that a girl of thirteen had been executed for killing her mistress, and a boy of eight hanged for setting fire to barns. These children, it was presumed, understood the difference between right and wrong, and therefore were classed as adults before the law.[41] Of course justice was severe, in its physical manifestations at least, for all Upper Canadians during the first half of the nineteenth century insofar as it followed British law and practice. Lewis listed twelve crimes that were still punishable by death in Upper Canada after the passage of the statute reducing the number of capital offences in 1833.[42] Imprisonment began to replace the harsher punishments earlier considered suitable for many offences, but the tendency to treat fairly young children more or less as adults before the law continued for some time after attitudes had begun to change. As late as 1859 school-age boys were still being sentenced to terms in the penitentiary at Kingston for the crimes of larceny and burglary.[43]

Children, as Strachan had observed earlier in the century, were also expected to enter the work force at a very young age. G. R. Cockburn, speaking as rector of the Model Grammar School in 1860, claimed to have been warned before coming to Toronto that there were "no boys in Canada, and that by some wonderful hot-bed process the child of the nursery was developed into the young man" virtually overnight.[44] Cockburn implied that this was not really true. But certainly among the poor in cities, and perhaps among all classes in rural parts of Upper Canada at that time, children who attended school were often "taken away" between the ages of twelve and fourteen "to assist their parents," as one report put it in 1860.[45] The practice was not yet considered unusual by many people.

But it began to be criticized. Educators especially seemed to feel growing qualms about exposing the young to the evils of possible "idleness" or to the demands of adult society as it might be encountered in the working world or in jails or penal institutions. The best place for children, they increasingly argued, was in institutions designed especially for them. For the majority, this meant schools.[46] Schooling would be made compulsory for young children; those in their teens would be encouraged by every possible means to remain in school, for longer and longer

37

periods of time. For if thistles and weeds inevitably grew when the early stages of childhood were left uncultivated, who knew what horrible growths might occur if children were neglected during their adolescence?

Clearly, as growing numbers of what Ryerson called "grown-up children" did stay in school, or did not work when they left school, this period of life seemed more and more problematic. Adolescence was of particular concern, as we have seen, to those who pressed for denominational colleges. "Grown-up young men" who were still living at home, or who had been working and were thus paying for their own education, were not much cause for alarm. But what of those who left home to go to college, without ever having had the steadying influence of adult commitments? Denominational college supporters argued that these years were the most critical in a person's life. At such a period, when youthful passions were strongest and temptations most powerful, young men could not be abandoned to the larger world without the most painful apprehensions. Ryerson cited the moral ruin of "more than one" who had come to Toronto "for the noblest purposes, but without the restraints and counsels of home, or the oversight and influence of church institutions," and had fallen victims to the city.[47]

As the tendency toward older children staying in school became more pronounced,[48] complications concerning their discipline inevitably arose. Did young men and women, or "grown-up children" who remained in school, have to be treated differently from younger children? Educators and parents were uncertain, and perhaps had different views on the subject. Ryerson thought that children under twelve could justifiably be suspended from school for disobedience, a thing which often occurred because of parental over-indulgence at home, implying that there was less agreement about older children.[49] The children themselves varied, as did the expectations of adults. As the grammar school master of Brantford pointed out in the late 1850s, there were boys at school who were "fairly their own guardians – in fact men," and these could safely be left to govern themselves. But this was not the case with all young men. The Brantford newspapers published the debates which ensued when an adolescent attending the Central School in that city was sent home by the same school master for what the latter took to be deliberate rudeness to his teacher in the form of remarks to a neighbouring student. Did teachers have the right to suspend older pupils? Whose word had most value, the pupil's or the master's? Who was the ultimate authority, the teacher or the parent?

The chief superintendent's advice was sought, as in many similar cases, and the letters back and forth on the subject were printed for the information of the public in 1859.[50]

Clearly a lot of people were very uncertain about the relationship of older children and parents to the teacher and the school. Boys and girls were no longer seen in pinafores and smocks, one reviewer noted in the correspondence over the Brantford school question; they were "young ladies and gentlemen," or they and their parents expected them to be treated as such.[51] What he failed to realize was his own reversal of the facts. It was not that more and more children were casting off their childhood dependence, but that more and more teachers and adults like himself expected children to remain in pinafores and smocks for far longer than they ever had before. What Charles Phillips has called the "sudden right to crude self-assertion" – the right to self-government claimed by many rural children when adult responsibilities came early[52] – was no longer acceptable to growing numbers of people in Upper Canada.

Nor were the unhappy conditions commonly experienced by many children, rural or urban. In the May, 1857, *Journal of Education* there appeared an unsigned article entitled "Old Children." In it the author referred to another kind of prematurely-aged child among those to be deplored. In addition to the boy or girl who was too old because of precocious manners, there were those who were too old because of their premature experience of poverty or cruelty, the article pointed out.[53] Reformers hoped that by treating children as special – that is by classing them as in particular need of protection and discipline – they could perhaps be saved from such early aging.

What was appropriate, or reluctantly permitted, for adults then, was no longer to be suffered for the young; it therefore seemed increasingly necessary to define the different stages of life and the point at which adult status was achieved. As the maverick politician, Robert Baldwin Sullivan, put it in a lecture which he delivered to the Mechanics' Institute of Hamilton in 1847, the life of a man was divided into epochs and the rules of conduct which applied to one period were "inapplicable" to any of the others. John Strachan meanwhile railed more pointedly against the corrupt appetite in the young for "unseasonable" knowledge to which some people pandered.[54] If children needed to be prevented from acquiring adult manners and unseasonable knowledge, they were clearly better off separated from adult society in schools. The schools themselves, it was increasingly thought, should be hived off – either physically with fences or by situating them as far as possible from busy, commercial or industrial locations.

How to deal with the growing gap between childhood and manhood was greatly complicated, if not entirely governed, by the whole question of sex. Many nineteenth century educators believed that the sexes should be schooled separately, especially when it came to adolescents, as the latter began to stay in school longer, and by the 1860s there were heated debates going on in Upper Canada on the subject of girls in grammar schools. Usually the argument for separating girls and boys was a moral one, the concern to suppress any sign of sexuality. It was the forwardness of girls in grammar schools and their physical contact with boys that alarmed Upper Canada's most famous grammar school inspector of the 1860s, George Paxton Young. He didn't like to see "big boys" chasing "big girls" around classrooms. However, Young also justified separate treatment by implied differences between the sexes. "There was a very considerable diversity," he argued, "between the mind of a girl and that of a boy; and it would be rash to conclude that, as a matter of course, the appliances . . . best adapted for bringing the faculties of reflection and taste to their highest perfection in the one" were "the best also in the case of the other."[55]

Yet, whatever the deeper reasons for separating boys and girls from each other and from the larger society, the stated goal for both was always the same: perfection. The possibility was constantly implied and frequently articulated. Educators saw as their goal the creation of almost perfect human beings, a generation better than the one which had gone before. If the child was born "innocent," such perfection was possible; through formal and orderly education children would be elevated from the grossness inherent in their physical nature; if such elevation proved impossible, as well it might if children were really as subject to the dictates of sensuality and self-indulgence as most educators implied, then restraint would be employed. Certainly, the animal passions could not be allowed to go their own way completely unchecked.

Such perceptions of the nature and needs of children implied a rather pessimistic opinion of society as a whole, and it is true that educators in this period increasingly felt that the social conditions to which children were exposed were unsavoury, that the transition from childhood to the real world held many dangers. They insisted that children attend school for longer and longer periods of time, partly, at least, in order to protect them on the one hand and prepare them on the other for the complex and troubled society which sooner or later, as Upper Canadians, they would have to confront.

NOTES

[1]Quoted in DHE, IV, 159. Hodgins notes that *The Monthly Review* was published briefly during the Sydenham period at Ryerson's suggestion.

[2]David J. Rothman, *The Discovery of the Asylum: Social Order and Disorder in the New Republic* (Boston, 1971), chapters 1-3, contains a good analysis of changing attitudes to deviance in the United States.

[3]The Colborne Memorial, 1848, Education Records RG 2 C-6-C, Provincial Archives of Ontario, Toronto, p. 4. (Hereafter cited as RG 2, PAO).

[4]Edwin C. Guillet, *In the Cause of Education: Centennial History of the Ontario Education Association, 1861-1960* (Toronto, 1960), p. 14.

[5]*Claims of the Churchmen and Dissenters of Upper Canada brought to the Test; in a Controversy between Several Members of the Church of England and a Methodist Preacher* (Kingston, 1828), p. 70.

[6]John Strachan, *A Letter to the Rev. A. N. Bethune, On the Management of Grammar Schools* (York, 1829), pp. 36-37.

[7]Ryerson, *Inaugural Address on the Nature and Advantages of an English and Liberal Education, delivered at the Opening of Victoria College, June 1, 1842* (Toronto, 1842), p. 23; "Permanency and Prospects of the System of Common Schools in Upper Canada, 1851," DHE, X, 38.

[8]Strachan, *On the Management of Grammar Schools*, p. 23; Ryerson, *Inaugural Address at Victoria College*, pp. 12-13.

[9]Rev. David Rintoul, *Two Lectures on Rhetoric, delivered in the Mechanics' Institute, Toronto* (Toronto, 1844) Part II, pp. 29-30; "The Schoolmasters' Social Science Association," *The Journal of Education for Upper Canada*, XIV (August, 1861), 117 (hereafter cited as JEUC); "School Organization and Discipline," in Charles Clarkson to Ryerson, 8 March 1871, RG 2 C-6-C, PAO.

[10]Ryerson, "The Importance of Education to an Agricultural, a Manufacturing, and a Free People, 1847," DHE, VII, 141; Walter Eales, *Lecture on the Benefits to be derived from Mechanics' Institutes* (Toronto, 1851), pp. 6-7.

[11]A. Potter and G. B. Emerson, *The School and the Schoolmaster: A Manual for the Use of Teachers, Employers, Trustees, Inspectors, etc. of Common Schools* (New York, 1842), pp. 24-25.

[12]Ryerson, "Canadian Mechanics and Manufacturers: An Address Delivered before the Mechanics' Institute, Toronto," JEUC, II (February, 1849), 18; Ryerson to Varden, 20 May, 1847, RG 2 C 1, Letterbook C, p. 378, PAO; "The University Question in a Series of Letters, 1861," DHE, XVI, 293-94.

[13]Ryerson, *First Lessons in Christian Morals for Canadian Families and Schools* (Toronto, 1871), p. 40.

[14] "Elements of Social Progress," JEUC, XX (April, 1860), 51.

[15] "Charge of Bishop Strachan to his Clergy and Laity in 1853," DHE, XV, 6.

[16] Ryerson, "A Lecture on the Social Advancement of Canada," JEUC, II (December, 1849), 184.

[17] "Dr. Wilson's Address to the Upper Canada Teachers' Association," JEUC, XVIII (October, 1865), 146.

[18] Report on a System of Public Elementary Instruction for Upper Canada (Montreal, 1847), p. 75.

[19] Annual Report for 1864, Part I, p. 26; and Wesleyan Methodism in Upper Canada: A Sermon Preached before the Conference of Ministers of the Wesleyan-Methodist Church in Canada (Toronto, 1837), p. 1.

[20] Wesleyan Methodism in Upper Canada, p. 1; Ryerson, Christians on Earth and in Heaven: the substance of a Discourse, delivered in the Adelaide Street Wesleyan-Methodist Church (Toronto, 1848), p. 14; Claims of the Churchmen and Dissenters, pp. 164-65 and 184-88; First Lessons in Christian Morals, pp. 64-65.

[21] Rev. Henry Esson, Strictures on the Present Method of Teaching the English Language, and Suggestions for its Improvement (Toronto, 1852), pp. 9-10; The Canadian Gem and Family Visitor, II (February, 1849), 43.

[22] The Colborne Memorial, 1848, RG 2 C-6-C, p. 3, PAO; "Dr. Wilson's Address," p. 148; Annual Report for 1864, Part I, p. 34.

[23] "Dr. Wilson's Address," p. 146; Ryerson, "Obligations of Educated Men," and "The Importance of Education to a Manufacturing and a Free People," JEUC, I (July, 1848), 193 and I (October, 1848), 300; and Annual Report for 1850, Appendix VI, No. 14.

[24] John Lalor, Esq., "Respect for Teachers the Interest of Society," JEUC, I (March, 1848), 80.

[25] Philippe Ariès, Centuries of Childhood: A Social History of Family Life (New York, 1962) translated by Robert Baldick, p. 119.

[26] For examples see JEUC for December, 1848 and June, 1854.

[27] Ryerson to Mr. Johnston, 4 March, 1847, RG 2 C1, Letterbook C, P. 460, PAO.

[28] "School Organization and Discipline," 8 March 1871, RG 2 C-6-C, PAO; "Summary of the Curriculum of Knox College, Toronto, 1848," DHE, VII, 267; Annual Report for 1859, Appendix A, p. 163.

[29] "Report on a System of Public Elementary Instruction for Upper Canada, 1846," DHE, VI, 163 and 174; Guillet, In the Cause of Education, p. 50.

[30] "School Organization and Discipline," 8 March, 1871 and John Armour to Ryerson, 7 February, 1851, RG 2 C-6-C, PAO. For negative usage of derivatives of the word "child," see "Annual Report of the Assistant Superintendent of Education on the Common Schools of Upper Canada, 1842," in Hodgins, ed., Historical and Other Papers and Documents Illustrative of the Educational System of Ontario, 1842-1861 (Toronto, 1912), V, 4, and The Governor of the Toronto Gaol to Ryerson, 4 February 1859, RG 2 C-6-C, PAO.

[31] Esson, Teaching the English Language, p. 10.

[32]James McLachlan, *American Boarding Schools: A Historical Study* (New York, 1970), pp. 54-56, notes criticism of Pestalozzian educational ideas during the same period in the United States. On the need to train the faculties, see "School Organization and Discipline," p. 6 and the *Annual Report for 1861,* Appendix B, p. 211.

[33]*Annual Report for 1855,* Part I, p. 23; "Dr. Wilson's Address," p. 146; Ryerson, *Inaugural Address at Victoria College,* p. 26; "School Organization and Discipline," p. 7.

[34]An examination of published local superintendents' annual reports from the late 1860s, when the subject had become an issue, reveals only five or six in any given year who were willing to express their doubts or opposition.

[35]*Annual Report for 1867,* Part I, pp. 8 and 30; *Annual Report for 1864,* Part I, p. 25.

[36]Ariès, *Centuries of Childhood*, especially chapters 3 and 4, and pp. 238-40.

[37]Strachan to Brown, December, 1818, in George W. Spragge, ed., *The John Strachan Letterbook, 1812-1834* (Toronto, 1946), p. 184; and *Centuries of Childhood,* pp. 39 and 128-33.

[38]Quoted in J. George Hodgins, ed., *The Ryerson Memorial Volume* (Toronto, 1889), p. 45. The comment was made in 1809.

[39]McLachlan, *American Boarding Schools,* p. 125.

[40]Rev. J. H. Harris, *A Sermon Preached at St. James' Church, York on Sunday, March 17th, 1833, in aid of the Sunday School Society for the Diocese of Quebec* (York, n.d.), p. 6.

[41]Israel Lewis, *A Class Book, for the Use of Common Schools and Families, in the United Canadas, entitled the Youth's Guard against Crime* (Kingston, 1844), pp. 20-22.

[42]The capital offences were treason, murder, petit treason, rescuing murderers, rape, carnal knowledge of a girl under ten, sodomy, robbery, burglary, arson, accessory before the fact to capital offences and refusal to disperse if apprehended in riotous assembly. Persons convicted of forgery or impersonation (crimes formerly punishable by death) could still be whipped or set in the pillory. *Ibid.,* pp. 73 ff.

[43]"Truancy and Juvenile Crime in Cities, 1859-1860, Charges of the Judges on the Subject," DHE, XV, 1.

[44]JEUC, XIII (August, 1860), 120.

[45]"Truancy and Juvenile Crime in Cities," DHE, XV, 2.

[46]Eventually reformers came to believe that there was a class of "delinquent" or "incorrigible" children for whom other institutions were necessary. The gradual development of the concept of juvenile delinquency and the founding of reformatories for delinquent children is described in Susan Houston's important study entitled "The Impetus to Reform: Urban Crime, Poverty and Ignorance in Ontario, 1850-1875," (Ph.D. diss., University of Toronto, 1974). See also, Houston, "Victorian Origins of Juvenile Delinquency: A Canadian Experience" in Katz and Mattingly, eds., *Education and Social Change,* pp. 83-109.

[47]"The Methodist Conference Memorial to the Legislature, 1859," DHE, XIV, 228, and "The University Question in a Series of Letters,

1861," DHE, XVI, 289.

[48]Michael Katz has documented this shift dramatically for the city of Hamilton in the decade between 1851 and 1861. During that period the "average school life" increased about three years, the leaving age increasing from between eleven and twelve to between fourteen and fifteen. "Who Went to School?" in *Education and Social Change,* pp. 271-93.

[49]Ryerson to Elias Burnham, 28 September 1849, RG 2 C1, Letterbook E, PAO, p. 51.

[50]Newspaper clippings enclosed in Peter D. Muir to Ryerson, 26 August 1859, RG 2 C-6-C, PAO.

[51]*Ibid.*

[52]Phillips, *The Development of Education in Canada,* p. 100.

[53]JEUC, X (May, 1857), 76-77.

[54]R. B. Sullivan, *Lecture Delivered before the Mechanics' Institute of Hamilton . . . On the Connection between the Agriculture and Manufactures of Canada* (Hamilton, 1848), p. 4 and "Dr. Strachan's History of King's College, from 1797 to 1850," n.d., DHE, IX, 90.

[55] "Inspector's Report and Suggestions with Respect to the County Grammar Schools of Upper Canada, for the year 1865," *Annual Report for 1865,* Appendix B, pp. 75 and 73.

Chapter 2

Upper Canada at Mid-Century: The Necessity of Progress

A school-house is no longer a matter of choice but of necessity. It is now pretty generally understood that, if a community desire its youth to keep pace with the march of events going on almost everywhere, it must educate them; to neglect to do this would be to make them pariahs in society – hewers of wood and drawers of water for their better educated neighbours.

The Stratford Examiner,
1868[1]

Educational innovation in the nineteenth century was associated not only with slowly changing perceptions about the nature and needs of children, but also with extremely ambivalent feelings about the surroundings they grew up in. Was Upper Canada a proper environment in which to raise the young? Increasingly, educators seem to have thought not. Alarmed by what they perceived to be the degeneration of political and social mores in their time, they joined a host of other reformers in an anxious quest for social improvement, in searching for the elusive "progress" that was to become so important a part of the Victorian world view.

The mid-century decades were not without stress in Upper Canada. The tragic debacle of the Mackenzie-Papineau rebellions, which temporarily wrote *finis* to the reform agitations of the 1830s, were a source of profound pessimism in the province. The forties, fifties and sixties brought, in their turn, equally severe dislocations in local commercial and political patterns, as Great Britain moved to free trade and British North America to responsible government and Confederation, against a background of growing hostility between French and English and Catholics and Protestants locally, and the rumblings south of the border that would culminate in the American Civil War. Periods of commercial growth were interspersed with periods of depression; canal and railroad-building drastically altered the fortunes of individuals and towns and were accompanied by new kinds of labour unrest; while urbanization and immigration, especially of the famine Irish, presented the province with social problems on a scale never encountered before.[2]

Anxiety to come to terms with what to many observers seemed a serious increase in social disorder resulted in the proliferation of all kinds of causes directed at the improvement of adults – from church reform to the movement for temperance in the consumption of alcohol. But for children (as for some deviant members of adult society) the basic solution proposed was an institutional one, their temporary removal from the larger society and education – or re-education – in schools. The assumption was that existing schools were inadequate, a perception, it should be noted, that did not necessarily reflect the opinion of the majority of Upper Canadians. It was, rather, the result of a particular collective mentality, the viewpoint of educators who believed that schools ought to be and could be better than the society which created them. Ideally, they were special environments for the raising of a generation of children who would be better than the generation that had gone before.

But that was not all, for the proposed expansion and improvement of formal schooling had more than one purpose. School promoters thus sought not only the eventual moral and intellectual elevation of Upper Canadians, but their economic development as well. If a second class position *vis-a-vis* the rest of the world was to be avoided, they argued, Canada had to join the continental race for commercial as well as social improvement. "Advance with the advancing," educators cried – or run the risk of slavery. The irony of their position was that many of the desired changes – the accelerated development of industry, the growth of commerce and cities – were intimately connected with the social disorders so frequently deplored by the most vocal of the promoters of schools. Few of them appeared to see any contradiction, however, between the search for material growth and prosperity in nineteenth century free enterprise terms, and the search for social order. Rather, they sought solutions to the social ills of their times in institution-building, in the creation of controlled environments which would contain, suppress or avoid what they found unacceptable in the wider society.

The concern with environment was reflected in debates about the kind of physical accommodation schools should provide, as educators became increasingly aware of the impact of the school's appearance and form on the behaviour and even the attitudes of the children. Efforts to improve the design of school buildings can be traced in part to the idea that good thoughts could only occur in beautiful surroundings. Also, as schools multiplied and became larger, their promoters became increasingly worried about the influence of the massive institutions which they had created on the children attending them. Egerton Ryerson, for example, concluded that boarding halls, such as those which he had helped found at the Upper Canada Academy and Victoria College, could be quite unfortunate environments for young boys. He also believed that when "masses" of children were schooled together, even in day schools, they could not be governed without "the presence of authority and the influence of fear," a situation which might not obtain with small groups of children.[3] But the need for schools in the first place was rarely questioned by their promoters, for the environment outside the schools, they thought, was even worse. Send the children to school young, advised Ryerson's assistant and Upper Canada's Deputy Superintendent of Schools, J. George Hodgins. For by the age of seven, he argued, they would already be corrupted by the street.[4]

The complaints of educators about their society focussed on four fundamental and interrelated problems that they perceived as especially threatening to the well-being and future stability of their society. One was the obsessive materialism that they attributed to Canadians and the consequent lack of interest among the majority of the people in the things of the mind or spirit. Equally dangerous, in their view, was the "ignorance" of the mass of Canadians. A third problem and one that was clearly related in their minds to the other two, was the apparent increase of crime in the province, especially among juveniles. Finally, promoters of mass education in Upper Canada dwelt on the fundamental lack in their growing community of public spirit, of collective energy and enterprise. Canadians, they argued, were too willing to be behind the times. They cared insufficiently about their collective future and seemed to settle for less than equality with their more enterprising neighbours.

The fear that physical or material need might propel not only individuals but the whole society into a state of barbarism had been a North American theme from the time of the earliest European settlements. It was a theme which apparently struck an

47

especially profound chord in the minds of mid-nineteenth century Canadian educators, who were afraid that their fellow men were so wrapped up in everyday material concerns that all others would be lost sight of. To Daniel Wilson, for example, it seemed entirely possible that "industry and zeal for the accumulation of wealth" might absorb "all other energies" in the New World. Wilson elaborated on this theme to the members of The Upper Canada Teachers' Association in 1865, urging them to stress moral and intellectual values in the schools – to prevent their being contaminated with the "dust and turmoil" of everyday working life.[5] The theme was echoed everywhere, in every decade and to many audiences. The family monthly known as *The Canadian Gem and Family Visitor* also saw the struggle for material prosperity as weakening the moral fabric of the society. "In the turmoil of business," the *Gem* exclaimed, "in the scramble for wealth and power, how are the affections neglected! How do we trample upon man's higher and nobler nature!"[6]

Two school superintendents, from Lennox and Lanark counties respectively, reported to Egerton Ryerson in the 1850s and 1860s that the desire for wealth pervaded the public mind. One of them attributed Canadian materialism to the way in which the pioneer environment affected immigrants. It was in "this new country," he believed, that the physical was exalted above the intellectual in man. In Upper Canada, or perhaps especially in his own remote county, parents were not sufficiently ambitious for their children and took them out of school too young, with the result that "animal passions" were resorted to, instead of the purer intellectual and literary pursuits that they might have grown to enjoy.[7]

Some commentators attributed the overpowering materialism not only to the place but to the times. All Upper Canadians, according to one of Canada's most educationally-oriented governors, should exert themselves, lest the material progress of the province should outstrip its intellectual progress, lest wealth and luxury should, "like rank and noisome weeds," spread over the surface of the entire society. The speaker was Lord Elgin, and he was congratulating the University of Toronto on the occasion of her first convocation as a secular institution in 1849. In an attempt to pour oil on troubled waters and to calm the bitter feelings that had attended this change in the status of the university, he warned of the danger of too much secularism or materialism. According to Elgin, Upper Canadians lived "in an age and in a condition of society, more favourable to the growth of what may be called 'acquisitive propensities,' to the exclusive growth of the commercial spirit than any . . . before in the history of the world."[8] Thus the wealth and material progress of the province produced concern as well as satisfaction. To some Canadians, at least, it seemed as if the whole society was perched on the edge of a dangerous abyss; that unless urgent measures were taken to elevate the minds and spirits of the general population, all efforts to bring civilization to the province might founder in the irresistible materialism of the place and times.

Educators were not consistent about the state of civilization in Upper Canada, however. There were times when Egerton Ryerson, for example, attempted to prove that all was well in the province, as in 1839 when he argued that in spite of the unrest that had culminated in rebellion two years before, the "general intelligence, morality and loyalty of the people" could not be doubted. Literacy and reading, he claimed on that occasion, were as widespread in the Home, Niagara and Gore Districts of the province as in any place in England. But in private letters of the same period, Ryerson appeared much less certain. To an American correspondent, he revealed his fear that Canadians were really "slaves," and that under the system of things as they then were, the morals and intelligence of the people would remain "on a level with their liberties."[9] Another Upper Canadian, looking back on the same period at a later date, held that the "educational condition" of Upper Canada had at the time of the rebellion been at its lowest ebb, with fully one-half of the children growing up in what he called "a state of semi-barbarism."[10] Material necessity, the pursuit of wealth and physical as opposed to spiritual goals, had led, in the opinion of many commentators, to a tragic neglect of the things of the mind. As a result, Canadians were typically uneducated and uncivilized – or to use their own favourite word – they were "ignorant."

Like the related complaints about materialism, comments on the subject of popular ignorance were not confined to the difficult period of the 1830s. Indeed, throughout the mid-century period people like Ryerson seem to have rarely passed up an opportunity to condemn publicly, as well as privately, what they saw as one of Upper Canada's most persistent and perplexing problems. In 1846, the newly appointed superintendent of schools wrote that he had not imagined that there was so little information among the people on the subject of education, "after so much boasting of high intelligence." Nearly one-half of the London school trustees, he pointed out on this occasion, were incapable of filling out the forms which he had provided for the annual school reports. Yet there was a desire for instruction.

With patience and perseverance, the people might be helped to improve themselves.[11] Within a year, however, even this note of optimism was fading, and local problems in the administration of the 1846 school law were attributed by Ryerson to the ignorance of the people. It had operated with success in some districts; it was therefore plain that where it had not been successful there was something wrong "in the state of society or in the administration of the law, or both." There was not "sufficient educational intelligence" among the people to carry out the law effectively, and what was worse, the people apparently preferred their ignorant and barbarous ways. They really did not want to be improved.[12]

Outright opposition to school reform was dealt with in the same way. Thus Ryerson was able to argue that the critics of educational innovation in the late 1840s were "reckless" and "ignorant," and condemned their ideas as essentially unworthy of consideration.[13] Finally, the superintendent's annual reports began in the 1850s to suggest, through the use of statistics, that certain localities were more guilty than others of the sin of popular ignorance. Percentages of the population that could neither read nor write were shown, along with the numbers of children not attending school, in any given district or municipality. Municipalities where no public lecture had been given by the local superintendent, which did not support free schools or were without educational apparatus like globes or blackboards, were also singled out for attention.[14] Such failures were clearly considered to be evidence of ignorance – ignorance which was all the more to be deplored because, most educators agreed, Canadian affairs required increasing knowledge and mental discipline; indeed the "most painstaking inquiry and comprehensive judgment."[15] The times demanded decision. What if Canadians were too uninformed to rise to the occasion?

But the need to counteract rampant materialism or to ensure intelligent decision-making in politics and the administration of government were not the only reasons for concern about the general level of civilization in the province. In Canada, as in Great Britain and the United States during the same period, "ignorance" began to be associated with crime. The Bishop of Toronto, John Strachan, made the connection in his annual charge to the clergy in 1844. The effective instruction of Upper Canadian children in schools, he stated on this occasion, would result in the comparative emptying of jails in the province, and relieve the courts of a good portion of their business.[16] Ryerson's defense of increasing state intervention in schooling was based on the same premise. To leave children uneducated, he argued gloomily, was "to train up thieves and incendiaries and murderers." Would it not be better to spend money educating the child, than punishing the culprit?[17] The shutting down of all common schools in Toronto in 1849 when the city council refused to levy the property tax demanded by the school board seemed to some educators to offer concrete evidence of the connection between crime and the lack of formal education. "In Toronto, the Common Schools are yet closed," The *Journal of Education* reported in May, "while juvenile crime increases and abounds beyond all precedent." By June, the schools had finally reopened. It was now to be hoped that their "moral and intellectual restraint" would counteract "the evil influences of a twelve months' training in the schools of indolence and vice" to which the youth of the city had been exposed.[18]

The *Journal* continued to labour the point throughout the fifties, and by 1860 was claiming statistical evidence in the form of the educational attainments, or lack of them, of the inmates of Toronto jails. It was reported that of 1029 male prisoners incarcerated over a certain period of time, 317 could neither read nor write, 202 read only, 496 read and wrote imperfectly and only a tiny group of 14 were able to do both reasonably well. The figures for the 1123 female prisoners studied were even more damning, at 483, 345, 196 and 1, respectively. Ryerson's assistant, J. George Hodgins, who was by this time largely responsible for what went into the *Journal,* had for some time been interested in supplying libraries to the jails of Upper Canada.

His efforts in this area showed, as did most discussion of the evils of ignorance in general, that ignorance and crime were by many people increasingly associated not only with each other, but with simple illiteracy or the inability to read or write.[19]

The notion that ignorance, or the lack of formal instruction in the arts of written communication, led to crime was carried to its logical conclusion in Ryerson's *Annual Report for 1857.* Ignorance was no longer merely a cause of crime – it was a crime. He equated ignorance not only with simple illiteracy, but also with idleness; that is with the failure to be properly occupied at home, at work, or more important, at school:

> If ignorance is an evil to society, voluntary ignorance is a crime against society . . . If idle mendicancy is a crime in a man thirty years of age, why is not idle vagrancy a crime in a boy ten years of age? The latter is the parent of former.[20]

It appalled school promoters, especially as more and more municipalities made common school education free after 1850, that numbers of children should "choose to grow up in ignorance and vice, without control or restraint, and in violation of the implied social compact between citizens and communities." And failing to educate a child seemed more and more a crime in the adult, as being uneducated seemed to verge on the criminal in the child.[21]

Materialism, ignorance and crime: these were the three chief and most clearly articulated complaints of mid-century school promoters in Upper Canada. Wallowing in the ignoble pursuit of wealth, unable to cope with the complexities of either responsible or local self-government, Upper Canadians seemed also be an increasingly lawless lot. The fourth and somewhat less tangible grievance concerned what Ryerson called "the state of the public mind." In 1840, he wrote to the governor that it was chaotic, "without any controlling current of feeling, or fixed principle of action in civil affairs."[22] What he was looking for was the elusive spirit of patriotism, in his view the fountain of all collective energy and enterprise. Occasionally he claimed that he had found it, as in 1847 when he argued that opposition to the school laws ran counter to the spirit of the majority of Upper Canadians, or in 1851 when he publicly rebuked that "unpatriotic spirit of Canadian degradation" in which a few of his countrymen indulged – apparently forgetting for the moment his own diatribes on the ignorance and depravity of the people. "It cannot be too strongly impressed upon the mind," Ryerson declared, "that it is on Canadian self-reliance, skill and enterprise – in a word, on Canadian patriotism – that depends Canadian prosperity, elevation and happiness."[23]

These were the characteristics which educational reformers hoped would replace the inertia and apathy which they clearly felt to be the real attributes of many Canadians – attributes which were observed even by foreign visitors like the Reverend James Fraser of Manchester, who in 1863 commented that the characteristic spirit of Canada's "sparse and anything but wealthy population" was "as far as possible removed from the spirit of enterprise." Victoria College's Principal Nelles, for example, worried about the "torpid minds" he encountered, while John Johnston, the local school superintendent from Hungerford in Hastings County during 1856, commented on the "lazy negligence" which he claimed pervaded all classes in that area, "teachers, trustees, parents and children alike."[24] Whatever their name for it, educators were clearly preoccupied with the problem and could not help comparing Canada's inadequacy in this regard to the energy and enterprise that were all too obvious elsewhere on the North American continent.

The apparently greater prosperity of the United States clearly represented both an ideal and a threat to these mid-nineteenth century Upper Canadians. Certainly they saw it as a fact of life from which there was no escape. The obsessive quest for material goods among individuals or families might seem sinful to educators, but the quest of nations for the same prize was quite another matter. That Upper Canada might not be able to match the burgeoning material prosperity of her powerful southern neighbour was a real and recurring fear.

Educators' comparisons of Upper Canada with the American states were not always favourable to the latter. Disgust with republicanism and with the manners and morals of Americans had from the beginning informed John Strachan's desire to promote better educational facilities in Upper Canada,[25] and Egerton Ryerson's early writings suggest that he too had been struck by the lack of civilized culture encountered on visits to the United States. He blamed the disruptions of 1837 in part on the influence of American school books and also had disparaging comments to make about the effects of slavery and racial prejudice on the American national psyche. Indeed, a major motivation in gradually setting up provincial controls over text and library books in Upper Canada was the hope of eventually ridding the schools of republican, chauvinist and anti-British literature from the United States, which many teachers and superintendents believed had had a pernicious influence on the minds of young Canadians.[26]

Dislike of the theatrical or racial overtones in American politics, or of the super-patriotism of American textbooks, however, still could not cancel out the genuine admiration that Ryerson and most of his contemporaries felt for the great economic and educational achievements of the American nation. And the two were clearly connected in their minds. Ryerson specifically attributed American prosperity to the superior conformity of schools, as well as churches, in that country to "the *wants* and *wishes*" of the majority of the people.[27] Good schooling, it appeared, led to collective wealth. This was his opinion in the 1820s, and when he became superintendent of schools, Ryerson continued, in spite of defensive statements to the contrary, to see the middle and northeastern United States as models for Upper Canada in the field of education. The opinions of American school promoters like Horace Mann and Henry Barnard, or Alonzo Potter and George Emerson, were frequently quoted in the *Journal of Education* and in Ryerson's annual reports to the legislature, along with those of famous British and European educators, and the schools of New England and New York held up as examples of what could be done to promote intelligence, enterprise and industry among the people of Upper Canada.[28] In addition, comparisons between American and Canadian school systems became a continuing preoccupation of the Education Office.

Sometimes, of course, comparisons were designed to show the essential superiority of the Upper Canadian system. It was pointed out, for example, that schools stayed open longer, teachers were paid proportionally more, and attendance was proportionally better in Upper Canada than in the state of New York by 1859. It was also noted that American schools were more subject to political interference, that American superintendents of education exercised more arbitrary powers, and that Upper Canadian school law was superior to "anything of the kind" in the United States.[29] The outspoken grammar school inspector, George Paxton Young, even came close on one occasion to saying that the fact that the American educator Horace Mann had believed in co-education was an excellent reason for preferring the segregation of the sexes in schools. Young was not convinced that Mann's views were the considered opinions of a disciplined, unprejudiced or sober mind.[30]

At other times, however, Upper Canadians showed their concern that they might not be able, in fact, to match the achievement of their American neighbours. As a report of an Education Committee of the Legislature had put it as early as 1833, no educator wanted Upper Canada to remain a "solitary and deplorable exception" to the "general improvement" that was taking place on the continent of North America.[31]

And in 1839, Ryerson, in spite of any reservations he may have had about the United States, had been able to argue that Upper Canadians should try to learn from their "powerful neighbouring rivals." This was a better course at least and one more likely to encourage the development of "intelligence and nobleness of mind" and produce real public advantage, than the creation of "thriftless jealousy and anti-commercial rancour by appeals to popular ignorance." The Colborne Memorial to the legislature of 1848 clearly expressed the same concern. Canadians ought to strive for equality with Americans and had to be careful not to drift into a permanently inferior position in the continental race for improvement. Ambivalence about the state of economic and social development marked most such statements. For Ryerson, however, it was basically a matter of more enterprise, more energy. If only Canadians would exert themselves, he argued in 1853, "Canada could be placed on a level, if not on an eminence above every State on the continent."[32]

The trouble was that one could not stand still. "No country, no community can with safety be stationary," Robert Baldwin Sullivan told his Mechanics' Institute audience in Hamilton in 1847. "To improve with the improving, to advance, to keep pace with the foremost" was essential. The only alternative fate possible to a nation was "to sink into contempt and poverty, or what is worse into slavery and dependence." Sullivan was worried about the "strange inactivity" of Canadians, which Americans falsely attributed to the monarchical form of government. Canadians had to show that this was not true, and, that if they were to compete with the United States, the spirit of enterprise had to be awakened. Twenty years later the *Stratford Examiner* was still talking in the same terms. A country could only advance or retrograde – and it was education that made the difference. As Ryerson put it on the eve of Confederation in 1867, Canadians had become the architects of their own future. Would they make themselves "a virtuous, intelligent, happy and prosperous people?" Or were they destined to become "the outskirt hewers of wood and drawers of water" to the neighbouring republic? Clearly, if they would avoid the latter fate, they could not afford to be ignorant.[33]

The complaints of Upper Canadian school promoters about their society in the end covered a wide range. The people were too involved with everyday material concerns, with their own material advantage, to seek intellectual and spiritual elevation. They were quite simply ignorant, and ignorance not only made for the inability to conduct public affairs with success, but led to crime. In addition, in spite of their individual materialism, the people were somehow collectively apathetic and unenterprising. If they wished as a nation to compete with the powerful and prosperous United States, something would have to be done. And most Upper Canadian school reformers would certainly have agreed with R. B. Sullivan that the monarchical form of government was not the source of weakness. The causes had to be sought elsewhere.

Insofar as educators analysed the ills of their society, they tended to associate them with two fundamental facts of contemporary Canadian life: rapid economic and social change, and the apparent failure of traditional patterns of child care and education. About the first, however, they were remarkably reticent. This was because they clearly regarded economic and social change not only as inevitable, but as entirely necessary and desirable. Many believed that the laws of nature demanded such change. "In any living system, physical or social, the arrest of development involves not only the cessation of vital action, but the destruction of vital power; and is at once a symptom and cause of decay," one of Ryerson's correspondents declared. There seemed little that one could do to prevent or change the course of fundamental social and economic development in the Victorian world.[34]

One of the most obvious and constant aspects of mid-nineteenth century change in Upper Canada was the continuing influx of new settlers into the province. After the original migration of Loyalist and post-Loyalist Americans before the War of 1812, British immigrants began to come in increasing numbers, and the mid-century years saw this immigration reach a peak, with the annual exodus from Great Britain to British North America averaging 46,000 people. Many Upper Canadians welcomed the great flow of "the redundant population" from the mother country, agreeing with R. B. Sullivan that, in the absence of local initiative, Canadian prosperity depended in large measure on continuing immigration. But doubts were also expressed. Many of the newcomers arrived poverty stricken and diseased, particularly during the period of the great exodus resulting from the Irish potato famine, and both their fate and their ultimate influence on the province were a source of grave concern in Upper Canada. In 1848 Ryerson claimed that arrivals in the province had numbered in that year nearly one hundred thousand, or approximately one-sixth of Upper Canada's population. Many of the immigrants would add to the intelligence and productive industry of the country, he admitted, but was this the character of most of them? The majority, according to the Chief Superintendent of Schools, were in fact notoriously lacking in skills and the inclination to work and, if their circumstances were wretched, their habits were more so. Their arrival had been "accompanied by disease and death," which might be, Ryerson predicted, possible "harbingers of a worse pestilence of social insubordination and disorder" to come. It was essential that this "untaught and idle pauper immigration" be prevented from undermining the laws and their administration in Upper Canada. Ryerson's solution for the problem of course was an educational one. Only the diffusion of education among the immigrants could counteract what was becoming an unfortunate influence on provincial affairs.[35]

By the mid-fifties, the number of arrivals had greatly declined, and those who came were on the whole more prosperous than their predecessors of the forties. Nevertheless, hard times in North America resulted in the return to Britain of many prospective settlers;[36] the overall improvement could not have seemed that substantial to many contemporary observers.

Immigration, however, was only one of the perceived causes of incipient social disorder in Upper Canada. Educators seemed increasingly to feel that the whole fabric of society was undergoing a profound change. And, to some extent, they associated contemporary social disorganization with accelerating urbanization. Ryerson's early writings, indeed, suggest a strong prejudice against the rising metropolis of Toronto, at this stage because of its connection in his mind with Toryism and the established church. Yet he was drawn to the capital, as he was later drawn to the metropolitan centres of Europe, in spite of the drunkenness, sabbath-breaking, and other "sins of cities" which were said to prevail there even in the thirties. His feelings were, and clearly remained, ambivalent. He wrote of his relief in 1830 at the prospect of moving his family from a certain "hateful corner" of the city to another part of it, but seemed very reluctant to give up Toronto altogether for the seclusion of a smaller town when, in 1842, his appointment as Principal of Victoria College required removal to Cobourg.[37]

The prospectus of Victoria when it was still known as the Upper Canada Academy suggests the dangers which some educators associated even with relatively small communities. In it, parents and guardians were assured that Cobourg, while affording all the advantages of a large commercial city, was entirely "free from their vices and scenes of allurement." To be on the safe side, however, the academy placed strict limitations on student contact with the townspeople. Frequenting taverns or groceries where intoxicating liquors were sold, or lounging about in any public place longer than business required, were forbidden, as were most excursions into town for any purpose whatever.[38]

Distrust of "the city," of course, was not a unique theme, either to the period or to Upper Canada. De Witt Clinton, a governor of New York and promoter of urban schools in the early nineteenth century, believed that great cities were and always had been "the nurseries and hot-beds of crimes." In 1840, *The Connecticut Common School Journal* expressed the opinion that city children were far more excitable than their rural counterparts and more easily persuaded to do both good and evil. Indeed, fear of the urban environment increasingly led many well-to-do Americans to send their children to boarding schools, safely situated, like the Upper Canada Academy, in the country and far from the cities which might corrupt them. In Nova Scotia, too, social critics like Thomas Chandler Haliburton and William Young wrote of the dangers of cities. According to Haliburton, they generated mobs, vice and want, which in turn could only produce "anarchy and bloodshed."[39]

Educators could not seem to help idealizing, in contrast, the advantages of the rural environment. Egerton Ryerson, for his part, compared the weakness of city boys and the superficiality of city girls to the vigour and modesty of young men and women from the country. He also praised the rural way of life. "Where can the bricks and mortar of a city present abodes of safety and enjoyment comparable with the rural residences of a peaceful, a virtuous and an intelligent population?" Ryerson asked the people of Upper Canada during one of his early tours of the province. He claimed, admittedly to a predominantly rural audience, that Divine Providence had "marked out Upper Canada for agriculture;" and that the manufacturing and commercial interests were "mere offshoots" of the farming interests.[40]

But no amount of lip-service to the importance of farmers, or the superiority of their sons and daughters, could hide the essentially urban orientation of the Chief Superintendent of Schools. He escaped to his country retreat near Lake Erie, or to his boat on Lake Ontario, more and more frequently as time went on, but his home base and the seat of his power, as he was fully aware, was the City of Toronto. "Our cities and towns are the centres and hearts of large sections of country and radiate influences for good or evil, which are felt over the whole area of surrounding circles," Ryerson told urban school trustees in an 1850 circular.[41] He increasingly recognized that certain cherished educational innovations like the division of schools into grades, or even the adoption of free schools, were more acceptable, or in some cases, only possible in the larger towns. Many of the new ideas in education were, in fact, clearly a response to what Ryerson and like-minded contemporaries felt to be the needs of cities and their growing masses of unemployed children. The uneducated vagrants increasingly referred to in the superintendents' reports of the 1850s and 1860s were plainly, in the minds of some educators at least, the children of cities. Daniel Wilson claimed in 1868 that the poor "street Arabs" who were the cause of so much concern during that decade were really only to be found in Ontario in the streets of Toronto and Hamilton. Whether or not this was true, most educators agreed that the problems of such children were connected with what they called "city temptation" and believed that their formal education or re-education was essential if they were to be saved, or if society were to be safe from their depredations.[42]

Yet in spite of the problems presented by the apparently increased visibility of the children of the urban poor during the middle of the nineteenth century, it would be difficult to see in Upper Canada of the 1860s or even the 1870s a highly urbanized or industrialized society. In 1849, Ryerson described it as one in which trades were still for the most part carried on "by isolated individuals, or in small shops." Thus he argued for the education of mechanics who were, or ought to be, entrepreneurs, and therefore needed more than the simple skills that factory operatives needed elsewhere. Things were clearly changing, however. Canada's competitive situation *vis-a-vis* the United States demanded that economic change be vigorously pursued. Ryerson argued that because native skills and industry had not been developed, the country remained a backwater, a prey to foreign adventurers who had little or no interest in its welfare. When would Canadians wake up to the fact that in "these hard times of sharp and skillful competition and sleepless activity," hard work was no longer enough, that as society advanced, education, as well as enterprise, were essential?[43] The two things went together. Commercial development and the rapid growth of cities may have presented Upper Canada with the problems of vagrant children and an apparent increase in certain kinds of crimes. But cities also meant opportunities, opportunities for more commerce and industrial development, and also for new approaches to schooling. Cities, for all their depravity, were essential to both economic and educational progress, as understood by most nineteenth century reformers of schools.

Upper Canadian school promoters thus tended to paint a somewhat contradictory picture of their society. They believed that vast numbers of Upper Canadians had come to the country ignorant; that the increasingly urban environment somehow encouraged their depravity; and that the growing competitiveness of the economy, the need for local self-government and the threat of crime, meant that Upper Canada could no longer allow them to remain in this state. But the glorious future held out for Canada was nevertheless one of growth: economic growth, the growth of population, cities and towns.[44] If rapid growth and change, immigration and urbanization were the root causes of apathy and social disorder in the province, most educators did not wish to dwell on this fact. These, after all, were the very changes that they were busy promoting.

When looking for causes, they tended to look elsewhere, placing the blame instead on human weakness and inadequacy. Increasingly they also blamed the traditional institutions of social and moral education, the churches, the family and the schools. Since progress, competition and social change were considered both desirable and inevitable, it was to these institutions that educators looked for solutions to the social stress and disorganization that they saw around them. Yet they felt that there was a great deal wrong with all three. Fundamental Christianity was swallowed up in the outrages of sectarian controversy, while neither families nor schools seemed sufficiently strong to cope with the new demands made on them.

The proliferation of denominations very much complicated educational debate in the nineteenth century; very often, indeed, it was also the case that educational questions were right at the core of denominational conflict. The opposition of Egerton Ryerson and his fellow Methodists to the Church of England in the 1820s and 1830s came in part from the belief, which they shared with reformers of other persuasions, that the church had retarded the progress of education in Upper Canada by its attempted monopoly. Anglicans like John Strachan, on their side, accused the Methodists and other "enthusiasts" of undermining true religion, education and the social order in the province. Eventually Protestants of all sorts tended to unite, as the separate school agitation got underway in the 1850s, in opposition to the role played by the Roman Catholic Church in Upper Canadian education. Rivalry among the province's churches and sects and the perceived difficulty, in a multi-denominational society, of granting special privileges to the members of any one denomination, led school men such as Ryerson to place less and less emphasis on the public role of the churches. More and more they tended to stress the privacy and separateness of the churches and their role as family institutions, and to look elsewhere for solutions to Upper Canada's most pressing educational problems.[45] Although many continued somewhat ambiguously to insist on an important role for religious institutions in the education of young men and women in residential colleges,[46] it was to the state and its public, supposedly non-sectarian common schools that reformers increasingly looked for the schooling of the majority.

Mid-nineteenth century school reformers were equally hard on the institution of the family. They urged on the one hand that it become a protective and private retreat for its members, and on the other that it relinquish a considerable measure of its control over children to schools. Perhaps the protective ideal was best expressed in Upper Canada by an artisan named Walter Eales, in a lecture to the Toronto Mechanics' Institute, which took place in 1851. In this lecture, the author stressed the importance of the artisan's home. Families, he explained, were the "arks" that sheltered mankind "from the raging tumults and storms of life." For husbands returning from work that was often among strangers, they provided an oasis of calm, while for children embarking on their own lives, they gave fortification against the coming encounter with the world. Egerton Ryerson, for his part, urged the household to improve itself, in order to live up to this ideal. The family ought to provide the "social enjoyments" that children needed, if the parents wished to protect their offspring from the "snares and dangers" of seeking such enjoyments abroad.[47] The ideal family was thus portrayed as a safe harbour in a dangerous world.

At the same time, however, school promoters attacked the family as educationally inadequate. Parents were criticized for failing to take the education of their children sufficiently seriously. Above all, they were urged to send their children more often and more regularly to school. As the *Journal of Education* put it in 1854, there were in Upper Canada selfish parents who, "on the slightest pretext or pressure of business," kept their children out of school, starving their intellects "in order to enrich their own pockets." The practice of employing children in this way was clearly less and less acceptable to many of the promoters of schools, above all in regions where, after 1850, common schooling had become free. By the mid-1860s Egerton Ryerson was arguing that parents should see their duty to have their children educated as more imperative than their obligation to see them clothed and fed.[48]

As school promoters became more critical of traditional institutions and their failure to meet the educational needs of Upper Canadian children, they gradually began to redefine the roles of these institutions in the nurture and education of the young. Increasingly, the formal training of children was seen to be the function less of families and churches, although these remained vital, than of the state, acting through a transformed system of public schools – schools that would now be defined as public institutions in the modern sense of the term, not just because they were publicly financed, but because they had a public function to perform. This function was the social, moral, intellectual and economic elevation of a generation of Upper Canadians who, improved through proper education, would be the equals of their neighbours and no longer mere "hewers of wood and drawers of water" for those better educated than they. In this way, the promoters of mass public schooling in Upper Canada attempted to deal with a world whose outstanding characteristics seemed to be competition, disorder and potential decline, to make sure that from the economic and social upheavals of the mid-century, Upper Canadians would emerge on top and take their proper place among the economically prosperous and morally advanced peoples of the western world.

NOTES

[1]"The Influence of a Good School House," JEUC, XXI (September, 1868), 136.

[2]For discussions of early labour unrest in Canada, see H. C. Pentland, "The Lachine Strike of 1843," *Canadian Historical Review,* XXIX (September, 1948), 255-77; and Steven Langdon, "The Emergence of the Canadian Working Class Movement, 1845-1875," *Journal of Canadian Studies,* VIII (May, 1973), 3-13 and (August, 1973), 8-26. A recent discussion of the Irish famine migration and its effect on Canada may be found in Kenneth Duncan, "Irish Famine Immigration and the Social Structure of Canada West," *Canadian Review of Sociology and Anthropology,* II (February, 1965), 19-40. The political, social and cultural climate of Canada in the early and mid-century years is described in the works of Gerald M. Craig, J. M. S. Careless and S. F. Wise. See especially Craig, *Upper Canada: The Formative Years, 1784-1841* (Toronto, 1963); Careless, "Mid-Victorian Liberalism in Central Canadian Newspapers, 1850-1867," *Canadian Historical Reveiw,* XXIX, (March, 1948) and *Union of the Canadas: The Growth of Canadian Institutions, 1841-1857* (Toronto, 1967); Wise, "God's Chosen People," in W. L. Morton, ed., *The Shield of Achilles: Aspects of Canada in the Victorian Age* (Toronto, 1968), "Sermon Literature and Canadian Intellectual History," in J. M. Bumsted, ed., *Canadian History before Confederation: Essays and Interpretations* (Georgetown, Ont., 1972) and S. F. Wise & Robert Craig Brown, *Canada Views the United States: Nineteenth-Century Political Attitudes* (Toronto, 1967).

[3]Ryerson to John Macaulay, 16 January 1850, RG 2 C1, Letterbook E, p. 107, PAO; *Annual Report for 1864,* Part I, p. 25.

[4]"Proceedings of the Annual Convention of the Ontario Teachers' Association, 1869," DHE, XXI, 296-97.

[5]"Dr. Wilson's Address," JEUC, XVIII (October, 1865), 147.

[6]*Canadian Gem,* II (February, 1849), 50.

[7]*Annual Report for 1856,* Appendix A, p. 144; *Annual Report for 1866,* Appendix A, p. 14.

[8]"Lord Elgin at the Toronto University Convocation of 1849," DHE, VIII, 263.

[9]Egerton Ryerson, *The Clergy Reserves Question; as a Matter of*

History – a Question of Law – and a Subject of Legislation; in a Series of Letters to the Hon. W. P. Draper (Toronto, 1839), p. 93; Ryerson to the Rev. Dr. Bangs, 10 May 1841, cited in Sissons, ed., *Egerton Ryerson,* I, 577.

[10]Rev. James Williamson, "Historical Survey of Education in Upper Canada," DHE, III, 298.

[11]Ryerson to W. Elliot, Esq., 31 December 1846, RG 2 C l, Letterbook C, p. 163, PAO.

[12]Ryerson to Hon. Hamnet Pinhey, 15 February 1848, RG 2 Cl, Letterbook D, p. 163, PAO; *Annual Report for 1847,* Part I, pp. 5 and 10; Ryerson to the *Globe,* May 1848, RG 2 Cl, Letterbook D, p. 232, PAO.

[13]"The Importance of Education to a Manufacturing and a Free People," JEUC, I (October, 1848), 292-93.

[14]See for example Table F in Part II of the *Annual Report for 1853.*

[15]"The Importance of Education to a Manufacturing and a Free People," JEUC, I (October, 1848), 292-93.

[16]"Bishop Strachan on the Common School Acts of 1841 and 1843," DHE, XVI, 270.

[17]*Annual Report for 1847,* Appendix 4, p.84; *Annual Report for 1848,* Part I, p.38.

[18]"School Architecture," JEUC II (May, 1849), 73; "Free Schools in the City of Toronto," JEUC, II (June, 1849), 96.

[19]"Educational Intelligence: Canada," JEUC XVI (March, 1861), 47; Hodgins to the Warden of the Municipal Councils of the Counties of Peel and York, 5 February 1856, DHE, XII, 90-91.

[20]*Annual Report for 1857,* Part I, p.47.

[21]"Educational Progress in Upper Canada," JEUC, VII (September, 1854), 148; "The Universal Education of the People," JEUC, X (January, 1857), 9.

[22]Sissons, ed., *Egerton Ryerson, I, 537-38.*

[23]*Annual Report for 1847,* Part I, p. 22; J. George Hodgins, ed., *Ryerson Memorial Volume,* (Toronto, 1889), p. 91.

[24]"Bishop Fraser's Estimate of the Upper Canada System of Education in 1863," DHE XVIII, 99; "Ontario Teachers' Association Convention in 1869," DHE XXI, 294; *Annual Report for 1856,* Appendix A, p. 146.

[25]Alison Smith, "John Strachan and Early Upper Canada, 1799-1814" *Ontario History,* LII (1960). See also the perceptive studies of Canadian opinion and ideology by S. F. Wise, cited in footnote 2.

[26]Sissons, ed., *Egerton Ryerson,* I, 15; *Claims of the Churchmen and Dissenters* (Kingston, 1828), p. 51; *Special Report of the Measures which have been adopted for the establishment of a Normal School; and for Carrying into Effect Generally, The Common School Act (9th Vict. Cap XX) with an Appendix, by the Chief Superintendent of the Schools for Upper Canada* (Montreal, 1847), pp. 14-15; "Lecture on the Social Advancement of Canada," JEUC, II (December, 1849), 122; *The School Book Question: Letters in Reply to the Brown-Campbell Crusade against the Education Department* (Montreal, 1866), p.11.

[27]*Letters from the Reverend Egerton Ryerson to the Hon. and Rever-*

end Doctor Strachan, published originally in the Upper Canada Herald (Kingston, 1828), p.30.

[28]See for example the *Annual Report for 1848,* Part I, p.33.

[29]*Annual Report for 1860,* Part I, p.14; Ryerson to Draper, 20 April, 1846; Ryerson to Hodgins, 16 October 1850, in Sissons, ed., *Egerton Ryerson,* II, 101-02, 199.

[30]*Annual Report for 1866,* Part I, pp. 36-37.

[31]DHE, II, 110.

[32]*The Clergy Reserves Question,* p. 122; The Colborne Memorial, 1848, RG 2 C-6-C, p. 2, PAO; Clipping from the Toronto *Examiner,* 23 February 1853, RG 2T, PAO.

[33]R. B. Sullivan, *Lecture . . . on the Connection between Agriculture and Manufactures . . .* (Hamilton, 1848), pp. 4-5, 35-36; JEUC, XXI (September, 1868), 136-37; Ryerson, *The New Canadian Dominion: Dangers and Duties of the People in Regard to their Government* (Toronto, 1867), p.7.

[34]J. K. Johnston to Ryerson, April 1859, RG 2 C-6-C, PAO.

[35]Helen I. Cowan, *British Immigration to British North America: The First Hundred Years* (Toronto, 1961), p. 200; "First Report of the Select Committee on Education, 1833," DHE, II, 143; Sullivan, *Lecture . . . on the Connection between Agriculture and Manufactures,* p. 11; "The Importance of Education to a Manufacturing and a Free People," JEUC, I (October, 1848), 299-300.

[36]Cowan, *British Immigration,* pp. 199-200.

[37]See *Letters to Strachan,* p. 29, and Egerton Ryerson to George Ryerson, 11 October 1830, in Sissons, ed., *Egerton Ryerson,* I, 125-26, 262. Sissons notes that the *Guardian* Office (which was also evidently Ryerson's place of residence) was at that time on March Street, dubbed later by Scadding "a thoroughfare of ill repute."

[38]*Circular of the Upper Canada Academy* (Cobourg, 1841), pp. 14-16.

[39]W. C. Bourne, *History of the Public School Society of the City of New York* (New York, 1870), p. 17; *The Connecticut Common School Journal,* II (January, 1840), 87-88; James McLachlan, *American Boarding Schools;* Wise & Brown, *Canada Views the United States,* pp. 39-40.

[40]Sissons, ed., *My Dearest Sophie,* letter dated 6 June 1866, p. 94; "The Importance of Education to an Agricultural, a Manufacturing and a Free People," DHE, VII, 142-44 and 148.

[41]*Annual Report for 1850,* Appendix VI, No. 14, p. 302.

[42]*Annual Report for 1847*, Appendix 3, p. 77; *Annual Report for 1849,* Part I, p. 52 and "Compulsory Education and the Repression of Juvenile Crime," DHE, XX, 263, 269. See also Susan Houston, "The Victorian Origins of Juvenile Delinquency," in Katz and Mattingly, eds., *Education and Social Change,* pp. 83-109.

[43]"Canadian Mechanics and Manufactures," JEUC, II (February, 1849), 19-20, 23; "The Importance of Education to a Manufacturing and a Free People," JEUC, I (October, 1848), 299.

[44]Unsigned editorial JEUC, VI (December, 1853), 182.

[45]See Alison Prentice, "Education and the Metaphor of the Family:

The Upper Canadian Example," in Katz and Mattingly, eds., *Education and Social Change,* especially p. 119; Sissons, ed., *Egerton Ryerson,* II, 268.

[46]Egerton Ryerson never quite resolved the contradiction between his promotion of state controlled elementary education and church controlled residential colleges. See "The Methodist Conference Memorial to the Legislature, 1859," DHE, XIV, 228; "The University Question in a Series of Letters, 1861," DHE, XVI, 289 and *Extracts from the Chief Superintendent's Report for 1857,* pp. 27-28.

[47]Prentice, "Education and the Metaphor of the Family," pp. 116-20.

[48]*Ibid.,* p. 118.

Chapter 3

Education and the Creation of a Respectable Class

Wherever the present school system has been for any time in successful operation, the effects are strikingly visible in the improved manners and conversation of the young, in their taste for reading, and their advanced state of preparation for the duties and business of life.

Rev. James L. Alexander,
Barton, Wentworth County,
1863[1]

The social and economic ambitions that accompanied Upper Canadian educational reform were rooted in the fear that an inferior status was in fact to be the fate of the country. Educators voiced similar fears on behalf of individual Canadians and their families, whose futures seemed often to be equally precarious. The times were unstable. All too easily, it appeared, even the affluent and comfortable could slip into poverty, dependency and disgrace.[2] On the other hand, school promoters genuinely believed that it was possible for individuals and families to rise in the world. Education was at once the best means to rise and the only real insurance against social and economic decline.

When they talked about schooling and status, school promoters did so at two levels. On the first, they offered schooling as an almost certain avenue to upward mobility, to individual as well as class betterment. On another, they promoted education itself as the sign and symbol of success. On this second level, formal schooling became a barrier, for, if with it one was sure to get ahead and join the respectable classes of society, the other side of the coin was that without it, a drop in social and economic status seemed almost inevitable.

These attitudes to the relationship between education and class reflected changing perceptions of social structure which seem to have occurred in most western countries during the nineteenth century. This was the transition from society perceived as a multi-level, hierarchical and rather static structure of interdependent ranks, to the idea that increasingly the community was made up of two great classes only, classes that were potentially if not actually hostile to one another. Harold Perkin, in his *Origins of Modern English Society,* points out that the former view of social relations was representative of a basically agricultural economy, geographically organized in small villages and towns, while the latter emerged with the development of the modern industrial nation and large cities. Where pre-industrial thought made much of the multitudinous and fixed "orders" of human society, and assumed considerable contact and dependency between people of differing ranks, many nineteenth century people were beginning to think of the world as divided into two increasingly alien camps: the respectable, proprietary or "middle" classes on the one hand, and, on the other, the propertyless lower classes or the labouring poor.[3]

The dualism inherent in Victorian educators' ideas about human and child nature was thus carried over into a world view in which fundamental distinctions were made not only between "civilized" and "savage" societies, but also within any given society, between the respectable classes and the lower orders. What school promoters contributed to this idea was that it was education, more than anything else, that made the difference. Their belief in this was fundamental to their belief in and promotion of schools. For in these schools lay the hope, they were certain, of individual and class as well as collective social advancement.

But the schools had yet another function related to class. For as nineteenth century educators came increasingly to see the world in this way, they also became more and more concerned about the potential for conflict between the two great classes of society. What was to prevent the poor from robbing or murdering the rich? Was there a real likelihood of class war and, if so, could it be contained? Their answer, once again, was to turn to the schools as the institutions best adapted to promote peace in the community, to foster good relations between rich and poor.

Educators, then, not only subscribed to the opinion that their society was divided into two great, mutually-hostile classes, but they also promoted it. By continually dividing the world into the "educated" and the "uneducated," they gradually enhanced the apparent value of their product, which was increasingly accepted by Upper Canadians as by other North Americans and Europeans in the mid-nineteenth century, as the best hope for individual and class improvement, as well as for the betterment of the nation at large.

The view that society is divided into social classes presupposes a set of values whereby members of different classes can be distinguished from one another. What were these values as far as the promoters of schools were concerned? How did they perceive class differences in mid-nineteenth century Upper Canada? There is no simple answer to such questions, for attitudes undoubtedly varied from one part of the province to another and the ideas of native British North Americans differed somewhat from those of recent arrivals from the Old Country. The educators themselves were by no means a homogeneous group, representing only one view of class. Nevertheless, it is possible to identify in their writings a number of central themes. And the most prominent of these, as well as a concern that was of overriding importance in mid-nineteenth century attitudes to education, was their interest in respectability. The word "respectable" appears over and over in their works as a positive value, while "want of respectability" was an absence to be deplored.

"Respectability", in its turn, had to be defined. Upper Canadian school promoters certainly associated the concept with a number of character traits, and were willing to argue that a "respectable" person was a person who was modest, honest or kind. But they also believed that, in order to distinguish the civilized from the uncivilized members of society, visible signs too were necessary; and that the promotion of such signs was one of the essential functions of schools. The manifestations of respectability that they praised and promoted were refined manners and taste, respectable religion, proper speech and, finally, the ability to read and write proper English. In addition, both the concept and actual possession of private property were sometimes portrayed as distinguishing not only civilized from savage societies, but within a given social order, the respectable from the lower classes.

It was John Strachan's attack on the respectability of Methodists which had so stung Egerton Ryerson in the 1820s. "I am far from undervaluing education, or speaking lightly of refinement," he had replied. "I believe these things to be the greatest earthly blessings that we can possess." Twenty years later, the *Journal of Education for Upper Canada* took up among its many other campaigns the promotion of good manners in Upper Canada. Articles dealing with the subject generally were printed along with specific advice on such matters as the use of calling cards, and readers were reminded that civil manners led to financial as well as social success. Bad habits acquired early in life, it was pointed out, could cause the loss of reputation later on; impressions were constantly being produced "by one's slightest actions." A local superintendent wrote to congratulate Ryerson in 1850 on the success of the *Journal.* It was promoting education among the people, he said, and education, in turn, was promoting not only their comfort but their "respectability."[4]

The relationship between schooling and refinement of manners was almost taken for granted, but occasionally educators tried to show how specific influences achieved the desired end. In his first extensive report on the Upper Canadian school system in 1846, for example, Ryerson cited both American and European authorities on the value of music in the common schools. It was agreed that it had great powers to "humanize, refine and elevate" whole communities. Attractive school buildings, classrooms and grounds were also considered essential to the development of taste. The Hamilton Grammar School authorities were among those who showed particular concern on this point in the late 1860s, and frequent references in the annual reports of grammar school inspectors and common school superintendents testify to their growing belief that unattractive buildings or squalid surroundings had a very unfortunate effect on the "taste" as well as the "feelings" of the scholars.[5]

The impressions made by people on the pupils was of course even more important than the impact of the physical environment. Ryerson deliberately solicited the occasional presence of gentlemen of "high public standing" at Victoria College as a way of influencing the "tastes and feelings" as well as the ambitions of the boys, and hoped that the publication of their remarks to the scholars would similarly influence the general public. Above all, educators were concerned about the impressions made by the teacher on his students. "We are creatures of imitation," a local superintendent pointed out, "and children especially will adopt more or less the habits and manners of those who are placed over them." Ryerson, in his turn, once cited a man's "gentlemanly manners and address" as the sole reason for recommending him over other possible candidates for a teaching post in Montreal.[6] Books also had class appeal. The mere presence of books was held to operate against "profanity and levity" by one Education Office correspondent, and another considered the bindings and illustrations of books as important as their contents in humanizing and refining the minds of young readers.[7]

The concern was quickly translated into direct intervention to regulate both the appearance and behaviour of children in schools. Some of the early schools had written regulations on these matters. The Upper Canada Academy, for one, ruled in 1841 that strict attention would be paid to the manners of the students and that spitting, writing on the walls and "slovenliness" were strictly forbidden. By mid-century similar efforts were clearly being made in the common and grammar school systems of the province. The work of John S. Tidey, the superintendent from Oxford County, was probably typical and was apparently effective. In 1861, Tidey reported a great improvement in the common schools under his supervision. Copy books were now kept clean and handwriting was generally more tasteful. As far as slate work was concerned, "unfinished figures at every degree of obliquity ploughed in the greasy dirt" were everywhere replaced by "neatness, parallelism and taste."[8] Great exertions had obviously been made by someone. But it was not just writing that had to be clean, neat and in good taste. Of far greater importance were the appearance and manners of the students themselves, as provincial and local efforts to regulate such things imply. At the Model Grammar School in Toronto, it was announced that "personal neatness" would be "insisted upon" and every effort made to "induce a high tone of feeling and to cultivate openness and manliness of conduct among the pupils." In 1867, rules governing all model schools in Upper Canada were published in the *Journal of Education.* The pupils were to present themselves at school "neat and clean in their persons and dress, with hands and face washed, hair combed, shoes polished, etc.," and all who failed to "exhibit the most marked attention to these particulars" would be sent home at once. Textbooks hammered home the theme. As Ryerson pointed out in *First Lessons in Agriculture,* a "dirty person cannot be a good Christian, apart from consideration of comfort and decency."[9]

His own concern with outward appearances sometimes worried Ryerson. In 1824, he admitted to himself that he thirsted too much "for the honours of the world," and throughout his life he sought a spiritual rebirth that was more than "the mere growth of intellectual and social culture." To his children, he expressed concern that while they aimed at what was "most accomplished and refined in the world," they should also seek and secure "above all things *conscious* adoption as children of God." It was important to him that his family avoid ostentation and snobbery, as well as spiritual shallowness, in the pursuit of respectability.[10]

But it was very difficult to distinguish religious from social attitudes, for the two were inextricably bound together in nineteenth century Upper Canada. To begin with, according to the prevailing ideology, a gentleman was almost by definition a Christian. This was certainly a major reason for the anxiety expressed on nearly every side to increase the "Christian character" of popular education during the mid-century years. Proper religious feeling, educators believed, led almost inevitably to proper behavior.[11]

The various denominations furthermore had distinct class associations. In the nineteenth century, the word "class" itself was often used to mean "denomination" or "sect" and, from the earliest days in Upper Canada, the opposition of established churchmen like John Strachan to Methodists and other radical sects was clearly informed by their disapproval of the social behaviour of non-conformists. True Christianity, Strachan had claimed in 1807, knew no class, but by this he must have meant that all were welcome in the true church as long as they didn't behave like "enthusiasts." Non-conformists, in his view, were unrestrained and even licentious; he was convinced that they sought power rather than true religious enlightenment. The Scottish schoolmaster was no doubt less prejudiced against what he called "the Scotch Church," but even among its members he doubted if any could be found "of sufficient standing and leisure" to become efficient members of the King's College Council in 1837.[12]

Ryerson was not dreaming, then, when he blamed Strachan in the 1820s for stigmatizing non-conformists as socially inferior. And Strachan only added insult to injury, apparently, by claiming that the more respectable non-conformists usually ended up joining the Church of England.[13]

The Methodists, along with other religious groups, fought back with every weapon they could find. In 1828 Ryerson's main concern was to prove that Anglicans had no real claim to superior status as a class. Did the church really believe that her members were less disposed "to profaneness, to gambling, etc." than others? Were they really "more exemplary, upright and pious than any other class in the community?" Comments made in the 1840s imply, however, that the barbs had in fact hit home; perhaps the Methodists and Presbyterians really were inferior. But was it fair to accuse them of a "want of science and literature" and then to deprive them of the means of obtaining the same? It was as if "a man were bound in chains, and was then reproached by his oppressors for being a slave."[14] The Methodists, meanwhile, spurred on by Ryerson and those who shared his feelings, worked hard to improve themselves. Ministers were charged with

71

the duty of keeping up with "the intellectual progress of society," and the soul-searching zeal of pioneer days was gradually played down in favour of the respect for family privacy and reserve associated with respectability. Piety in childhood, Ryerson observed in 1854, was better than the reformation of the adult, and respectable family religion, therefore, better than revivalism. From the forties on, Ryerson also seemed anxious to make his peace personally with the Church of England. He wrote to Draper on the eve of his appointment as Chief Superintendent of Schools that he would do all that he could to see that leading Anglicans obtained that consideration in the school system which "their intelligence and standing in the community" justly warranted. While such a statement carried no obligation whatever, it indicated a willingness at least to develop more amicable relations with his former enemies, for the sake of peace or power.[15]

By the time he was appointed superintendent, the Methodists were well on their way to leaving their lower class status behind them, and Ryerson's attention shifted to other matters. The great religious issue of the 1850s was the pressing problem of separate schools, which to many Upper Canadians was also a class issue. The Roman Catholic Bishop, Alexander Macdonell, had complained as early as 1830 that the Catholics of Upper Canada, "for want of education," were made "hewers of wood and drawers of water" to people who themselves had come to the country adventurers and beggars. He had even warned the authorities at home of the possible disgust that might be felt by an upper class missionary confronted with "the manners and habits of the lukewarm, selfish and semi-barbarous Catholics of Canada." The image was no better in the 1840s, when his nephew, Angus Macdonell, was soliciting funds for the College of Regiopolis. Roman Catholics, the latter argued in 1846, were still the poorest people in the province, and none too loyal, as a result of the poverty and injustice that many had suffered under British rule in Ireland.[16]

Egerton Ryerson shared Macdonell's view of the situation and, to some extent, even his sympathy for the Irish or at least for the Irish in Ireland. He was also convinced that it was only through education that Roman Catholics could improve their social and economic position in Upper Canada. But it was Ryerson's opinion that the Catholic Bishop of Toronto, the French aristocrat Armand de Charbonnel, had, from the time of his arrival in the province in 1850, pursued a course that was bound to deprive his co-religionists of any hope of improvement. This course was his persistence in demanding more and more privileges for Roman Catholic separate schools.

If Catholics insisted on promoting these schools, Ryerson wrote to Charbonnel in 1852, they doomed themselves and their descendents "to a hopeless inferiority in comparison with other classes of their fellow citizens," to a "state of vassalage and degradation" in a free country. The public schoolhouses of Upper Canada, he argued, were equally the property of all classes within the community and should be used as such. Finally it was to the advantage of Roman Catholics to attend the common schools in Toronto particularly because, although they made up a quarter of the population there, they paid only a twelfth of the taxes. This was true, in spite of the fact that "the wealth of the Roman Catholics, in proportion to their numbers, compares as favourably with that of the Protestants in the City of Toronto, as in any other municipality in Upper Canada." The Roman Catholics, it would then appear, were not really poorer than anyone else. They were merely determined to bring lower class status and poverty on themselves, by attending separate schools. If they became "hewers of wood and drawers of water" to their fellow citizens instead of rivalling them in "intelligence, mental power, enterprise, wealth, individual influence and public position," in Ryerson's view, they had only themselves, the church and the separate schools to blame.[17]

The church ignored Ryerson's predictions and campaigned vigorously for the separate schools. Especially in the cities, they increased in number throughout the 1850s and, by 1857, even Ryerson had accepted them as an inescapable fact.[18] But his acquiescence occurred against a background of continuing strife. Throughout the mid-century years, Protestants and Catholics alike sought arbitration for local disputes from the Chief Superintendent of Schools, and some of these disputes ended with the anger of the contestants from both sides directed at himself.

In one such case, a Protestant school superintendent allegedly persecuted a group of recent Roman Catholic immigrants, first by attempting to foist on them a missionary of his own church as teacher of their new school, and then by refusing to pay the provincial money to the Roman Catholic teacher that the trustees had chosen to replace his man. The priest who had paid the Catholic teacher out of his own pocket became involved in a lengthy and increasingly irate correspondence with Ryerson over the whole issue, and concluded that no justice was to be had for Roman Catholic schools in the province. But, on an earlier occasion, the shoe had been on the other foot. In this case, Roman

Catholics allegedly hired a gang of vagrants to swing the vote in a local school board election to their side, and failing to accomplish this, not only caused all the furniture in the school room to be broken up, but succeeded in depriving the Protestant teacher of his fair share of the provincial money by returning 314 children for their new separate school, when the census had shown only 173 Roman Catholic children in the section. The Protestant teacher claimed to have received no sympathy from the local superintendent and despaired equally of getting justice from the provincial Education Office.[19]

Ryerson's usual response when first confronted with crises of this sort was that ignorance of local circumstances disqualified him to judge the situation fairly, and that he would have to be more fully informed in order to give useful advice. But of the fundamental cause of such disturbances he was quite certain, and on a number of occasions he said what he thought. The Roman Catholics, he argued, usually were too poor and ignorant to run their own schools. In Lower Canada, the separate schools were more successful, as he informed the Governor-General confidentially in 1858, because the Protestants to whom they belonged were "more intelligent and more wealthy," and knew better "how to proceed and manage their affairs" than did the Upper Canadian Roman Catholic supporters of separate schools, especially in the rural parts of the western province:

> This poverty and ignorance on the part of a great portion of the supporters of Separate Schools in Upper Canada is not so apparent, or so much felt, when they are associated with other classes of the inhabitants in the management of local affairs; but when they stand out isolated from other classes, as they do in Separate School matters, from the intelligent counsel of Local School Superintendents, and the co-operation of Municipal Councils, their inexperience and incapacity become perfectly obvious.[20]

The point was made publicly in the *Annual Report for 1858*. If the Roman Catholic separate schools were "of little account," it was because their supporters were "less concerned and energetic in the education of their children" than the supporters of public schools.[21] The proper solution to poverty and ignorance was education, but Ryerson doubted its value when the poor and ignorant tried to run their own schools.

In the meantime, as we have seen, respectable religion was pushed in the common schools, partly as a result of the apparent reluctance of the churches to do the job themselves, and partly because of charges from both Protestant and Roman Catholic groups that the schools were "Godless." During a brief period in 1862, when Ryerson seemed tempted to support the idea of separate government-financed charity schools for all denominations willing or able to instruct the poor, the chief superintendent admitted that all religious instruction must be sectarian in the sense that it was given by a member of some sect. But nevertheless he and his supporters steadfastly claimed that the opening and closing prayers and Bible reading that the Education Office and local superintendents pressed on the schools were essential, and that the common schools remained "non-denominational" because by law no child was compelled to participate in such exercises.[22]

At least a few contemporary observers, however, thought otherwise and most historians would agree that it was active Protestantism in mid-century schools which drove the Roman Catholic Church to insist on a separate system.[23] John A. Murdock, from Lanark County, was probably one of the few local superintendents who attempted to reverse the trend in Upper Canada, arguing that there was "very little sense" in forcing religious exercises on anyone, since separate schools arose from trustees insisting on opening and closing prayers against the wishes of Roman Catholic parents. Ryerson, on his side, claimed that Protestant religious activities in the schools were the result rather than the cause of Roman Catholic withdrawal.[24]

Whatever the answer to this conundrum, it is clear from mid-nineteenth century discussions of the whole separate school question that respectable religion, education and status all went together, and that all three were only to be obtained in respectable schools, which to many Protestants and certainly to Egerton Ryerson did not include the separate schools of the Roman Catholic minority. Renewed agitation on the subject in the 1860s resulted in a heated statement from the chief superintendent in 1865. The separate schools, he had concluded by this time, were an "incubus" on the Roman Catholic population of the province. The youth who attended them were not only excluded from the advantages of better schools, but were "deprived of those springs of mental development, activity and energy" which came with the opportunity to compete with other youth of the land. The result was that "inferiority of mental culture and development" was stamped forever upon the mass of the community that was thus isolated.[25]

If the right sort of schooling and respectable religion, manners and appearance constituted important avenues to status, it did not escape the notice of educators that the right sort of language was another. A lower class position was clearly associated in their minds with "inferior" patterns of speech as well as the inability to read or write. Consequently, pressures for "improvement" in the arts of speech and written communication became intense. They were exerted on all of the people associated with the schools – pupils and teachers, school trustees and superintendents alike. All were urged to aspire to uniform, improved standards of English pronunciation and writing.

Egerton Ryerson devoted a large part of his inaugural address at Victoria College in 1842 to a discussion of the power and prestige that came with correct and fluent speech. It was essential, he told the Victoria students, that they aim for "purity and propriety" in the use of the English language. Through serious study and the reading of the classics, Ryerson explained, they could look forward to achieving not only a correct and elegant style, "but that rich variety of language" which gave one man "so great an advantage over another:"

> Speech is the great instrument of intercourse between man and man; and he who can speak well, both in public and in private, on all subjects in which he may be concerned, possesses a power more enviable and formidable than that of the sword; he possesses an empire over *mind*, the more admirable as it is entirely voluntary, – the more elevated as it is the force of reason in man's immortal nature, – the more formidable as it controls the very springs of human action. Knowledge itself cannot properly be said to be power, without the appropriate power to communicate it.[26]

In his first report on the school system, written a few years later, the superintendent of schools took a slightly different tack. Language was still important, but "pompous spouting" and rigidity of grammar were to be avoided as unnatural, for language was not founded on grammar but the reverse. Common school children ought first to be taught to speak and write their native language properly – afterwards they might be taught to use it with elegance and force. Certainly at a later date the Reverend James Porter agreed, as a result of his experience as superintendent of schools in the city of Toronto, that little more could be expected in the speech of common school children than "simple accuracy." Grace and elegance were beyond most of them.[27] But some account must also be taken of a growing preference on the part of Ryerson and many of his contemporaries for the natural and the plain, for a common form of expression to which all classes, in theory, might aspire.

For the artisan no less than the scholar was urged to seek a higher station in society. This supposed that he too would take instruction in "the grammar or structure of his native tongue," Ryerson argued, since he presumed that no one thought that "the mechanic, any more than other professional men, should be a murderer of the QUEEN'S English all the days of his life." If artisans wished to live up to the ideal of respectability, they had to strive for respectable English. But above all, they should not allow poor English to ruin their children's chances to get ahead. Incorrect or vulgar speech would "constitute an impassable gulf between the mechanic's sons and those rewards and positions of power and usefulness" to which they might aspire. Similar logic was applied to the farmer, and presumably to his sons. Shouldn't a farmer be able to speak his mother tongue "as well as any lawyer?" Ryerson asked.[28]

The campaign for improvement was carried on everywhere. By 1852, the Methodist conference had passed a resolution to the effect that no one should be received as a preacher who was not "well acquainted with the Grammar of the English language." The respectability of the church would be sought in part through the proper speech of its ministers.[29] School textbooks were also chosen with a view to improving the speech of school children. Dr. Thomas Rolph had argued as early as 1836 that American spelling books, dictionaries and grammars should be eliminated because they taught an "anti-British dialect and idiom," and among the reasons given by Ryerson in 1864 for preferring the Irish national readers to any others for Upper Canada, was their emphasis on correct "accentuation" and "intonation."[30]

A knowledge of grammar and good pronunciation was increasingly considered the key to success in the teaching profession, and shortcomings in this area interpreted as evidence of unsuitability for the occupation. The superintendent for the District of Gore in the late 1840s, Patrick Thornton, was especially sticky about this, and refused to grant certificates to people whose pronunciation he found "inaccurate," or who lacked "sufficient" grammar. In the case of a Mr. Wetham which came to Ryerson's attention in 1850, Thornton was especially annoyed because this "ignorant" teacher had kept out the qualified man that he, in his capacity as local superintendent, had sent to the people. Thornton refused to give Mr. Wetham a certificate or his share of the provincial fund.[31] Local superintendents continued in this vein throughout the 1850s and 60s. One cannot know if Thornton or Dr. M. F. Haney, the superintendent of schools from Humberstone in Welland County, were typical, but the latter at least certainly knew what he liked and what he did not like, and made detailed comments on the subject in 1864. He reported to Ryerson that even teachers with degrees in arts sometimes exhibited language that was "full of mispronunciations and grammatical errors," and urged that more pressure be brought to bear on teachers to improve both their pronunciation and grammar. "I like to hear the English language spoken in all its purity," said Haney. "I do not like to hear "*done*" and "*seen*" used for the past tense of "do" and "see", nor do I like to hear "*dooty*" and "*Institootion*," and "*but what*" used for a conjunction." That the pupils were to improve went without saying. The Reverend George Blair from Durham County felt that it was a serious mistake to let children get away with "national peculiarities in the utterance of vowel sounds," or "provincialisms."[32]

But the provincial Education Office had been pushing this for years. At the Normal School, a Mr. McArthur was suspended in 1849 as a result of an argument that started over the refusal of a professor to understand his pronunciation of the word "mean," the student evidently having said "mane"; and Ryerson included in an appendix to his annual report of 1854 a statement by Massachusetts Commissioner of Schools Barnas Sears that the common school had succeeded in ridding immigrant children of their Irish brogue.[33]

The *Journal of Education* gave somewhat contradictory advice to its readers. In 1849, it was pointed out in its pages that conversational powers were a deception; a host of famous men were quite deficient in "that fluency which often fascinates a promiscuous circle." But three months later the *Journal* advised that correct speaking was of critical importance to the average man. There was no one "however low in rank" who could not "materially benefit his financial condition" by speaking well, especially if at the same time he cultivated "such morals and manners as correspond with good words."[34] Once again, it was simplicity that was sought, the common denominator of a plain but grammatical English. Readers were advised to avoid the extremes of pomposity or too much elegance and fluency on the one hand, and vulgarity on the other.

The written as well as the spoken word was important. As the society became more and more dependent on written communication, a fact to which the educational system itself contributed in no small measure with its increasing reliance on written forms and instructions, the ability to write correctly became even more important than proper speech. Written examinations gradually replaced the oral questioning that had once done for the selection and certification of teachers, and grammar school inspectors pressed for provincial written entrance examinations for the grammar schools.[35] Ryerson also had a tool with which he could assess the relative merits of local superintendents and teachers with whom he was in correspondence. The above-mentioned Patrick Thornton suffered somewhat as a result, for Ryerson wished to know why, in the case of a widow named Mrs. Merry, the superintendent from Gore had felt justified in depriving her of her salary, when her letters to the Education Office did not "disadvantageously compare" with Thornton's own, and in fact were better composed and written than many he had received from more fully qualified teachers. Correspondence with the Education Office was examined for grammar and spelling, and the mistakes occasionally underlined, presumably by one of the chief superintendent's assistants or by Normal School Principal Robertson for quick identification by Ryerson. As Robertson pointed out in a memo to the latter in 1859, "the wording" of a Mr. Gallivan's letter, which had been dealt with in this way, "would scarcely entitle him to a second class certificate" and he doubted, on the basis of the letter, if Gallivan should be accepted at the Normal School.[36]

But if the pen was mightier than the sword, it was also a weapon that was available to everyone – everyone, that is, who could read and write. And if the accusation of poor grammar, spelling or pronunciation was increasingly hurled at teachers, they in turn used it with great effect against trustees and parents. In the 1830s it was common among the educated to make fun of the illiteracy of Upper Canadian legislators, but by mid-century one could almost imagine that the only people who could not read and write correctly in the province were common school trustees. Over and over again Ryerson heard from teachers on the subject. Perhaps no one was so incensed as Henry Lively, a disgruntled school-master who in 1846 was about to give up teaching after nearly fourteen years in the occupation in Upper Canada. The trustees in the Brantford area, Lively charged, were brutal, ignorant and lacking in discernment. These "ignorant boobies" not only dictated to the teacher the management of his school, they even insisted upon "an erroneous pronunciation of words." But, above all, many could themselves neither read nor write. Local superintendents also complained, as did E. William Cunningham, from Camden East in Addington County. He pointed out in 1862 that there were still some trustees who could not sign their own name. While conceding that this was not the general situation, he felt that one should not be surprised that, where it did prevail, trustees selected teachers who were cheap rather than teachers who knew how to run a school.[37]

In the schools themselves, superintendents, grammar school inspectors and interested parents, teachers and trustees turned to the question of English grammar and spelling with a vengeance. As Seabury Scovil, of Yonge and Escott Rear, Leeds County, reported in 1862 with what was probably the understatement of the century, "more attention is paid to the study of English grammar than formerly." Grammar was to be taught, in theory, in a natural way, avoiding rote learning and emphasizing ordinary usages, but it was to be increasingly stressed in both the common and the grammar schools. The grammar school inspectors noted with alarm that many teachers and children, even in the schools under their jurisdiction, did not really know their own language and concluded that the subject of English grammar was defectively taught in both kinds of school. In the grammar schools, possibly, it was too much sacrificed to the study of the classical languages. Things had come to a pretty pass when the English grammar of the students was actually better in the separate schools of the City of Hamilton than in the local grammar school, as one inspector was astonished to discover.[38]

It became a goal of the inspectors and the Education Office to make the ability to speak and write English correctly the primary criterion for admission into the grammar schools, and later to the high school and collegiate institutes created by the School Act of 1871. As early as 1850, an "acquaintance" with English grammar along with geography was added to the knowledge of reading, writing and arithmetic formally required for admission into the provincial Normal School.[39]

There appears to have been bitter debate on the local level. In one school section, a trustee marched into the school and forbade the teacher to teach his child *"that grammar"* as it was *"useless stuff."* In another, an argument developed over whether or not a teacher qualified to instruct the children in grammar should be hired. The majority in the school section were satisfied with the three R's only, but evidently some families who wanted their children taught grammar were very unhappy as a result.[40]

The ability to read and write and cast accounts had long been the basic goal for the students of common schools. But in the traditional schools, nevertheless, a great deal of the instruction had been oral, and only in the schools of the elite had intensive instruction in grammar of any kind been the rule. The growing emphasis on spelling and grammar, standards of speech and written communication for common school pupils signalled a growing belief in the importance of these things for everyone. The development of a provincial education system itself was accompanied by a proliferation in written communication on an almost unimaginable scale, based as it was on an ever-increasing flow of information between the provincial office and authorities on the local scene.

Educators promoted what they thought was a standard grammatical English. Included in their definition of what was acceptable seemed to be a pronunciation that was neither "lower class," American nor Irish; spelling and grammar that accorded with norms set in Department of Education-authorized spellers and grammars; and handwriting that was appropriately slanted, regular and neat.

That people should become anxious and ashamed when they lacked correct knowledge of language was the express intention of many educators. "Bad spelling is discreditable," the *Journal of Education* announced in 1853; and the year before Chief Justice John Beverley Robinson had predicted, in an address at the opening of the new Normal School buildings in Toronto, that literacy would eventually become so widespread that those unable to read and write would feel in a very inferior position.[41] As Ryerson once wrote to a Mr. William Mitchell, if the householders and landholders in a section insisted on electing illiterate trustees, it was they themselves who would have to bear "the disgrace," as well as the consequences of it, while the superintendent of schools from Oxford County, John Tidey, believed that the gradual development of a feeling of inadequacy in the people of a particular community in his county was a good sign. He noted in 1853 that they were not a reading people, being of humble origin. But among them were a few with "better education" whose example had the salutary effect of promoting among their inferiors not only "an admiration of mental attainment," but "a feeling of degradation for the want of it, and a desire to see remedied in their children" that which had been "so lamentably neglected in themselves."[42]

If the desire for improvement was the key to better language, and hence a more respectable social standing, it was also the key to the right approach to property. The very concept and existence of private property was what distinguished savage from civilized societies, according to opinions cited by Ryerson in his 1877 textbook on the *Elements of Political Economy*. The savage thought only of his daily wants, and saw no need for acquiring property.[43] It was also respect for private property that most clearly distinguished the respectable from the lower classes, according to many educators. One of the chief complaints made about the poor of Toronto in the 1860s, for example, was that they had little or no sense of property, tending to regard the region around them as "a kind of common" from which their children might pick up whatever they could, "towards the satisfaction of their very inconvenient cravings."[44]

Just as property was the mark of civilization, so too was the desire to acquire it. This urge, according to Ryerson's text, was co-existent with the dawn of intelligence in the individual. The savage knew little, and therefore wanted little; but as his knowledge increased, so did his desire for exchange. Ryerson believed therefore that there was a definite connection between education and the consumption of goods:

> A family or neighbourhood that never goes from home, or never opens the door of knowledge, will make but few exchanges, and remain stationary, and relatively retrograde from year to year, if not from generation to generation; but every one knows how the desire of exchange is awakened even in the bosom of a child the moment he enters a toy shop; how the desire of a reader for books is enkindled by his passing a few minutes in a book store; how the desire for a multitude of objects is created by reading and travel in our own and other countries.[45]

Such views were to be found at every level of opinion. According to Lord Elgin, the prosperity of the province was dependent in a great degree on the spread of intellectual culture, and the proof of prosperity was in the importation and sale of goods, especially of luxury items. David Mills, who was superintendent of schools in Camden, Chatham and a number of other localities in Kent County, observed in 1857 that the development of school libraries had had an important effect in "awakening new wants" among the people, wants which were not specified, but which he clearly felt were desirable in that they countered that "pernicious and immobile conservatism" which resisted all change, whether good or bad.[46]

The right to property soon followed the desire for it. In the history of societies, ownership of the land came with the application of labour to the land, or the development of agriculture, according to the Ryerson textbook on political economy. Even in savage societies, the savage had exclusive rights to his bows and arrows and to the game he had killed, proving that "he whose labour creates a value acquires the right of possessing it." The lessons that Ryerson drew from this opinion were essential to his whole concept of social order. The first was the general conclusion that human labour was the "true and only source of wealth." The second was that the "French Communist" or, as he put it, any other "war on property," was "a war against the first elements of civilization."[47] Finally, if the right to property came with labour, all who laboured ought in theory to be able to acquire some. Ryerson did not deny this, and, in fact, in an article published in 1852 stated that it was a principle of nearly all societies that each labourer ought to be assured "the fruits of his own industry." But, conversely, he who did not labour had the right to nothing; no man should expect to prosper without sweat.[48]

Certainly the possession of capital or property was what all men ought to aim for, in the opinion of an economist cited in Ryerson's 1877 text, although only "according to their position," a rather important qualification. The possession of property was not only equated with civilization, but was also the means of acquiring civilization. Property enabled a father to educate his children and to raise their condition above his own.[49]

As always, he returned to formal education. People were told to seek education, for education was the road to wealth; now they were told to seek wealth, as the means to a better education. A spiral of consumption was being set up. The more you had of one, the more you could get of the other. Whatever people sought, however, it ought to be "according to their position," or as befitted their current station in the social order, for no one should aim too high or for too much. It was in the striving rather than in the possession of "riches" or "exalted station" that real happiness was to be found.[50]

It was with this contradictory advice that Ryerson and many of his more education-oriented contemporaries attempted to reconcile the old with the new, a traditional hierarchical and comparatively static social order with a more fluid society, in which all were exhorted to advance. Education meant wealth and power and ought to be within the reach of every Upper Canadian, argued the *Canadian Gem and Family Visitor* in 1849.[51] Whether or not they truly thought this was so, educators at least agreed that education and wealth and power were intimately associated. Even "the lowest class of agriculturalists and mechanics," Ryerson claimed, could look forward to a better life and higher status as a result of schooling. The *Journal of Education* cited examples of men who had risen from being beggars, peasants, bricklayers and copying clerks to become leaders in their societies, and quoted an ambiguous statement from an English journal to the effect that while education was intended to elevate the character but not the station of the industrious classes, the former would inevitably lead to the latter.[52] In Canada, explained a local superintendent of schools in 1860, there was nothing wrong with the son of a poor man or labourer aspiring to an education and station above that of his parent, as this was quite in accord with the fact that "distinctions of wealth and birth" were disappearing.[53]

The message that Upper Canadian school promoters were attempting to get across in the end was this: he who sought "education" could join the ranks of the civilized and respectable classes of society, for schooling was intended to provide, or lead to the acquisition of, literacy, respectable speech and manners, respectable religion, and even real property. But the converse of this was that he who missed or ignored the opportunity for advancement through the right sort of schooling was doomed to an almost hopeless inferiority. He who did not go up, in the competitive nature of things, would almost certainly go down, to swell the ranks of the lower classes and the poor.

NOTES

[1] *Annual Report for 1863,* Appendix A, p. 126.

[2] On the fear of downward mobility in England during the same period see R. S. Neale, *Class and Ideology in the Nineteenth Century* (London, 1972), especially chapter 1. The instability of economic life and social status in one Upper Canadian city emerges in Michael B. Katz, *The People of Hamilton, Canada West: Family and Class in a Mid-Nineteenth Century City* (Cambridge, Mass., 1975), chapter 4.

[3] Harold J. Perkin, *The Origins of Modern English Society, 1780-1880* (London, 1969).

[4] *Claims of the Churchmen and Dissenters* (Kingston, 1828), p. 74; "Good Manners," JEUC, I (November, 1848), 334-35; Simon Newcomb to Ryerson, 17 May 1850, RG C-6-C, PAO.

[5] Egerton Ryerson, *Report on a System of Public Elementary Instruction* (Montreal, 1847), pp. 126-30; "The Hamilton Grammar School," JEUC, XX (March, 1867), 56; "The Inspectors' General Report on the State of the Grammar Schools in 1856," DHE, XII, 328.

[6] Ryerson to the Hon. W. H. Draper, DHE, IV, 220-21; *Annual Report for 1864,* Appendix A, p. 34; Ryerson to the Rev. Dr. Mackie, 30 July 1849, RG 2 C1, Letterbook E, p. 19, PAO.

[7] R. M. Merry to Ryerson, 23 May 1850, RG 2 C-6-C, PAO; *Annual Report for 1863,* Appendix A, p. 34.

[8] *Circular of the Upper Canada Academy,* (Cobourg, 1841), pp. 16-

17; *Annual Report for 1861,* Appendix A, p. 184.

[9]". . . Model Grammar School . . . Regulations for Ordinary Pupils," JEUC, XIV (September, 1861), 137; "General Rules and Regulations . . . (for) . . . the Model Schools . . . ." JEUC, XX (May, 1867), 84; Egerton Ryerson, *First Lessons in Agriculture* (Toronto, 1871), p. 199.

[10]Hodgins, ed., *The Story of My Life,* p. 34; Ryerson, *Christians on Earth and in Heaven* (Toronto, 1848), p. 15; Sissons, ed., *My Dearest Sophie,* pp. 61, 131, 170.

[11]Ryerson, *Report on a System of Public Elementary Instruction,* p. 150.

[12]See S. D. Clark, *Church and Sect in Canada* (Toronto, 1944); John Strachan, *The Christian Religion Recommended to his Pupils* (Montreal, 1807), p. 31; G. W. Spragge, ed., *The John Strachan Letterbook* (Toronto, 1946), p. 222; "Strictures of the Rev. Dr. Strachan on (the) Appeal of the Hon. William Morris to the Colonial Minister," 4 December, 1837, DHE, III, 91.

[13]*Letters from Ryerson to Strachan* (Kingston, 1828), p. 34.

[14]*Ibid.,* p. 29; "Dr. Ryerson's Historical Criticism of Mr. Draper's Speech Against Mr. Baldwin's University Bill of 1843," DHE, V, 59.

[15]"Reply of the Methodist Conference to an Address of the British Conference, 1853," DHE, XI, 15; Ryerson, *Scriptural Rights of the Members of Christ's Visible Church* (Toronto, 1854), p. 10; "Correspondence on the University Question, 1843-44," DHE, V, 105.

[16]Franklin A. Walker, *Catholic Education and Politics in Upper Canada,* pp. 21-23; Angus Macdonell to the Provincial Secretary, 25 April, 1846, DHE, VII, 271.

[17]Ryerson to Bishop Charbonnel, 13 March and 12 May, 1852, in *Copies of Correspondence Between the Roman Catholic Bishop of Toronto and the Chief Superintendent of Schools on the Subject of Separate Schools* (Quebec, 1852), pp. 8, 24-25; Ryerson to Rev. J. M. Bruyre, 22 December 1856, *Dr. Ryerson's Letters in Reply to the Attacks of Foreign Ecclesiastics against the Schools and Municipalities of Upper Canada* (Toronto, 1857), p. 48.

[18]*Special Report on the Separate School Provisions of the School Law of Upper Canada and the Measures which have been adopted to supply the School Sections and Municipalities with School Text Books, Apparatus and Libraries, by the Chief Superintendent of Schools* (Toronto, 1858), p. 16.

[19]*Copies of Correspondence between the Chief Superintendent of Schools for Upper Canada and other Persons, on the Subject of Separate Schools* (Toronto, 1855), pp. 209-26; John Hopkins to Ryerson, 10 September 1846, RG 2 C-6-C, PAO.

[20]"Confidential Report to the Governor-General, 14th January 1858," DHE, XIII, 253.

[21]*Annual Report for 1858,* p. viii.

[22]"Draft of Bill, relating to Vagrant and Neglected Children in Cities and Towns, 1862," DHE, XVIII, 180; *Annual Report for 1866,* Part I, p. 9.

[23]See for example, Phillips, *The Development of Education in Canada*, pp. 310-12. Similar conclusions have been reached regarding the Protestantism of public schools in the United States during this period: David Tyack, "The Kingdom of God and the Common School," *History of Education Quarterly*, VI (Fall, 1966).

[24]*Annual Report for 1862*, Appendix A, p. 102; *Extracts from the Chief Superintendent's Report for 1857*, p. 28.

[25]*Remarks on the New Separate School Agitation, by the Chief Superintendent of Education for Upper Canada* (Toronto, 1865), pp. 17, 20-21.

[26]Ryerson, *Inaugural Address at Victoria College* (Toronto, 1842), pp. 11, 14-15.

[27]*Report on a System of Public Elementary Instruction*, pp. 55, 80, 108, 112, 129; *Annual Report for 1864*, Appendix A, p. 58.

[28]"Canadian Mechanics and Manufactures," JEUC, II (February, 1849), 17; "Educational Features of the Provincial Exhibition of 1856 . . ." DHE, XIII, 38.

[29]Sissons, ed., *Egerton Ryerson*, II, 252.

[30]"Statistical Account of Upper Canada, 1836," DHE, II, 346; *Annual Report for 1864*, Part I, p. 11.

[31]Patrick Thornton to Ryerson, 20 February 1850, RG 2 C-6-C, PAO.

[32]*Annual Report for 1864*, Appendix A, p. 34; *Annual Report for 1865*, Appendix A, p. 19.

[33]H. Y. Hind to Ryerson, 3 August 1849, RG 2 C-6-C, PAO; *Annual Report for 1854*, Appendix G, No. 113.

[34]"Conversational Powers," JEUC, II (March, 1849), 43; "Correct Speaking," JEUC, II (June, 1849), 82.

[35]*Annual Report for 1851*, Appendix B, p. 213.

[36]Ryerson to Patrick Thornton, 19 August 1848, RG 2 C1, Letterbook D, p. 271; Memo appended to a letter from J. Gallivan to Ryerson, 9 November 1859, RG 2 C-6-C, PAO.

[37]The *Courier*, 16 January 1836, DHE, II, 277; Henry Lively to Ryerson, 27 October 1846, RG 2 C-6-C PAO; *Annual Report for 1862*, Appendix A, p. 107.

[38]*Annual Report for 1862*, Appendix A, p. 100; *Annual Report for 1861*, Appendix B, pp. 215 ff; *Annual Report for 1868*, Part I, pp. 29-31; *Annual Report for 1865*, Appendix B, p. 79.

[39]*Annual Report for 1869*, Appendix A, p. 7; Minutes of Proceedings of the Board of Education for Upper Canada and the Council of Public Instruction for Upper Canada, 12 April 1850, RG 2 B, Vol. 2, p. 113.

[40]Joseph H. King to Ryerson, 12 July 1850; John Flood to Ryerson, 4 November 1850, RG 2 C-6-C, PAO.

[41]"Learning to Spell," JEUC, VI (November, 1853), 175; "Ceremony of Opening the Normal School Buildings, 1852," DHE, X, 282.

[42]Ryerson to Wm. Mitchell, 25 February 1847, RG 2 C1, Letterbook C, p. 256, PAO; *Annual Report for 1858*, Appendix A, p. 53.

[43]*Elements of Political Economy* (Toronto, 1877), p. 129.

44*Annual Report for 1866,* Appendix A, pp. 55-56.

45*Elements of Political Economy, pp. 67 and 81-82.*

46 "Lord Elgin and Education in Upper Canada," JEUC, VII (October, 1854), 165; *Annual Report for 1857,* Appendix A, p. 198.

47*Elements of Political Economy,* pp. 67, 72-73, 16.

48"Political Economy – A Branch of Public Education; A Lecture Delivered by the Rev. Dr. Ryerson," JEUC, V (September, 1852), 131.

49*Elements of Political Economy,* p. 129.

50Ryerson, *First Lessons in Christian Morals* (Toronto, 1871), pp. 82-92.

51JEUC, II (February, 1849), 53.

52*Report on a System of Public Elementary Instruction,* pp. 10-18; "Self-Made Men," JEUC, I (February, 1848), 64; "The Benefits of Education Dependent upon Good Education," JEUC, VII (July, 1854), 112.

53*Annual Report for 1860,* Appendix A, p. 192.

Chapter 4

Occupations in Transition: The Danger of Downward Mobility

> Does a man wish his sons to swell the dregs of society
> – to proscribe them from all situations of trust and duty
> in the locality of their abode – to make them mere
> slaves in the land of freedom? Then let him leave them
> without education, and their underfoot position in
> society will be decided upon.
>
> Egerton Ryerson, 1848[1]

The nature of work underwent a major transformation in the nineteenth century. The basic change was from the pre-industrial condition in which artisans, farmers, merchants and professional men were frequently self-employed or worked with only a few others, to the "modern" situation in which large factories, businesses or bureaucratic organizations employ the majority of workers. Under earlier conditions, the work place was often the household; sons frequently followed the occupation of their fathers; wives and daughters could and did participate in the remunerative work of the household; and apprenticeship or service was the usual introduction to an occupation. Each small village or regional society was perceived as a relatively fixed hierarchy of ranks and orders, based on the local structure of occupations. It was as these general conditions of employment seemed increasingly threatened that observers began to be alarmed by the prospect of a general breakdown in the traditional ordering of society.

While Upper Canada at mid-century was still a pre-industrial society in many ways, there were many signs of things to come. For one thing, the building of canals and railroads, lumber camps and mills, as well as urban development generally, had created opportunities for the employment of large numbers of people in one place. Secondly, unsatisfactory working conditions and wages had already resulted in the first uses of the strike. Although in 1849 Ryerson said that trades were still "for the most part carried on by isolated individuals, or in small shops,"[2] nearly all discussion of the occupational structure implied that this situation could not last. For the present generation, the old patterns might perhaps endure; for the next, an unpredictable future was the only certainty, and it was this problem that school promoters were trying to understand and solve. With the gradual disappearance of apprenticeship, how were fathers to secure the futures of their male children? With the disappearance of the old "stations" and "orders," how was a person's place in society to be determined? The answer, as always, was through schooling.

An analysis of types of labour made by Egerton Ryerson in 1852 suggests the dualistic approach that many Upper Canadians increasingly took to the subject of work. There were two basic kinds of labour, according to this statement: "rude, simple or uneducated," and "educated." Ryerson believed that the two would never be equal:

> No man thinks of placing the same value upon the labour of a gate keeper and of a master in agriculture; or the labour of a hodman and a master-builder in architecture; or of a messenger and manager in a mercantile establishment; or of a monitor and head manager of a school; or of a cryer and judge of a court.

The outrageous attempt to place the two kinds of labour on a par, he hoped, had been discarded in Upper Canada. On another occasion, Ryerson distinguished "discovery," which included passing on what was discovered, from "invention" or the contrivance of something new. But both, once again, were to be distinguished from "operation," – the kind of labour which occupied "by far the most numerous classes of society."[3]

Statements relating specific occupational groups to social status tended to be vague and contradictory. In 1842, for the students of Victoria College, Ryerson distinguished "the professional pursuits" from the "ordinary duties of life." Other educators went on about "the higher duties of life," compared with the "humbler" or "common avocations." There was sometimes projected in fact a strong suggestion of distaste for certain kinds of work. According to the Mechanics' Institute lecturer, Walter Eales, the "extremes of majesty and meanness" met in the nature of man, and the meanness was quite clearly manual labour, or man's involvement with "the soil, the oar and the loom." There were other educators, however, who found special virtue in manual occupations. A case in point was H. F. Sifton, whose 1859 request to Ryerson for the use of the Normal School for evening singing classes was accompanied by the remark that the members of choral societies ought to be drawn from the working classes, "as being more constant and persevering in their efforts, as well as more healthy in their constitutions."[4] The difficulty in interpreting these statements is one of definition. Who exactly were the "working classes" and from whom were they being distinguished? What were "the humbler avocations" in Upper Canadian society, and what were the "higher departments of life?"

The older view, and one that many upper class immigrants no doubt brought from Britain to Upper Canada, was that there were certain kinds of work that upper class people did not do. But the traditional distinctions, like that which prevented gentlemen from doing manual labour, were increasingly hard to maintain in a society in which at least some who thought of themselves as gentlemen found themselves involved in such labour.[5] Ryerson and many of his fellow school promoters were bent on relating class to occupation in quite another way: by distinguishing educated from uneducated work. As Ryerson oberved in 1842, it was upon knowledge and skill that one's ultimate status in society depended. An English education, he told those assembled for his inaugural speech at Victoria College, destined a man for ordinary duties; a classical and scientific background, on the other hand, enabled him to pursue the professions, and was essential for success in "any of the higher employments" to which one might be called. What was more important, knowledge and skill were now "the *fruit* of *labour*, and not the *inheritance* of *descent*."[6]

In addition, educators observed and were alarmed by a tendency on the part of the classes to separate from one another. The traditional class dependency was disappearing. In an article on the obligations of educated men, which appeared in the *Journal of Education* during its first year of publication in 1848, Ryerson attempted to recall the dependency that he believed was so essential to social order. The principles of mutual obligation, he argued, ought to pervade all ranks and classes of society, and impinged no less "upon the peasant in his lowly obscurity than upon the Sovereign in the magnificence and responsibility of Empire." An educated man, Ryerson went on, was anyone who knew more than his neighbour; and educated men had special obligations to others.[7]

It was not easy for Upper Canadians to abandon the old idea of society as a hierarchy composed of many mutually-dependent ranks and orders. People like John Strachan believed that a relatively fixed social hierarchy was essential to human happiness; that a man who got "above himself" was destined to suffer the ravages of envy, melancholy, hatred and chagrin. At mid-century, Ryerson still referred to the various "stations and orders" and "ranks" of society; the levels in Upper Canada ranged in 1849, according to the chief superintendent of schools, from the statesman at the top of the scale to the day-labourer at the bottom.[8]

As always, Ryerson seemed to straddle two worlds. The very word "class" was used by him to delineate religious groupings, or even distinctions of sex or age, as much as those of social or occupational status, and the plural "classes" usually preferred to the singular "class," with its implications of class exclusiveness or solidarity.[9] In fact Ryerson seems to have made an almost conscious effort to discover or rediscover diversity in the occupations and social relations of men. The variety that appeared in nature and "in the productions of the mineral, vegetable and animal kingdoms," he declared in 1849, had its counterpart in "the diversities of human genius, condition and employment." Men were adapted for a number of different pursuits. But there was nevertheless the suggestion of disaffection and potential conflict in such diversity. In the variety, there was "endless beauty," but the beauty consisted largely in "the adjustment of the several parts to produce unity of effect." Failure to adjust to one's place or role, it was implied, was unnatural as well as unbeautiful.[10]

When educators talked more specifically about the occupations of men the same ambiguities kept appearing. The working world was divided by them into a number of occupational categories, but these were not sharply delineated. There were gentlemen, who included "gentlemen of leisure" and "gentlemen of the several professions,"[11] as well as holders of public office. There were merchants, mechanics or artisans, and farmers, but some of these could apparently be gentlemen as well. There were labourers and servants. Then, there were also women, and some women were ladies. Within these categories there were, of course, many more specific trades, professions and occupations. The overwhelming impression given by the school promoters, however, and by Ryerson above all, was that the specific calling was increasingly less important than what one did within the calling. One could go up or down. One could be educated and *become* a gentleman (or a lady, although this was less discussed and clearly less understood by the educators themselves) or one could fail to do so, either remaining lower class or sliding imperceptibly into the lower reaches of the social order.

The definition of a "gentleman" was clearly a subtle matter. Egerton Ryerson, who believed that he shared the values of "the middle classes of society," also considered himself a gentleman, and wished his son to become one. But not everyone in this category met with his approval. Confiding his hopes and fears for his son Charles in a letter to his daughter, Ryerson expressed concern and not a little impatience on this point. "I am determined," he wrote Sophie from Paris in 1867, "not to spend money to make an *idle* & free-living gentleman out of him." Clearly there was more than one kind of gentleman, and a true gentleman was neither idle nor free-living. On another occasion, Ryerson revealed his definition of a "private conversation," which was that a gentleman did not disclose to the public the contents of one. More than once, he accused public enemies of failing to live up to the code of gentlemanliness. George Brown, ardent reformer, editor of the Toronto *Globe* and frequently violent critic of the superintendent of schools, was thus attacked in 1859. In the course of a long and stormy public life, Ryerson pointed out, he had come into conflict with "men of all orders and professions." But he had never had to do with anyone "holding the rank of gentleman" who was as unscrupulous as George Brown. The implication was clearly that Brown was no gentleman, in fact, even though this was his ostensible status.[12]

The *Journal of Education* took a great interest in the subject of what constituted gentlemanly behaviour and offered opinions from sources on both sides of the Atlantic. A gentleman was "slow to surmise evil" because he never thought it. A gentleman subjected his appetites, refined his taste and subdued his feelings. He was gentle, modest and generous. A gentleman was "slow to take offence," and never bet. He would neither "trample on a worm nor cringe to a king." A gentleman deemed "every other man better than himself."[13] Such emphasis on the behavioural aspects of gentlemanliness could only democratize the concept. Anyone might aspire to become a gentleman just as anyone might aspire to respectability, provided he had the opportunity to acquire the right characteristics and the will to avoid the wrong ones. It was education that made the difference. Education began the gentleman, according to the *Canadian Gem*. After that, "reading, good company and reflection" completed him.[14]

Similarly, professional status was no longer entirely a question of occupation or rank. Medicine, the ministry, the army and the law were still the major professions, but formal education and a code of behaviour were increasingly emphasized for those who aspired to become truly professional. To a promoter of higher education like John Strachan, the unfortunate part of having to train students of medicine or the ministry by apprenticing them to doctors or parsons was that the practice tended to reduce these liberal professions to "a kind of trade." A university training was essential if medical practitioners, for example, were to attain to any proficiency. Strachan also commented unfavourably on the illiteracy of army officers in Upper Canada. He clearly believed that formal education was an essential prerequisite of professional status. Appropriate remuneration was also not without importance and Strachan complained more than once that the annual salaries of parsons in the province were "totally inadequate." It was obvious that a clergyman could not "maintain that respectable position in Society" that was essential to his usefulness, on the £150 a year that he received in 1815, Strachan noted. The reason was that "a common servant" earned "more than half that sum."[15]

Egerton Ryerson carried on the campaign for professional improvement. It was the culture of the mind that made the man, he argued, not the profession; it was his education that made the difference between "the boor and the scholar, the statesman and the peasant." It was unfortunate that among individuals of supposed professional rank in Upper Canada, many failed to live up to the ideal. Ryerson complained at his inaugural address at Victoria College, in 1842, of the fact that the province was overrun by "swarms of unlettered pettifoggers and quacks." It would really be better, he argued at the time, to have a few learned jurists and physicians, than an overabundance of illiterate so-called professional men. A few years later Ryerson had equally unkind words for the public servants of Upper Canada, whose inadequacy he blamed largely on old-style patronage. The result was a proliferation of incompetents – "a chainwork of functionaries" – when what was needed was knowledge, justice and generosity in the ordering of public affairs. Ryerson pointed out that it was possible to fill the public offices of the country with uneducated persons or with office-seekers from the Old World, clearly disastrous solutions, both of them. Then, there was the possibility of educating "a privileged class" through college, not an entirely unacceptable idea in 1842, and when he was speaking to the students and faculty of Victoria. But when Ryerson's thoughts were directed to a wider public in the late 1840s this too was rejected in favour of a still more democratic approach. The whole society

93

would be educated, and public servants selected according to merit.[16]

But however important the public services and the professions, and however based on merit the selection was in either case, it was no good if everyone aspired to these callings. By 1867, Ryerson was worried that Canadian youths were too much interested in the learned professions, and too little in "what are termed the industrial pursuits." He urged the people to be more practical. The "three great branches of industry," as he had outlined them in 1846, were commerce, agriculture and the mechanic arts.[17] Each branch had its problems, but all were related to status and to education.

Commerce was discussed the least. Young men seemed to be attracted to it in sufficient, if not overwhelming, numbers. The major complaint was that men of business thought too little of the "treasures and pleasures of the mind." There were also comments about those "rival publishers and itinerant book vendors" that many educators felt were such a plague to the schools, which implied a definite lack of sympathy with certain branches at least of the commercial world. Education Office personnel, certainly, had few kind words for the many booksellers who complained about having to share the rapidly growing school text market with the Education Department's equally rapidly expanding School Book Depository, a sort of public mail order house, which supplied authorized texts, library and prize books to local school boards at reduced prices. Opponents of Egerton Ryerson's who happened to be merchants seem to have come in for more than the usual amount of scorn; one is left with the impression that it was enough to point out that a critic of the Education Office was "a wooden ware merchant" to demonstrate his utter disqualification for discussing educational affairs, in the opinion of the chief superintendent. Merchant critics of the provincial Book Depository were accused of selfishness and irresponsibility and of seeking monopolies and profits at the expense of public improvement. Yet at the same time, Ryerson purported to believe that the responsible merchant was an important person in Upper Canada. His textbook on political economy, with its definitions of "agents of exchange" and explanations of the value of retail merchandising to the community, was no small contribution to the attempt to create a better image for businessmen in the 1870s and 80s.[18]

Educators seemed to feel that there were more problems in the other two branches of industry, the mechanic arts and farming, for these occupational groups appeared to be declining, both in status and opportunity. In the case of the former, confusion about the nature of the occupations themselves suggests the rapidly changing state of affairs. What were artisans really? Were they in the same category as factory operatives? Were they members of the labouring classes? Or were they businessmen?

The answer was that they could be any one of those things. What they could no longer do, in the opinion of many educators, was stay where they were. Much was said in the mid-nineteenth century that implied an improving status for the artisan, but much was also said that implied the reverse. Ryerson argued, for example, that each Canadian mechanic ought to combine "in his own person, the qualifications and skill" of both the "manufacturing superintendent" and the "operative" as these terms were understood in Europe, since in Upper Canada mechanics continued to be largely self-employed or to work in small shops rather than in large manufacturing establishments. The politician R. B. Sullivan, in a talk to the Mechanics' Institute of Hamilton in 1847, said that mechanics were or ought to be businessmen, and urged them to become involved in new enterprises and to expand their operations. Walter Eales worked on the development of a better class image when promoting Mechanics' Institutes in Toronto during the same period. If machines were a threat to the status of the artisan, he pointed out, it was important to remember who had invented machines in the first place, and that was the working man.[19]

All three were suggesting that something more than ordinary skill was essential if artisans were to maintain their position in society. Why should the mechanic be "a mere operative at his bench, or anvil," Ryerson wanted to know in 1842, "when by the higher powers of a cultivated mind, he might equally contribute to his country's wealth and advancement?" But it was not just the opportunity to contribute or advance that Ryerson put forward; there was also the threat that if one did not advance, one would fall behind. It was clear, he argued in 1849, that mechanics would never attain "the educational advantages and social position" that were due to arts and manufactures, "without asserting the rights of their order, and the hitherto neglected interests of their trades."[20] These interests were to seek schooling, for Ryerson was convinced that a dark future awaited mechanics who failed to educate themselves and their children.

Like Eales, whose ideal working man was a potential inventor, Ryerson's ideal worker was one who understood the processes and the principles involved in the construction and operation of machinery. It was his ambition that the teaching of the natural sciences in the common schools should promote this object, and science lectures at the Normal School were intended to deal not only with mechanical principles, but with their applications to specific manufacturing processes. In 1853, Ryerson attempted to explain this concerted attack on what he believed to be the ignorance of the average worker engaged in manufacturing. The mechanic who was knowledgeable would advance; he would promote industry and manufacturing in Canada. But the one who did not cultivate learning would decline. A "prey to animal passions," he would be left behind, to remain, presumably, a "mere operative" all his life.[21] In this way Ryerson promoted the view that individual artisans would eventually find it hard to maintain their independence or status in Canada. No doubt his words reflected a very real situation as well. As a painter turned teacher-in-training confided to the chief superintendent in 1859, if he had been able to support his family "in a respectable manner" by his craft, he would never have enrolled in the Normal School.[22]

The Reverend David Rintoul, lecturing to the Mechanics' Institute of Toronto on the subject of rhetoric in 1844, took a slightly different tack. The education of the artisan in his view was no more than necessary compensation for an "inferior life and work," created in Rintoul's opinion by the growth of capital and the consequent division of labour, which reduced the worker to boring, repetitive tasks, often in an unstimulating environment. For the city worker, especially, education was essential to counteract the terrible effects of purely mechanical labour in a confined space.[23]

Whatever the reason for the education of the mechanic – his elevation from inferior work, or compensation for having to do it – it was essential that this education take place in schools. This was the message of Ryerson's lecture, the "Nature and Importance of Education to Mechanics," delivered in 1853. Apprenticeship alone doomed a man to the "fate and temptations of hopeless inferiority for life." Ideally, trade schools would be developed to train Canadian architects, engineers and "mechaniciens," so that the province need no longer be a prey to foreign adventurers in these fields. But in the meantime, the mechanics ought to send their children to the common schools.[24]

The state of agriculture presented an even greater problem to educators. Ideally, the educated artisan could become an entrepreneur or businessman. What had the fates in mind for the farmer? There was a tendency among the young to abandon farming, a superintendent of schools from Hastings County com-

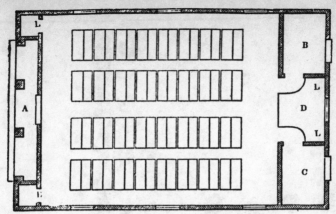

PLAN 9.—GROUND FLOOR.—FIG. II.

A. Front Entrance.
B. Girls' entrance and lobby, fitted up with mats, scrapers, hooks and shelves.
C. Boys' entrance, ditto.

D. Teacher's platform.
L. Cases for library.
E. Closets for apparatus, &c.

PLAN NO. 10.—END AND SIDE PERSPECTIVE, WITH GROUND, ETC.—FIG. I.

Mid-nineteenth century ideas about education were nowhere more concretely embodied than in the campaign for improved school houses, plans for which were made available to local trustees through the *Journal of Education* and later in a small book on the subject by J. George Hodgins. Above, view and plan for a small rural school. Hodgins, *The School House: Its Architecture, External and Internal Arrangements . . .* (Toronto: Department of Public Instruction for Upper Canada, 1857), p. 54.

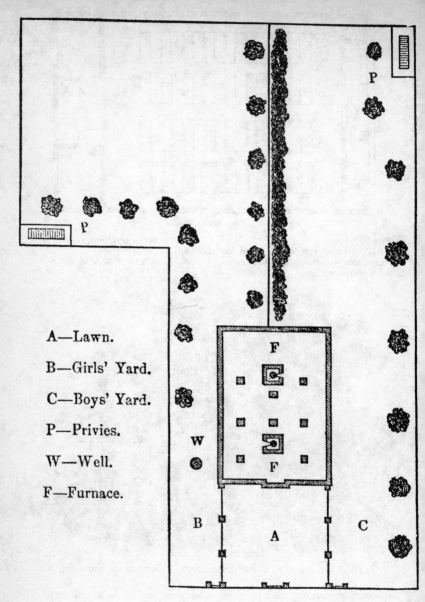

A—Lawn.

B—Girls' Yard.

C—Boys' Yard.

P—Privies.

W—Well.

F—Furnace.

PLAN VIII.—OUT GROUNDS.—FIG. II.

Segregation of the sexes was carefully provided for, even in the school yard. *The School House*, p. 32.

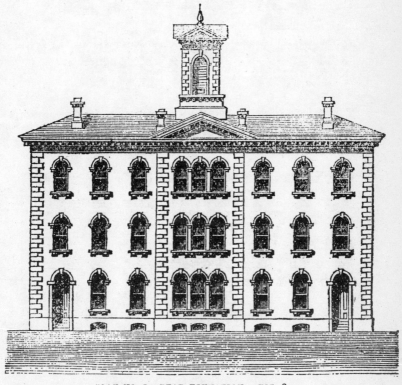

PLAN NO. I.—REAR ELEVATION.—FIG. 3.

An elaborate three storey urban school. Each floor was to be governed by one master and four assistants. *The School House,* p. 12.

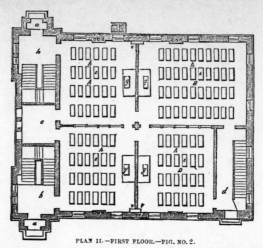

PLAN II.—FIRST FLOOR.—FIG. NO. 2.

A. Girls' intermediate or Superior School room.
C. Boys' intermediate or Superior School room,
B. Boys' Primary.
D. Girls' Primary.
aa. Outside Porches for boys and girls.
bb. Cap and cloak rooms for boys or girls.
e. Teacher's' or gallery, room.

d. Entrance to Primary School and cap room
    with stairs to boys' upper room.
e. Seats for two pupils each.
f. Flues for warm air.
g. Teachers' desk.
h. Passages two feet wide.
v. Ventilating flues.

Primary, intermediate and superior grades as well as sexual segregation were possible in the larger urban school. Hodgins' commentary on school rooms like the above included instructions on exactly how scholars were meant to circulate in the halls and spaces between the desks. *The School House*, p. 14.

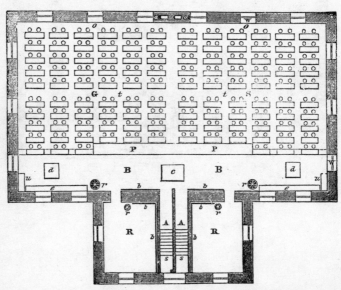

PLAN IV.—THE SECOND STORY OF A GRAMMAR OR UNION SCHOOL, ETC.—FIG. 4.

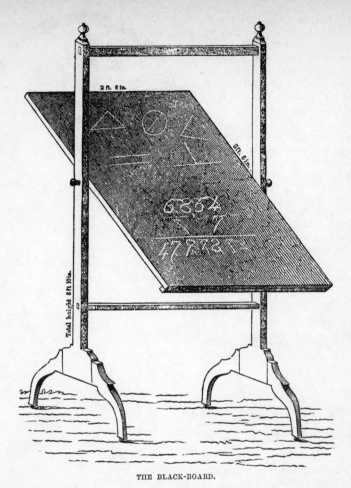

2 ft. 6 in.

3 ft. 6 in.

Total height 6 ft 10 in.

THE BLACK-BOARD.

COMPOSITION BLACK-BOARD.—For twenty square yards of wall, take three pecks of mason's putty (white finish), three pecks of clean fine sand, three pecks of ground plaster,

Along with improved school houses, the Education Department promoted the latest in furnishings and equipment. Above, a design and instructions for a home-made blackboard. *The School House*, p. 82.

◄ Despite concern about overcrowding, as long as seats were separate and ventilation good, school reformers had no trouble visualizing schoolrooms accommodating one hundred or more scholars. *The School House*, p. 19.

101

also enable the teacher to impart some knowledge of astronomy. Globes are generally constructed in pairs, and though the terrestrial is more useful, and better calculated to impress the true idea of the thing represented, than the celestial, yet both will be found highly advantageous.

A hemisphere globe supplies a want long felt, viz.: An illustration, which any child can understand, of the reason of the curved lines on a map, and shows how the flat surface is a proper representation of a globe. Two hemispheres are united by a hinge, and, when closed, a neat little globe is presented; when opened, two maps are seen, showing the continents, as if through transparent hemispheres.

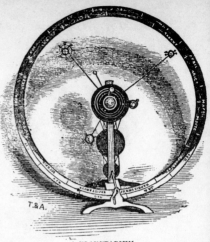

A PLANETARIUM.

THE TELLURIAN, OR SEASON MACHINE.—As a useful accompaniment to the globe and maps, in the study of geography, we notice the tellurian, or season machine. Among

THE TELLURIAN.

the most difficult phenomena presented to the minds of children, are the changes of the seasons—the revolutions of the moon around the earth, and the earth around the sun—and the subject of tides. These and several others, may be illustrated and explained by the aid of this machine. The science of geography, in its common acceptation, includes, with "a description of the surface of the earth," some account of its physical phenomena—of its people, manners, customs, religion, and laws; and of its relation to the other parts of the solar system. In this view, the study of the earth's motions and changes, although belonging to the science of astronomy, might properly be classed among these subjects to be taught in the school.

ASTRONOMY.—The apparatus to which we refer, for the study of the science of astronomy, consists of the Orrery, or model of the planets, revolving in their various orbits

ORRERY.

The Education Department promoted the use of scientific apparatus, which could be purchased through its "educational depository." *The School House,* p. 90.

BALANCING BAR.   INCLINED BOARD.

Climbing the ladder, the rope, and the inclined board, are all calculated to add strength to the limbs, activity and health to the body, and variety to the exercises of the play-ground. They can be provided for at slight expense, and be found, in common with other similar arrangements, to increase love school, by rendering it attractive. No gymnastic apparatus combines greater variety of healthful and pleasant

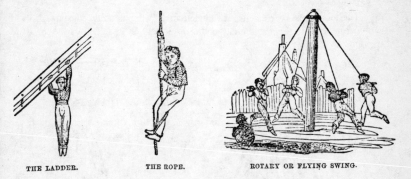

THE LADDER.   THE ROPE.   ROTARY OR FLYING SWING.

If schools were to become more up-to-date and efficient, they were also to be made more attractive, in this case by the provision of gym equipment for the boys. Educators were also responding to the belief that physical exercise had to be promoted, to offset the damaging effects of long hours of confinement in school. *The School House*, p. 118.

BLACK-BOARD BRUSH OR WIPER.—To save time and promote cleanliness, every p[...]
should, when at the board, be provided with a wi[...]
to clean the board and prevent as much as poss[...]
the dust from flying through the room. A com[...]
sized sheep's pelt would afford a sufficient numbe[...]
the kind represented in the cut, for an ordinary sch[...]
The skin should be cut in pieces eight inches [...]

BRUSH OR WIPER.

and five wide, and be carefully tacked, woolly side out, on a block a little smalle[...]
size. If the block is two or two and a half inches thick, it can be trimmed up so a[...]
form a handle out of the same piece. These wipers will last a long time, and if prop[...]
made and used, will not cut or scratch the boards or wall.

The Conical Brush or Wiper is a very superior article, and is sufficiently expla[...]
by the engraving. A wiper of some kind
should be provided, and its use insisted on
in every school. The filthy practice of
using the edge of the hand, or the cuff of
the coat for this purpose, should never be tolerated.

CONICAL BRUSH OR WIPER.

The School House, p. 84.

V. CALISTHENICS FOR GIRLS.

Though girls neither require the same robust exercise nor rough sports, to devel[...]
their frames and fit them for the duties of life, as boys, yet the system of educa[...]
which omits or slightly provides for their physical
training, is most radically defective. In addition to
such of the apparatus already enumerated, and others
proper for both sexes, those more peculiarly adapted
to their wants should be provided. In this point of

DUMB-BELL.

view, light dumb bells are best calculated, if properly used, to strengthen the arms
expand the chest.

The long back-board is also well calculated to expand the chest and give lithe[...]
and grace to all the movements of the arms and bust. The variety of attitude[...]

TRIANGLE.

BACKBOARD.

For girls, less energetic calisthenics were recommended. *The School House,* p. 119.

104

plained in 1865. It was essential therefore to "elevate the business... to its real standard." His proposed solution was to introduce a work on agriculture into the common schools. Ryerson did just this when he published in 1871 his text entitled *First Lessons in Agriculture, for Canadian Farmers and their Families,* but this effort was by no means the first to improve the status of farming. Robert Baldwin had complained of the Draper University Bill, in 1845, that a major fault was its omission of a chair of agriculture at the proposed provincial university. Agriculture, Baldwin claimed, "far from its being considered an inferior occupation... ought to be looked upon, as it really was, the noblest and most exalted of them all." A special interest in the subject was also taken by Governor-General Elgin, who offered his opinions on farming at an early Normal School prize-giving, in 1849. Like Baldwin, Elgin deplored the tendency in Upper Canada "to elevate the several professions above the agricultural pursuits." He had been appalled to discover that a Canadian farmer, who said that he would "make a man" of one of his sons, had meant by this that he intended to make of him a minister, a doctor or a lawyer. To be a farmer was obviously not so respectable.[25]

It became a mission of the Normal School and of the Education Office, therefore, to promote the respectability of agriculture. Ryerson's text was part of the effort. H. Y. Hind, the Normal School professor who was later to become famous as a geologist and explorer, lectured the teachers-in-training on the science of agriculture, prizes were offered in the subject, and an experimental garden developed in the Normal School grounds. The Education Office sent "educational exhibits" to agricultural fairs, and pointed out in circulars to local school officers that education was "at the foundation of all intelligent agricultural pursuits."[26] Ryerson also attempted to put across the idea in his speaking tours of the province. A lecture entitled "The Importance of Education to an Agricultural People" was repeated in dozens of towns and villages across the province during the late 1840s and in the 1850s, and was also printed in the *Journal of Education* for edification of its readers. In this lecture, Ryerson claimed that farmers in Upper Canada were increasingly proprietors of their own land, a fact which in itself should indicate that theirs was no longer a "servile" occupation. Agriculture, he went on, was the most important branch of human industry, and "agriculturists" were, and were likely to remain, "the people" of Canada. But, as Ryerson held in a companion lecture on education and mechanics, the Canadian farmer needed the intelligence of the overseer, as well as the practical skills of the farm labourer, to succeed.[27] Traditional skills were not enough for the farmer who aspired to land ownership and respectability.

Farmers, like mechanics, were therefore urged to send their children to school. Although some predicted that schooling would teach rural children to despise the occupations of their fathers, Ryerson argued that this did not have to be the case. Certainly there was a kind of "so-called" education which alienated the recipient from agriculture, and excited contempt for it, but using "education" for such a course of instruction was a misnomer, and an abuse of the children on whom it was inflicted, he believed. Certainly also, some farmers' sons would leave agriculture to enter other professions, but such changes should not be dictated by "any supposed meanness in the farm-house, as mere menagerie, – or in the Farm, as a place of cattle labour." They should be governed by the same considerations that governed the choice of any noble pursuit, including agriculture. In his *First Lessons in Agriculture,* Ryerson viewed the work of the farmer as no more offensive than that of the chemist, the surgeon or the advocate; "It is not what is worn, or what attaches from without, that defiles or degrades the farmer; it is that which is wanting, or comes from within." The independent farmer was the backbone of the nation. It was he who was the best material guarantee of its "freedom and virtuous prosperity."[28]

The message was perhaps more clear than was intended. The ideal farmer was the educated agriculturalist, the reader of books on horticulture. He owned his own land, and was independent and prosperous. But there was little apparent hope for the mere agricultural labourer or farm servant, and a strong suggestion that the physical aspects of farming really were degrading. One would have to look beyond the dirt and the work clothes to find the real man within, for the real man was not the farmer, but someone or something else. The purpose of such propaganda was to take away from farming, or the mechanic arts or indeed from any occupation or profession, whatever special meaning they might have had to the people whose occupations they were. The ideal of gentlemanliness was, in theory, applicable to all professions and occupations. As Ryerson put it, "it is the *man* and not the *profession* which constitutes the character."[29]

About "common labourers" or the "labouring classes," school promoters were clearly not very hopeful. Yet, in the case of those who were lowest on the occupational scale, the school men still tried to put the emphasis on the man, rather than on his work. Ryerson, in 1846, divided labouring men into three sub-groups;

"agricultural labourers," "manufacturing labourers" and "general labouring classes," and cited a Poor Law Commissioners' Report from England as proof that schooling was important to all three. In England, according to the report, the best educated working men managed "to live in the most respectable manner."[30] Two decades later, the chief superintendent could find few respectable workers among the labouring classes of England: he described them as the most vicious and degraded in all of Northern Europe. Why? Ryerson's answer was predictable. The English workers were the most degraded because they were also the least educated. As an article reprinted in the *Journal of Education* from the Port Hope *Watchman* pointed out in 1850, manual labour itself did not "deaden and paralyse the powers and faculties of the mind." If manual workers were rude and ignorant, it was because they lacked education.[31]

Ideally, schooling would lift labourers out of their rudeness and ignorance; but it must not, on the other hand, alienate them from their occupations. The "menial trades and employments," Ryerson claimed in a sermon in 1865, were in fact more necessary than all the others. A nation could get along without astronomers and philosophers, or artists and musicians, but it could scarcely manage without day labourers, woodchoppers and ploughmen; it was just as in the natural body – the "rudest parts" were the most useful.[32]

Like the respectable mechanic, farmer or labouring man, the respectable servant seemed to be in an anomalous position in nineteenth century Upper Canada. In England, servants may have at one time included all wage earners; they certainly included all wage earners or apprentices who were resident in the households of their masters or employers.[33] Similarly, in Upper Canada, the category clearly included more than those employed exclusively in domestic work. Thus, one finds nineteenth century "farm servants," and servants who were messengers or clerks, as in references to the servants of the Education Office.

The status of servants, however, never seems to have been very high in provincial society. In the early days, Ryerson tried to rebuke those who suggested that service implied great inferiority, and when someone said that they only took the *Christian Guardian* for their servants to read, replied that he and his friends were "edified and pleased" to read what might also interest their servants. But if he liked the idea of service, Ryerson did not like that of servility; the right kind of education, for example, prompted the mind to independent thinking and action and discouraged "servile imitation." And by the 1870s, Ryerson was deeply resentful of Dr. Daniel Wilson, who in his investigations of the Education Office, tended to treat the superintendent of schools as a "master" would a "servant."[34]

The *Journal of Education* seemed bent on a campaign to undermine service as an ideal. The attitudes of a servant, the *Journal* noted in 1853, were inappropriate to the man who wanted to get ahead in the world. According to an article reprinted from an American source on how to rise in business, he who wished ultimately to become a master ought to "be something more than a servant;" he should identify his interests with those of his employer. The status of servant was also one which increasingly bothered ambitious teachers, as they pressed for higher salaries, greater power and a more respectable position in society. School promoters did not think that teachers should be on a par with "common servants" or, for that matter, with labourers or wage-earners of any kind.[35]

The belief in a man's "calling" was gradually abandoned in Upper Canada as ideologists stressed education, manliness and gentlemanliness and downgraded the particular occupations or professions. So too the ideology of service gradually fell into disfavour. The category "public servant" and the ideal of public service remained. Except for these usages, however, the term "servant" was eventually reduced to its modern meaning of "domestic," increasingly applied to women only, or abandoned altogether. In 1860, Egerton Ryerson was perhaps still interested in the respectability of his household servants, but their punctuality, economy and willingness to oblige seemed to interest him even more.[36]

The position of domestic servants, and eventually of teachers also, as the teaching of the very young gradually evolved into an almost exclusively female occupation, was complicated by Victorian attitudes to women as a class. No work could have status if performed by a class of people who, by virtue of their sex, seemed to lack that very commodity. Women, most Upper Canadian school men seemed to believe, were by definition subordinate to men. Significantly, Egerton Ryerson called on women, children and servants together to accept their position in society. "Wives, submit yourselves unto your husbands . . . Children, obey your parents . . . Servants, be subject to your Masters," was his textbook exhortation in 1871. Husbands, fathers and masters, on their side, were to love their wives and treat the children and servants with justice.[37]

Since concern about the declining status of certain occupations was discussed by school promoters almost entirely in terms of the male need to succeed and the loss of manliness inherent in the uneducated state, it is not immediately obvious how the occupational position of women was to be affected by education. The basic assumption that emerges from most discussions of the education of girls in mid-nineteenth century Upper Canada is that all women would marry. The education of women, it followed, was designed to improve their chance to marry well, and their ability to perform their future roles as wives and mothers. It was also made clear that a young woman possessing the ideal attributes or educational "ornaments" could expect to enhance the status of her future husband and therefore to help him to rise in the world.

Charles Duncombe was the first Upper Canadian school promoter to devote space to a consideration of "female education." His concern was ostensibly the training of women to become teachers, a process which he believed would be equally "advantageous to the cause of education and to the happiness and ornament of society." Duncombe deplored the ephemeral character of most female schooling, the lack of any guarantee that girls' schools would continue to exist over the years, or that competent teachers could be secured for them. "Thus," Duncombe complained, "the character, the conduct and the continuance of those who are so extensively to mould the character of the future wives and mothers of this Province are almost entirely removed from the control of those most deeply interested."[38]

Duncombe's approach is interesting for several reasons. One is the apparent ease with which he passed from the consideration of training female teachers to a quite different concern, namely the importance of a good education for those who were to become wives and mothers. The emphasis was characteristic for his time, and seems to be based on a second assumption, that is that the education of women ought to be in the hands of women. As an anonymous critic of Upper Canadian education pointed out in the late 1840s, the fact that girls were to be educated assumed that there would be female teachers to instruct them.[39]

In the final analysis, it is plain that the basic concern of both the anonymous writer and Duncombe was less the education of women, in general, than that of "ladies". What was wanting, Duncombe argued, was a "uniform course of education adapted to the character and circumstances of females, to correspond with what is done in colleges for young gentlemen." He referred obliquely to the status that education might confer on women, by raising the problem of what "title of honour" ought to be conferred on girls who completed such a course of instruction. Academic titles, he seemed to feel, were "in bad taste and would provoke needless ridicule and painful notoriety except to those who propose becoming Teachers." Could there be an increase in status without a title? Duncombe believed that, should an appropriate course of study be established for women, it would simply prove "an Honour and an advantage to young ladies to have it known that their education was thus secured." Like medical and theological schools, female colleges would tend to "elevate and purify" even if they could not succeed in abolishing all "stupidity and empiricism."[40] To Duncombe, then, the possibility that education might elevate the status of women was not out of the question. But, except for women going into teaching, the basic occupation ascribed to women was nevertheless that of wife and mother. The "most important and peculiar duty of the female sex," was "the physical, intellectual and moral education of children."[41]

Ryerson's approach to women's role was generally less idealistic. The 1871 treatise on agriculture hardly sentimentalized the duties of mothers. If children were unwashed, disorderly and disobedient the mother was to blame. They could, after all, be clean, orderly and obedient. "The wife and mother is most responsible for all these," he observed in this text aimed at farmers, their families and rural common school children.[42]

If women worked outside the home, it is clear that their contribution was generally regarded as an inferior one; and if their labour was valued at all by most mid-nineteenth century Upper Canadians, this was because it was cheap. Division of labour was economical, said the chief superintendent of schools, because it allowed for the performance of those parts of a given operation not requiring the "strength of manhood" or "the skill of a trained workman" by inferior workmen or by women and children. The same reasoning applied to the employment of female teachers. Ryerson criticized the educational authorities in Dalhousie for providing that moneys be distributed equally among the teachers, making no distinction between men and women, although the responsibilities of the former were usually greater. On the other hand, one suspects that much of the abuse that the Education Office hurled at school trustees for hiring "cheap teachers" in this period was really meant to apply to female teachers. All were not as enthusiastic as Duncombe about women in teaching. Egerton Ryerson certainly avoided, until the mid 1860s at least, the kind of rhetoric which exalted women in the nineteenth century as superhumanly endowed with a special talent for teaching the very young. If women had any special role to play as far as

Ryerson was concerned, it was in the home rather than in the schools or in the larger society.[43]

Where women were found in the wider world, the superintendent of schools did attempt to be just. He saw no legal reason, for example, to prevent female heads of households or freeholders from exercising the vote in school board elections in 1851. And he came to the defence of at least one female teacher, a widow with a large family, whom he suspected was being unfairly deprived of part of her salary by a local superintendent in 1848.[44]

But if he was prepared to be reasonable about specific women whose role outside the household was already determined by virtue of widowhood, property ownership or employment, Ryerson and many of his fellow school promoters were reluctant to admit women as a class to the status that went with education. Under Ryerson's leadership, indeed at his instigation, co-education at the Upper Canada Academy came to an end with its translation to Victoria College in 1842, and women were not readmitted for thirty-six years.[45] A similar attempt to limit the opportunities of women came with a move by the Education Office to exclude them from full participation in the grammar schools in the 1860s. A Council of Public Instruction regulation of November, 1865, provided that girls could enter grammar school on passing the appropriate examination, but excluded them from the classical course which was a prerequisite for entry into the university or the professions. They were, in theory at least, to be restricted to the study of English and French as far as languages were concerned. Grammar school apportionments would have to be based on the number of male students in each school, since females would not be taking the prescribed course. In 1866, a new regulation provided that a girl taking the classical course could be counted as half a boy, for purposes of the provincial grant. But the battle did not end there, for Ryerson, with the blessing of the government, continued to press for the complete exclusion of girls, or second-best, their total non-recognition for financial purposes. In 1869, the Education Department had to admit defeat on both points, however, and actually acceded to the demand for the admission of girls on equal terms with boys, as well as their equal recognition if taking the classical course, for purposes of the grant.[46]

On one level the arguments for Ryerson's position were reasonably straightforward. It was assumed that the classical grammar school course ought to be strictly a preparatory course for university and the professions and was, therefore, "not at all adapted for girls," who, it was assumed, were not interested in either. Ryerson further claimed that many parents sent daughters to grammar schools for an English education simply because, as fee-paying institutions, they were more socially acceptable than common schools, most of which had become free by the mid-1860s. He also thought that school authorities crammed the grammar schools with girls not because of any interest in the girls, but in order to get more than their fair share of the provincial money.[47] No doubt there was an element of truth in all of these accusations.

But, as I have suggested earlier, the felt need to segregate the sexes went much further than such technical arguments would admit. Common school architecture and pedagogy as well as Education Office advice throughout the period insisted on separate entrances, separate playgrounds, separate seating and even separate recitations for boys and girls, "except in the primary department, and there too when practicable." And where most of the students were adolescents, as increasingly seems to have been the case in the grammar schools, segregation seemed more important still. As Ryerson pointed out to the trustees of a school in Clinton when they complained about the rules governing the admission and status of girls in grammar schools, mixed classes were simply undesirable.[48]

The most detailed defence of this attitude appeared in a lengthy statement in George Paxton Young's Grammar School Report for 1865, which reappeared in the *Journal of Education* in 1867. Young observed that there was no evil that he could see in the co-education of little children. But in the grammar schools, "girls of 15, 16 or 17 years of age" were "associated with boys of the same age." There was probably little the matter with this also, provided the schoolmaster possessed "weight of character," and in fact, such schools were like families or well-regulated social circles, where contact between the sexes was considered normal and salutary. The trouble was that out of a hundred grammar schools, there were always a few whose teachers did not possess the necessary authority, and in these schools undesirable things took place. Girls were apt to be subjected to the rough sports of boys, and to "a familiarity of treatment" which might "blunt their instinctive feelings of a delicate reserve."[49]

But this was not all that bothered Young. What was really worse was that some girls – young women who had enjoyed "no domestic advantages" – were quite without the feelings of delicate reserve previously described as instinctive to the class. These girls were drawn into an "unfeminine rudeness of behaviour" towards the schoolmaster. "They were ignorant of their lessons, but seemed to assume that as they were young ladies, he had no right to presume to be displeased with them; they were pert and bold." It was Young's feeling that girls who were thus "destitute of refinement" became even more insolent or sullen at having their self-love wounded in the presence of boys. And the same presence meant that the disrespect shown to the teacher would have more permanently damaging effects on character, although on whose character is not quite clear.

What was being said, effectively, was that women, like men, belonged to two classes. There were ladies, whose delicate reserve was best maintained in the protective environment of the family, or well-regulated social circles. This same delicate reserve also ensured the proper deference, should real ladies find themselves in grammar schools, or in society generally. But ladies were ill-adapted for the various professions open to gentlemen, to the rough games of boys, or even to higher education. Young women who did attend grammar schools endangered their status as ladies.

For those girls without "character" in the first place, the damage was less easy to explain, unless the real issue was the possible contamination of the young gentlemen involved. Women, educators seemed to be saying, were a class in themselves, and many women were low and vulgar. It was improvement that was sought, and in sexual segregation, school promoters hoped to achieve such improvement. Better that grammar school boys not know that girls could be "pert and bold," and that young women in general be separated from young men. Suddenly, private schools that practiced sexual segregation were taken to represent "the feeling of the community" and public educational authorities urged to follow their example.[50]

Egerton Ryerson's education of his own daughters best illustrates his personal ideal of the female role. They were sent to a convent to learn French, and even studied Latin. Sophie, the only daughter who survived adolescence and the boarding school experience, was further educated by travel with her father in Europe and social contacts with respectable people. Ryerson's letters to her leave no doubt that the behaviour and status of a lady was what he had in mind for her. He pointed out that while ladies did not drive carriages in Toronto, it was not considered amiss for them to do so in the country. On the other hand, ladies did not travel alone on freight steamers.[51] The respectable lady occupied her days with visits and drives, shopping, a little learning and household duties. The occupations of employed women who were not ladies, or even of employed ladies, were rarely if

113

ever discussed by leading Upper Canadian school promoters. The education of girls in the public system, if referred to at all, was most frequently discussed in very negative terms.

The pattern which emerges from educators' discussions of the occupations and education of men and women in Upper Canada clearly confirms Harold Perkin's analysis of the changing attitudes to social class in the nineteenth century. It was no longer a person's inherited rank or even necessarily his occupation which determined status, according to most of the school men, although the latter was obviously important; it was, increasingly, his education and social demeanour. For a man, it was upon "knowledge and skill" that ultimate status depended, and these in turn were the fruit of labour and not inheritance. And by skill, few school promoters meant manual dexterity. What mattered was that a man become a true gentleman, and any man who worked hard at it could in theory achieve this goal. To be a lady, it would appear, one had to accept the protection of a gentleman, or cultivate "delicate reserve," or both. It was clearly better for a lady not to be employed outside the home at all.

The inner achievement and outward appearance of gentility were purportedly considered appropriate goals for all types of people. But on the subject of education and occupations, school promoters were extremely ambivalent. Over and over again, people writing about education assured their readers that schooling would not alienate people from their work. Labourers, farmers, men and women who would dirty their hands were necessary in Upper Canada. But they ought to be educated nevertheless. As the *Journal of Education* noted in 1857, in Great Britain it was now recognized "that even the educated soldier is better than the uneducated – that the educated labourer is more valuable to himself and others than the uneducated – that the educated citizen, and mechanic, and farmer, has immensely the advantage over the uneducated."[52]

Grave warnings were issued, on the other hand, of the danger of downward mobility and loss of status to those who failed to seek education. Ryerson warned those present at his Victoria College inauguration that intellectual poverty was "the most despicable of all pauperism" and an invitation to social disaster. To the public at large, he had even more ominous things to say. The man who left his sons uneducated did them irreparable harm. He would live to see them become the underdogs, the very "dregs" of Upper Canadian society. He who did educate his children, however, conferred on them one of the greatest of gifts – the gift of power. "I do not consider respect for existing authority to be the sole object of education," Ryerson wrote to Bishop Charbonnel in 1852. The schools would fail in their mission if they did not develop all the intellectual powers of a man, teach him self-reliance and "instruct him in the rights as well as the duties of man."[53]

That power was an essential part of what Ryerson and many of his contemporaries sought through education emerges over and over again. There was pleasure – great pleasure – in "the very consciousness of power" which knowledge bestowed, the chief superintendent told the mechanics. Learning gave a man power over time as well as space. Thus, the ideas and sentiments of one man might eventually become those of his family, his neighbourhood, his country and even of succeeding generations. Significantly, education and power were masculine. The intellectual student grew up into "masculine maturity and vigour;" the college graduate appeared as *"a man;"* and the purpose of educating boys was to impart to them a "manly and Christian energy." Classes as well as individuals could expect to gain power through education, for "the power of each individual, or of each class of individuals in the community," was "in proportion to their intellectual and moral development."[54]

Yet if all were encouraged in theory to seek the status, property and power that went with education, it was not really expected that all would achieve it. Education had another function besides the elevation of a respectable or "middle" class in Upper Canada. This was the related one of providing a safe and disciplined lower class, the necessary labourers over whom those who had bettered themselves could exercise their newly won power.

NOTES

[1]"The Importance of Education to a Manufacturing, and a Free People," JEUC, I (October, 1848), 297.

[2]"Canadian Mechanics and Manufactures," JEUC, II (February, 1849), 19-20.

[3]"Political Economy – A Branch of Public Education," JEUC, V (September, 1852), 133; *Elements of Political Economy*, (Toronto, 1877), p. 35.

[4]Ryerson, *Inaugural Address at Victoria College* (Toronto, 1842), p. 9; DHE, I, 177; *Circular of the Upper Canada Academy* (Cobourg, 1841), p. 3; Walter Eales, *Mechanics' Institutes* (Toronto, 1851), pp. 6-7; H. F. Sifton to Egerton Ryerson, 25 July 1859, RG 2 C-6-C, PAO.

[5]G. P. de T. Glazebrook, *Life in Ontario: A Social History* (Toronto, 1968), p. 37.

[6]*Inaugural Address at Victoria College*, p. 9.

[7]"Third Annual Address to the People of Upper Canada, by the Chief Superintendent of Schools," and "Obligations of Educated Men," JEUC, IV (January, 1851), 2, and I (June, 1848), 160, 163-64.

[8]S. F. Wise, "Sermon Literature and Canadian Intellectual History," in J. M. Bumsted, ed., *Canadian History before Confederation*, p. 268; "On the Social Advancement of Canada," JEUC, II (December, 1849), 183.

[9]On the use of the plural and class terminology in general, see Perkin, *The Origins of Modern English Society*, p. 218.

[10]"On the Social Advancement of Canada," JEUC, II (December, 1849), 181. Asa Briggs explains the tendency to return to the language of grades and ranks, to talk about "an almost endless series of social gradations," in the 1850's and 1860's, as part of the struggle to re-define class ideology in this period. See "The Language of 'Class' in Early Nineteenth Century England," in A. Briggs & J. Savelle, eds., *Essays in Labour History*, (London, 1967) pp. 69-73.

[11]"On the Social Advancement of Canada," JEUC, II (December, 1849), 181.

[12]Sissons, ed., *Egerton Ryerson*, I, 562; *My Dearest Sophie*, p. 114; Ryerson to the Editor of the *Provincialist*, 19 February, 1848, RG 2 C1, Letterbook D, pp. 165-66, PAO; *Dr. Ryerson's Letters in Reply to the Attacks of the Hon. George Brown* (Toronto, 1859), p. 17.

[13]"The Gentleman," and "A Word to Boys," JEUC, II (June, 1849), 90-91; II (October, 1849), 159.

[14]*Ibid.*, II (February, 1849), 49.

[15]An article in the *Christian Recorder*, July 1819, attributed to Strachan, DHE, I, 159; George W. Spragge, ed., *The John Strachan Letterbook* (Toronto, 1946), pp. 5, 74.

[16]"The Importance of Education to an Agricultural, a Manufacturing and a Free People, 1847," DHE, VII, 143; *Inaugural Address at Victoria College*, p. 25; "On the Social Advancement of Canada," and "The Importance of Education to a Manufacturing and a Free People," JEUC, II (December, 1849), 181; JEUC, I (October, 1848), 296.

[17]*Annual Report for 1867*, Part I, p. 39; *Annual Report for 1868*, Part I, pp. 24-25; *Report on a System of Public Elementary Instruction* (Montreal, 1847), p. 191.

[18]"On the Social Advancement of Canada," p. 181; Ryerson to the Hon. James Leslie, 21 September 1850, "Returns Relating to the Receipts and Expenditure of (the Department of Education of) Upper Canada," Appendix L.L.L. *Journals of the Legislative Assembly of the Province of Canada*, Appendix No. 7 to the Eleventh Volume; *Special Report on the Separate School Provisions of the School Law of Upper Canada* (Toronto, 1858), pp. 29, 44-47; *Elements of Political Economy*, p. 82.

[19]"Nature and Importance of Education to Mechanics, 1853," DHE, XI, 45; Sullivan, *Lecture. . .on the Connection between Agriculture*

and Manufactures... (Hamilton, 1848), pp. 12, 18-21; Eales, *Mechanics' Institutes,* p. 4-5.

[20]*Inaugural Address at Victoria College,* pp. 24-25; "Canadian Mechanics and Manufactures," JEUC, II (February, 1849), 25.

[21]*Ibid.*, p. 20; Ryerson to Rintoul, 5 February 1847, RG 2 Series B, Letterbook A, p. 16, PAO; "Nature and Importance of Education to Mechanics, 1853," DHE, XI, 42.

[22]Robert Ridgeway to Ryerson, 16 August 1859, RG 2 C-6-C, PAO.

[23]Rev. David Rintoul, *Lectures on Rhetoric,* II, Appendix, Note A, pp. 43-47.

[24]DHE, XI, pp. 40 ff.

[25]*Annual Report for 1865,* Appendix A, p. 17; "Speech of the Hon. Robert Baldwin on the Draper University Bills of 1845," DHE, V, 187; "Agricultural Prizes at the Normal School," DHE, VIII, 261-62; "Address of Egerton Ryerson to the Governor-General, Normal School Opening, 1851," DHE, X, 6.

[26]Circular to Local Superintendents, Trustees and School Officers in the Counties West of Toronto, 1 September 1857, RG 2 Series Q, PAO.

[27]"Educational Lectures of the Provincial Exhibition of 1856, and Address by Doctor Ryerson on Agricultural Education," DHE, XIII, 36-38; "Nature and Importance of Education to Mechanics, 1853," DHE, XI, 45.

[28]"Address...on Agricultural Education," DHE, XIII, 36, 39; *First Lessons in Agriculture* (Toronto, 1871), pp. 11-12.

[29]"Address...on Agricultural Education," DHE, XIII, 38.

[30]*Report on a System of Public Elementary Instruction,* p. 15.

[31]*A Special Report on the System and State of Popular Education on the Continent of Europe, in the British Isles, and the United States of America, with Practical Suggestions for the Improvement of Public Instruction in the Province of Ontario* (Toronto, 1868), p. 107; "Education and Manual Labour," JEUC, III (February, 1850), 20.

[32]"A Good Man, Full of the Holy Ghost," 1865, in Samuel G. Phillips, ed., *The Canadian Methodist Pulpit: A Collection of Sermons* (Toronto, 1875), p. 47.

[33]D. V. Glass, *London: Inhabitants within the Walls* (London, 1966), p. xx; Peter Laslett, "Market Society and Political Theory," *The Historical Journal,* VII, (1964), 152.

[34]Sissons, ed., Egerton Ryerson, I, 438; Ryerson to Charbonnel, 24 April 1852, in *Copies of Correspondence between the Roman Catholic Bishop of Toronto and the Chief Superintendent of Schools, p. 17; Dr. Ryerson's Defence: Educational Department Fifth and Last Paper,* Broadside, (187?).

[35]"Rules for Young Men to Rise in Business," JEUC, VI (November, 1853), 165; Alison Prentice, "The School Promoters: Education and Social Class in Mid-Nineteenth Century Upper Canada," (Ph.D. diss., University of Toronto, 1974), chapter 8.

[36]*My Dearest Sophie,* p. 10.

[37]Ryerson, *First Lessons in Christian Morals* (Toronto, 1871), pp. 15-16.

[38]*Doctor Charles Duncombe's Report upon the Subject of Education* (Toronto, 1836), p. 38.

[39]*Remarks on the State of Education in the Province of Canada . . .by "L"* (Montreal, 1848).

[40]*Duncombe's Report*, p. 40.

[41]*Ibid*, pp. 40-41.

[42]*First Lessons in Agriculture*, p. 173.

[43]*Elements of Political Economy*, p. 53; *Annual Report for 1847*, p. 6. On Ryerson and women teachers, see Alison Prentice, "The Feminization of Teaching in British North America and Canada, 1845-1875" *Social History/histoire sociale*, VIII (May, 1975), 10.

[44]*Annual Report for 1851*, Appendix C, No. 8, pp. 177-78; Ryerson to Patrick Thornton, 19 August 1848, RG 2 C1, Letterbook D, p. 271, PAO.

[45]Sissons, ed., *Egerton Ryerson*, II, 15-16; *Annual Report for 1867*, Part I, p. 32.

[46]Walter N. Bell, *The Development of the Ontario High School* (Toronto, 1918), chapter IX, "The Admission of Girls;" Sissons, ed., *Egerton Ryerson*, II, 510. For a discussion of the grammar school question, see M. V. Royce, "Arguments over the Education of Girls – Their Admission to Grammar Schools in this Province," *Ontario History*, LXVII (March, 1975).

[47]"Chief Superintendent's Remarks on the Grammar Schools," JEUC, XX (May, 1867), 81-82. See also the *Annual Report for 1866*, Part I, pp. 26-29.

[48]"School Architecture," JEUC, IV (January, 1851); *Annual Report for 1847*, Appendix 3, p. 79; *The Grammar School System of Ontario, A Correspondence between the Board of Trustees of the Clinton County Grammar School and the Rev. Egerton Ryerson, reprinted from the Clinton New Era* (Clinton, 1868), p. 7.

[49]*Annual Report for 1865*, pp. 74-75; "The Education of Grown Up Boys and Girls Together," JEUC, XX (May, 1867), 81-83.

[50]*Ibid*.

[51]*My Dearest Sophie*, pp. 33, 39-40, 212.

[52]Rintoul, *Lectures on Rhetoric*, II, p. 46; *Remarks on the State of Education. . .by "L"*, p. 53; Unsigned editorial, JEUC, X (January, 1857), 8.

[53]*Inaugural Address at Victoria College*, p. 26; "The Importance of Education to a Manufacturing, and a Free People," JEUC, I (October, 1848), 297; Ryerson to Charbonnel, 24 April 1852, *Copies of Correspondence between the Roman Catholic Bishop of Toronto and the Chief Superintendent of Schools*, p. 17.

[54]"Canadian Mechanics and Manufactures," JEUC, II (February, 1849), 20; *Report on a System of Public Elementary Instruction*, p. 56; "The Object of a Collegiate Education," JEUC, VII (July, 1854), 120; *My Dearest Sophie*, p. 40; "Address. . .on Agricultural Education," DHE, XIII, 39.

Chapter 5

The Integration and Invigoration of the Labouring Classes and the Poor

One of the most formidable obstacles to the universal diffusion of education and knowledge is class isolation and class exclusiveness – where the highest grades of society are wholly severed from the lower in responsibility, obligations, and sympathy ... and where the men of liberal education regard the education of the masses as an encroachment upon their own domains, or beneath their care or notice. The feeble and most needy, as also the most numerous classes, are thus rendered still feebler by neglect, while the educated and more wealthy are rendered still stronger by monopoly.

Egerton Ryerson, 1851[1]

The gradual forging of a middle class consciousness had its counterpart in changing attitudes to the working classes and the poor. Many school promoters had begun to feel that the lower classes were becoming isolated, that they were no longer cared for as they had once been by the well-to-do. The condition of the poor, furthermore, seemed to weigh increasingly on their consciences as a problem which required a systematic response from society as a whole. In addition, there was the related fear of open and violent conflict, as the gulf between rich and poor seemed to widen and the labouring classes appeared more and more conscious of their degradation and isolation.

On the whole, educators lacked any real awareness of their own role in widening the gulf between the classes. Yet their message, the enhancement of the individual and the family by education, and the opportunities for property and position education would bring, certainly had that effect. Nor did they realize the extent to which they had idealized relations between rich and poor in pre-industrial village society.² What they saw as a worsening situation was really, at least in part, the development of a new ideal in class relations. More and more, class friction was to be contained by institutions structured to take the sting out of face-to-face contact between the "haves" and the "have nots." The school promoters saw themselves essentially as the makers of peace. Education would be made free, and all children brought into the schools. This would bind the classes together in a common enterprise and their children in a common history of having been schooled together.

Part and parcel of the vision of social harmony through education was the view that the educational system ought not to be tainted with party conflict, sectarianism or politics of any kind, and the somewhat contradictory belief that the social cement of Christian teaching, despite its undoubted sectarian nature, was nevertheless an essential part of public education. The poor would be taught the values of Christian love, order, property, correct social behaviour and even independence. The end result would be social peace, and the prosperity and progress of all classes.

Dislike of political and social controversy is a recurring theme in the writings of nineteenth century educators, many of whom came to believe that public debate of any kind was fundamentally alien to the values of peace and good order. Among the reasons that Egerton Ryerson gave for this belief, one of the most telling was that social agitation injured the economic interests of the country. In a "state of public unsettledness," he wrote from England just prior to the rebellion of 1837, commercial and public credit suffered, as did agricultural interests. General improvements were impeded, property declined in value, and potential immigrants of the wealthier sort were discouraged from coming to Canada. The "social happiness" was interrupted and sometimes destroyed. Bad news from home, Ryerson claimed, was leading the most intelligent men in England to view Upper Canada as "on a par with the South American semi-civilized Republics," where property itself was unsafe. He had found it difficult to make them see the difference.³ In 1842, when Ryerson accidentally met and conversed with his long-time enemy John Strachan for the duration of a carriage journey, the occasion gave rise to reflections on how much better it would be if those engaged in religious or political controversy met privately before they entered into "the arena of public disputation;" how many more reasons there were, Ryerson reflected, "for agreement than for hostility in the general affairs of a country," even among those who differed most widely on various points of doctrine and policy.[4]

But Ryerson's controversial labours did not end in 1842 as much as he might have wished them to; nor did conflict disappear from Canadian society as a result of behind-the-scenes agreements between gentlemen. In fact, social warfare became more intense as the decade wore on, and the stresses and strains of bad times combined with racial antagonism and the news of revolution in Europe to produce violence and disorder in the Canadas. The unrest culminated in riots and the burning of the Parliament buildings in the spring of 1849. The same year, as it happened, was also one of great uncertainty for the Upper Canadian school system. It was in the summer of 1849 that Ryerson offered his resignation over the passage of the abortive Cameron School Act, a law which the chief superintendent believed had the potential to frustrate his plans for provincial uniformity and control of the school system. He saw the passage of the act as the culmination not only of personal attacks on himself by his enemies, but also of a conspiracy to widen the gulf between the classes by the enemies of social harmony.[5]

In the autumn of 1849, Ryerson delivered "A Lecture on the Social Advancement of Canada" to the Mechanics' Institute of Toronto and Niagara, which was subsequently published in the *Journal of Education*. In it he warned of the dangers of political and social agitation. "Social restlessness," Ryerson argued in this fundamental statement of his beliefs, would never lead to social advancement. The dismemberment of society was not improvement, nor could revolution ever be progress. He deplored the actions of those who would sever the relations of the classes to one another, especially attacking "the gentlemen of leisure and of the several professions" who had wrapped themselves up in a "selfish exclusiveness," forgetting the bonds that tied them to the rest of society and particularly to the more numerous working classes. Any arrangement leading to the isolation of the classes, Ryerson argued, was dangerous. If this was so in the domestic circle, it was equally true in the larger family circle of a neighbourhood or country, and most especially in a new and comparatively feeble country. Upper Canada had no superfluous strength to waste on the suicidal business of "social warfare."[6]

Ryerson particularly objected to the newspapers which, in his opinion, exaggerated existing conflict, when they ought to have tempered it. Although differences of opinion had to be expressed, what was wanted, he believed, was the "manly discussion" of "gentlemen," not the personal abuse which was so often seen "hissing through the columns of a perverted press."[7] By 1852 public discussion of any kind seemed to have become intolerable to the chief superintendent. He chided the Roman Catholic Bishop, Armand de Charbonnel, for airing his grievances in the newspapers before appealing to the appropriate legal authorities, a practice which Ryerson argued could only lead to lawlessness and anarchy.[8]

Distrust of public controversy inevitably led educators to distrust political parties. Ryerson himself, from the mid-1830s on, claimed to be politically neutral, describing himself as "a sort of break-water – resisting and checking the conflicting waves of mutual party violence" in the province.[9] But political parties did not disappear from the Upper Canadian scene any more than did social conflict or newspaper attacks on personalities; indeed, it has been claimed that by 1845, public life in the united provinces was "essentially conducted" in partisan terms.[10] Ryerson was forced to work with whichever group was in power at any given time, but he was never completely happy with the party system. In 1867, in an address prompted by the imminent confederation of the Atlantic and central provinces, he once again rebuked the "partyism" which he believed endangered the very existence of the new Canadian nation. Partyism drove able men from public life, attracting in their place "partisans and sharpers," who deceived and corrupted the people and plundered them "for their own party and selfish purposes." This contagion, Ryerson said, spread to other young men of the land and to other classes of the community, until the public taste became vitiated, society divided and convulsed and the primary elements of civil and social progress "paralysed and corrupted." The worst effect was on the reputation of the state. Government ought to represent justice, honour and virtue, but was deprived of all three when the people came to see it as the tool of party domination.[11]

The perception of a society convulsed by social and political controversy led to the desire to do something about it, and in this area school promoters tended to focus on those whom they thought suffered most from social isolation – the very poor. Since many of them saw the failure of existing educational patterns as a chief cause of both class alienation and poverty, the more effective schooling of the labouring classes and the poor seemed to them both the obvious and most desirable solution to these problems. Other possible approaches, in fact, were beginning to be seriously questioned. John Strachan, for example, argued in 1828 that the spending of vast sums by the parishes of

England on the maintenance of life in the poor simply caused these classes to degenerate; they were deprived of hope. Egerton Ryerson came to have similar feelings. Like many others in his period, he seemed increasingly to question the usefulness of official charity, especially as it was seen to operate in countries like England and Ireland, sharing a widely held view that poor relief only degraded those who received it. It was pauperism, or having to live off charity, not poverty, that many nineteenth century reformers seemed to believe was evil.[12]

The poor were not to be neglected, however. "It is the poor indeed," Ryerson wrote in 1846, "that need the assistance of the Government, and are the proper objects of its special solicitude and care; the rich can take care of themselves."[13] But the poor should not be assisted by simple relief, or, for that matter, by government interference in wages. Thus in the 1877 *Elements of Political Economy* Ryerson upheld the view that government interference constituted "meddling despotism" that could only "fill the land with robbery, injustice and ruin." Nor were the poor or the labouring classes to organize themselves in order to find their own solutions. In the same book, the question was put rhetorically: "Is not free competition then the true Regulator of Wages in a Free Country?" The answer was simply "Yes." Combinations among either capitalists or labourers were not only unjust, they were useless.[14]

The only acceptable solution was to educate the children of the poor. One of the grand objects of the school system in Upper Canada thus became the prevention of "pauperism" in the province by the reduction or elimination of class exclusiveness in the schools. Ryerson felt that the different classes should be "not rivals, but fellow-helpers; not aliens, but members of the same body." Arbitrary class distinctions, as he put it in his Mechanics' Institute lecture of 1849, were "impediments to the social advancement of the country," and if allowed to prevail, would cripple and paralyse its energies for the common welfare.[15] It was the job of the schools to prevent such social paralysis.

Class conflict and "arbitrary" (presumably inherited) class distinctions were to be eliminated, but not the classes themselves, for the labouring classes were clearly as essential to the social structure as were their middle class brethren. What Ryerson and many of his contemporaries wanted was the traditional class deference that could still be found in Switzerland, where according to a contemporary traveller, (whose opinion was corroborated by Ryerson) the "intermixture of classes" was "wonderfully divested of the offensive familiarities which would

123

infallibly arise from it in less educated countries." Youth respected age and the poor man his wealthy neighbour. In addition it was to be hoped that the poor man would begin to respect himself. The educators were not interested, once again, in attacking poverty, so much as the attitudes of the poor. "Cringing beggars" and "paupers" would, they hoped, give way to a respectable and self-respecting class of labouring people, as a result of education.[16]

The general way in which schooling would divest social relations and poverty of their offensiveness was best described in the annual report for 1852 of R. S. Henderson, the Superintendent of Schools for the City of Kingston. Henderson complained of a widening gulf between the classes coupled with a noticeable lack of what he called "community of feeling," "oneness of interest" or "unity of sentiment" between rich and poor. Schooling, he argued, would bridge the gulf. It would be the "lever" that would

> not only show the deformity of vice, but elevate the social state of the poor – assimilating them in habits, thoughts and feelings to the rich and educated – giving them the same intellectual tastes and pleasures; and embuing them with the same sentiments and feelings.[17]

Class conflict would be eliminated, in other words, by getting the lower classes to take on the values of the higher.

Of primary concern was the necessity of actually involving the educated or well-to-do classes in mass schooling, for it was one of Ryerson's chief grievances in the 1840s that their interest had gradually been withdrawn. "If the wealth, the rank, the intelligence" of a community were arrayed on the side of progress, he argued in 1849, "the ignorance and apathy" which existed among the masses would soon be "penetrated and dispelled." The rich had been too selfish. It had been their "unnatural and unpatriotic separation" from the common school which had caused its "inefficiency and alleged degradation." The opinion was echoed in 1856 by Toronto superintendent George Barber, who attributed the failure of the common schools under his jurisdiction to the "*total absence of all interest* in the Schools by the affluent and influential portions of the community."[18]

Various practical means were proposed to remedy the situation. The creation of the Superintendent's Office in 1841 and the re-creation of a provincial Board of Education in 1846 were considered major beginnings. In addition the School Act of 1846 made the clergy of all Christian denominations, as well as judges of the district courts, wardens, councillors and justices of the peace into common school "visitors" by virtue of their offices in the community. Ryerson also clearly intended the district superintendents of 1846, and the army of county and local superintendents made possible by the School Act of 1850, to represent the wealth and education of the community in the schools. Over and above such official involvement, the wealthy and educated were also called upon to take an individual interest. Clergy and parents were urged to seek out the ignorant in their neighbourhoods, "to gather to the school, from the highways and hedges, the prodigal children of their prodigal brethren." "To educate the children of all classes," Ryerson pointed out, required the "individual as well as the official co-operation of all classes."[19]

The involvement of the wealthy in the education of the poor was to take place in other ways as well. The first was by levying local taxes on property, to cover all costs over and above provincial and other grants, that had in the past been borne by rate-bills levied on the parents of those children attending the schools. The idea was introduced in the Draft Bill of 1846 and again in the ambiguous School Act for Cities and Towns of 1847, but it was clearly embodied in the law for the first time for the whole of Upper Canada with the passage of the School Act of 1850. By this law, trustee boards throughout the province were recognized as corporate bodies having full powers to levy taxes in the districts they represented, and thus to make the schools free by placing the burden of their support on property. In rural areas, ratepayers voted annually on whether or not to adopt this means of raising money, while in cities and towns the power of decision was vested in elected boards of trustees.

That the idea of tax-supported schooling was not easily adopted by everyone is clear from the debates which ensued on the subject in local ratepayers' and school board meetings, as well as in the journals of the period,[20] but strong pressures were brought to bear in favour of free schools by their promoters. Among the arguments put forward on their behalf, apart from the general one that they involved the rich in the schooling of the poor, was the contention that they lifted the taint of pauperism from those parents who could not afford to pay for the education of their children. All children would attend of right, as free citizens; thus no child would have to bear the stigma of being educated as a "pauper" or a "neighbourhood charity."[21] It was Ryerson's opinion in the 1840s that the rate-bills were the most frequently alleged grounds for keeping children from school. Lifting these rates only for the poor did no good; the wealthier parents were unduly burdened and the poor ashamed to have their children singled out as objects of charity.[22] The obvious answer, in his view, was simply to eliminate the rate-bills on parents altogether.

One of the more vigorous supporters of this argument was Dexter D'Everardo, the School Superintendent for the District of Niagara. No man, D'Everardo claimed in 1850, was so poor that he could not pay a 3 or 6 shilling tax for a cow, or "what other little property" he might possess. The effect of paying the school tax on the poor but educated man was bound to be the restoration of his self-respect, his independence and consciousness of the right to participate in municipal affairs. As far as the poor uneducated man was concerned, his need was even greater, according to William Frazer of the Eastern District. It was "a species of oppression and cruelty," Frazer wrote to Ryerson in May of 1849, "to shut the school door against the helpless children of the toiling poor, who in preparing the comforts of the rich," had "enough and far more than enough to do to feed and clothe their children." The poor parent had neither the will nor the ability to make adequate educational provision for his children, according to Frazer, yet simple justice demanded that his children be schooled.[23]

Free schools were intended to lead to social harmony in other ways. Educators believed that a just system of school taxation would demonstrate that common interests were more important than individual ones and bring members of the community together. Most important was the predicted effect on the children, for not only were the rich to be involved in the common schools through taxes on their property, they were also to be persuaded to let their own children attend the improved tax supported schools. In 1852, Ryerson claimed that this was already the case in the major cities of the province:

What is taking place in our chief cities will, I trust, be witnessed in the remotest municipalities of Upper Canada – the children of "the rich and the poor meeting together," and under the protection and blessing of God "the Maker of them all," imbibing the first elements of knowledge at the same fountain, commencing the race of life upon equal terms, and cultivating feelings of mutual respect and sympathy, which, while they in no respect intrude upon the providential arrangements of order and rank in society, divest poverty of its meanness and its hatreds, and wealth of its arrogance and selfishness.[24]

The essential economic relationships, the orders and ranks of society were not to be disturbed; they were "providential." What free schooling was to change were the attitudes of the classes to each other. The poor would lose their envy, and the rich their exclusiveness.

School promoters argued that in school sections where all supported and sent their children to the same school, "mutual affection" was almost inevitable. The practical knowledge taught in common schools was held out as a catalyst that would bind the different classes of society into closer mutual dependence and friendship, while even the traditional public examination was portrayed as a sort of community festival which drew the people of a school section together.[25] It was the belief of the Chairman of the London School Board in 1860, that the Upper Canadian school system would eventually break down all distinctions "between the mechanic and the millionaire," at least from an educational point of view.[26]

If the school system was to encourage the development of social harmony, it had to be above politics, and school promoters endeavoured to prove that a non-partisan school system was a divinely-inspired necessity. They were equally quick to suggest that the divisions of party came from the devil, and that such divisions represented death to the school system. The "virus of party spirit," Ryerson argued, was poisonous to the interests of education; the "clangour and jostling of party conflicts" were its "funeral knell." Education always perished in the social storm, but grew and bloomed and bore fruit in the "serenity and sunshine of social peace and harmony."[27] Education, then, not only led to social harmony; without social harmony, it appeared, one could not have education. In such statements the priorities of educators were subtly reversed, and the creation or preservation of a harmonious educational system was itself revealed as a goal perhaps even more fundamental than the "social harmony" which was supposed to result from it. The means were beginning to overtake the end.

In this vein, reminders on the subject of politics seemed constantly necessary, lest political antagonisms disrupt the school system. In 1845, teachers were informed by the Education Office that they should "neither countenance nor permit their pupils to discuss matters connected with religious or political opinion." In the summer of 1850, a warning went out to the wardens of the new counties to avoid mixing politics with education. Local superintendents should not be men who were active in politics; the entire superintendency of the school system, in fact, "should be perfectly free from the spirit or tinge of political partisanship." In this way, its influence, "like the genial light and warmth of the sun," could be employed for the "equal benefit of all without regard to party, sect or colour." The same principle was applied to the *Journal of Education*, from which "all controversial or disputatious subjects" were excluded as a matter of policy,[28] and to the authorization of school books. With respect to the latter, the reasoning of the Council of Public Instruction became a matter of considerable dispute in the 1860s, and Ryerson's defence of a Council decision between two textbooks on Canadian history is worth quoting at some length:

> The "Summary of Canadian History," published by Mr. Campbell, was confined to *Canada*; and, as far as relates to Upper Canada, since 1815, it was a bald and partial rehash of old party disputes between individuals, parties, governors, and assemblies, which should not be taught in any school, if remembered by anybody, without an account of the progress and institutions of the country, which ought to be taught in the schools. Mr. Hodgins' little book was "Geography and History of Canada, *and of other Colonies of the Empire*;" it was written nine years ago in the true spirit of Confederation, contained nothing which any sect or party could object to; was written in the proper school book style and spirit, narrated the progress of the country and its institutions, and taught Canadian youth that there were other British Provinces in North America besides Canada's with which we have affinity and interest.[29]

As in every other sphere of the school system, approved textbooks were designed to spread the doctrine of social harmony and progress, and to ignore or suppress the facts of social and political conflict.

Blandness and uniformity in the treatment of sensitive subjects, then, was the educators' prescription for the promotion of social harmony. Politics was certainly a sensitive subject; so too was religion.

In 1847, Ryerson argued that all were agreed on the "absolute necessity of making Christianity the basis and cement of the structure of public education." Religion, most school promoters believed, was essential to social order; secular learning without it was like "a steam-engine without its safety valve."[30] The Council of Public Instruction attempted to put this maxim into practice by making regulations in October of 1850, which, as amended in 1855 and 1857, required that all common schools have opening and closing exercises consisting of the Lord's Prayer and reading from the Scriptures, and that the Ten Commandments be taught.

Similar rules were written for the grammar schools after their incorporation into the general school system in 1853. Christianity, it was officially laid down in connection with the latter regulations, was the basis of law and freedom, as well as the cement and ornament of society.[31]

The Education Office put pressure on teachers and trustees by requiring information about religion in the superintendents' annual reports. Were the schools opened with a prayer? Was the Bible in use? To what church or denomination did the teacher belong? Ryerson summarized the answers in his annual reports and attempted to show, in answer to those critics who claimed that the schools were Godless, that in fact they were getting more religious all the time. That the pressure worked can be seen from the local reports themselves. A typical one, which was reprinted in the March, 1855, *Journal of Education*, claimed that "all the public schools," in a certain unnamed Upper Canadian city were "now opened and closed by the teacher reading aloud a portion of the Scriptures and the Lord's prayer;" and that in almost all cases, the children voluntarily repeated the prayer with the teacher.[32]

There was, as has been shown, strong opposition to this trend on the grounds that such exercises and Bible readings constituted a blatant Protestant intrusion into the schools. But Ryerson and his supporters continued to maintain that they were indispensable and that the public schools remained non-sectarian since, in theory, children could opt out of participating in the prescribed exercises. "Special religious training and nurture," an 1859 Education Office circular argued, were still very much the preserve of the pastor and the parent. Nevertheless, as I have suggested earlier, it is probable that insistence on religious exercises in the common schools was largely responsible for increasing Roman Catholic demands for separate schools.[33]

Ryerson always regretted the legislation that had created the right to separate schools in 1841, and claimed that he had not been responsible for any of the laws that made their extension possible. But by the late 1850s, even he had come to believe that the separate schools' right to exist could not be challenged. The chief superintendent defended them at this point on the grounds that they had few ill effects on the "national" or state system; that the rights extended to the Protestant minority in Lower Canada could not be denied to the Roman Catholics in Upper Canada; and that, once granted, corporate rights could not be taken away. But the telling argument, when it came to class relations, was his view that it was important for Upper Canadian

Roman Catholics to realize that they lived in a society where all classes enjoyed equal rights. The privilege of separate schools constituted more than equal rights, in Ryerson's opinion, but he argued that it was better to "lean on the side of indulgence than to give any pretext for complaining of persecution." In his annual report for 1857, Ryerson implied that the rights of separate schools were very much tied in his thinking, despite numerous earlier and later denials, to his concern to defend the existence of denominational colleges and their right to financial assistance from the state. He may have found it hard to defend one and not the other. But the argument that Ryerson used most tied the existence of separate schools to the well-being of the common school system. He described the separate schools as a kind of "safety valve" for the explosion and evaporation of those feelings of hostility and alienation which, he believed, would otherwise be arrayed against the national schools. The requirements of social harmony within the school system demanded indulgence and the possibility of separation for the minority.[34]

For all his efforts to defend the separate schools against those who would have abolished them outright, Ryerson was never completely comfortable with them. He believed, as we have seen, that separate school children were condemned to social inferiority because the separate schools themselves were bound to be inferior. Perhaps even more crucial was his feeling, which became especially strong in the 1860s, that the safety valve idea might be wrong. All along he had argued that the "tendency of the age" was towards co-operation among religious classes "rather than isolation and estrangement from each other." Yet the overriding reason for co-operation, in the end, was the more fundamental fact that life itself was really a battle. It was therefore essential that all classes start as much as possible on an equal footing, and with the sentimental and religious bonds that a common schooling could provide. If they did not, Ryerson believed, the danger was that those made inferior by inferior schooling would resort to violence and crime to obtain their ends.[35]

By the late 1850s and 1860s, some educators suspected that in Toronto, the Roman Catholic population made up "five-sixths, if not nine-tenths, of the juvenile vagrants and criminals of the city."[36] A second link, between Catholicism and violence, in the minds of many, was made with the upsurge of Fenianism at the close of the American Civil War. Were local criminal activity and violence products of Irish Catholic separate schools? Ryerson began to think that perhaps this was so. When Roman Catholics were deprived of the opportunity to make friendly contact with the Protestant majority in youth, he argued, they were more likely to be alienated from society as adults. By 1865, Ryerson was predicting disaster. He listed the dangerous feelings and actions that were bound to result from the exclusion of Roman Catholic youth from the mainstream. Such isolation produced

> envy, then hatred of the more successful and prosperous classes, then mutual consultations and excitements to revenge their imaginary wrongs, and relieve themselves of their deeply felt but self-inflicted evils; and then, among the more daring and least scrupulous portion of such isolated community, the combinations and conspiracies of Fenianism – the employment of brute force to obtain power and wealth, which can only be legitimately obtained by the exercise of virtue, intelligence and industry.[37]

Whatever the merits or weaknesses of the separate schools in reality, or the variations in Ryerson's opinion of them, the message was always the same: a major purpose and function of the school system was the prevention of violent solutions to the problems of class inequality.

If the school system was designed to encourage attitudes of brotherly love and harmony, it was also intended to produce discipline in its lower class graduates. During his European tour of 1845, Ryerson expressed his admiration for the schools of Amsterdam, where the poor were instructed cheaply, without the use of the rod, but with perfect order.[38] School regulations published during the mid-century years stressed punctuality, orderly conduct and industry, while the whole school system seemed designed to create order and uniformity where before there had been none. Among the goals of the system was clearly the development of the practical habits and values that were held to be necessary to all working men in an urban, industrial economy. Local superintendents and school trustees stressed the disciplinary theme. Perhaps, like the school authorities in Collingwood in 1858, they purchased a bell to encourage punctuality in the children and to prevent latecomers from disturbing the harmony of the classroom. In increasing numbers of schools around the province, children who came late began to find the school door locked, a situation which led to much dispute, particularly in rural areas where distances between home and school were long.

The Reverend George Blair of Durham County lectured the local populace on the importance of discipline in the schools, arguing that it was "the most important lesson" that could be taught, and one without which all other lessons are "comparatively useless."[39] But it was not an easy lesson. An article in the *Journal of Education* sympathized with teachers attempting to reduce to orderly conduct children who had never been confined in their lives before:

> Little, restless, wandering things, that have roamed here and there at will, must be taught to sit still. Little irritable and pugnacious spirits . . . must be made quiet . . . You must not expect to do in a moment what can only be done in a week. Habits of order, obedience, attention, are not the mushrooms that spring in a dewy morning, but trees that have grown in many a day of sun and shower.[40]

Sympathy was also expressed for the teacher attempting to inculcate these habits in the coarse and unmannerly by Victoria College Principal Samuel Nelles in an inspirational address to the Teachers' Association of Ontario. The job was a hard one, he said, but the rewards were great, for the "ruder the materials on which we work, and the more repulsive the surroundings, the greater our praise." In the hands of the teacher alone was the wand of the enchanter, by which savages were "transformed into men."[41]

The alternatives to schooling and inculcating discipline in the poor, educators believed, were crime and its associated costs to society. They felt no qualms, therefore, in describing a school system as "a branch of the national police," designed not only to "occupy a large portion of the rising population," but also "to support and restrain many of the grownup population."[42] As Edward Scarlett, from Northumberland County, put it in 1863, common schools were the "cheapest form of moral police" that could be established in any country. Toronto School Superintendent George Barber simply argued that school houses were better public investments "than Penitentiaries or jails."[43] A similar view had been expressed slightly differently by the superintendent of schools in the Eastern District in 1849. He summed up educational reform with the argument that schools were probably the easiest and cheapest as well as the best response that the community could make to the perennial problem of poverty. All communities would have "to drag along with them a certain number of poor and helpless," he pointed out. The "most pleasant," and "cheapest and most effectual way" of reducing this number, and enlightening the minds of the children of the poor, was to educate them. The result would be useful members of society who might even support their own indigent parents. The result of not educating them, on the other hand, was that most would "continue in the same degradation of their parents and so always accumulate the common burden which property in some sense or other must bear."[44]

That it was "property" that would benefit in the long run from the education of the poor became axiomatic. Free schools were the rich man's security, according to an 1848 editorial in the *Journal of Education*. Over and over again, Ryerson pointed out that the payment of a tax by the rich for the schooling of the poor was recognized in enlightened Massachusetts and in those European countries "where the value of education was understood," as the best means of safeguarding property and even of enhancing its value. And his opinion was echoed in statements by other Upper Canadian educators. The investment in education, they believed, guaranteed the safe possession of the taxpayer's goods, for a disciplined and moral working class would not steal or rise up against property.[45] Critics might claim that the free school system was a kind of socialism or communism, but they were wrong:

> In no country is private property held more sacred, and more effectually protected than in the countries of Free Schools, – Prussia, Switzerland and the New England States of America. Socialist newspapers do not exist in any free school state of America; they only exist in states where the system of free schools has not yet formed and developed the popular mind.[46]

In a country of free schools, the argument went on, all property would be worth more. Ryerson claimed that the value of land, especially, was "maintained or increased" by the "labor, enterprise and intelligence" of those who lived in the surrounding neighbourhood. Education, therefore, was a good community and national, as well as individual, investment. "Whatever ... tends to develop the physical resources of a country, must add to the value of property; and is not this the tendency of the education of the people?" Ryerson wanted to know. Indeed, the chief superintendent was entirely willing to admit that mass education was really of more benefit to the propertied than the poor; that the "balance of gain financially" in the long run, was on the side of "the wealthier classes of the community."[47]

After the inculcation of appropriate social morality, schooling had the further task of developing industry in the poor. Ryerson's explanation of this point in *Elements of Political Economy* has a very modern ring about it. The true way of assisting the poor, according to the argument put forward in this book, was "to make them agents in bettering their own condition ... to supply them, not with a temporary stimulus but with a permanent energy."[48] Apathy and listlessness would be conquered in the schools, which would instil industry and vigour in the labouring classes, a vigour which was essential to the health of society. The favoured metaphor was one of growth. As the sap rose from the ground in the vegetable world, Ryerson argued, so it was in the structure of human society. With "a stagnant lower class" no community could be well, no country powerful or strong.[49] The schools would conquer lower class apathy for the good of all.

Thus it was the whole society, in the long run, that was to benefit from an integrated and invigorated class of labourers in Upper Canada. The poor would gain power and "the unmeasured power of their intelligence and enterprise" would soon be "added to the resources of their country." An added bonus deriving from the social harmony developed in the schools was the more rapid advancement of society towards the ultimate goal of collective control over nature:

> Is not education in fact the power of the people to make all the resources of their country tributary to their interests and comforts? And is not this the most obvious and prominent distinguishing feature between an educated and an uneducated people – the power of the former, and the powerlessness of the latter, to develop the resources of nature and providence, and make them subservient to human interests and enjoyments?[50]

It was through his technology, the power of mind over matter, that man would make "the great store-house of nature minister to his wants, tastes and pleasures." His technology, furthermore, was the chain that would bind the different classes of society and even the nations and continents into "mutual dependence."[51] It was thus that education would ultimately lead to a final resolution not only of class differences, but even of the conflict between nations and empires.

NOTES

[1]"Permanency and Prospects of the System of Common Schools in Upper Canada," *Annual Report for 1850,* Appendix II, p. 215.

[2]For a discussion of the breakdown of these relations in Reformation England see Lawrence Stone, "The Disenchantment of the World," *The New York Review of Books,* XVII (December, 1971), 19.

[3]Quoted in R. G. Riddell, ed., "Egerton Ryerson's Views on the Government of Upper Canada in 1836," *Canadian Historical Review,*

XIX (December, 1938); Sissons, ed., *Egerton Ryerson,* I, 319.

[4]*Ibid.,* II, 7-8.

[5]J. M. S. Careless, *The Union of the Canadas: The Growth of Canadian Institutions, 1841-1857,* chapter 7; J. Harold Putman, *Egerton Ryerson and Education in Upper Canada,* p. 149.

[6]"A Lecture on the Social Advancement of Canada," JEUC, II (December, 1849), 178-181.

[7]*Ibid.,* p. 181.

[8]*Copies of Correspondence between the Roman Catholic Bishop of Toronto and the Chief Superintendent of Schools on the Subject of Roman Catholic Separate Schools* (Toronto, 1852), pp. 16-17.

[9]Sissons, ed., *Egerton Ryerson,* I, 193-97, 539-40; II, 66.

[10]P. G. Cornell, *The Alignment of Political Groups in Canada, 1841-1867* (Toronto, 1962), p. 19.

[11]Egerton Ryerson, *The New Canadian Dominion: Dangers and Duties of the People in Regard to their Government* (Toronto, 1867).

[12]J. L. H. Henderson, *John Strachan, 1778-1867* (Toronto, 1969), p. 43; *Annual Report for 1848,* p. 36.

[13]*Report on a System of Public Elementary Instruction* (Montreal, 1847), p. 20.

[14]*Elements of Political Economy,* pp. 107-08, 117.

[15]"On the Social Advancement of Canada," JEUC, II (December, 1849).

[16]*Report on a System of Public Elementary Instruction,* pp. 18-19.

[17]*Annual Report for 1852,* Appendix A, p. 130.

[18]"Duty of Public Men of All Classes in Reference to Common Schools," JEUC, II (May, 1849); *Annual Report for 1848,* p. 37; *Copies of Documents relating to the Common Schools of the City, forwarded by the Board of School Trustees to the City Council* (Toronto, 1858), p. 14.

[19]*Extracts from the Chief Superintendent's Report on Education in Upper Canada for the Year 1857* (Toronto, 1859), p. 49.

[20]For a discussion of the free school debate, see Peter N. Ross, "The Free School Controversy in Toronto, 1848-1852," in Katz and Mattingly, eds., *Education and Social Change,* pp. 57-80.

[21]*Annual Report for 1852,* Part I, p. 16.

[22]*Annual Report for 1848,* p. 36.

[23]Dexter D'Everardo to Ryerson, 30 April 1850, RG 2 C-6-C, PAO; William Frazer to Ryerson, 29 May 1849, RG 2 C-6-C, PAO.

[24]*Annual Report for 1848,* p. 37; *Annual Report for 1852,* Part I, p. 17.

[25]*Annual Report for 1847,* Part I, p. 17.

[26]*Annual Report for 1860,* Appendix A, p. 192.

[27]"Third Annual Address to the People of Upper Canada," JEUC, IV (January, 1851), 1.

[28]*Forms, Regulations and Instructions for Making Reports, and Conducting all the Necessary Proceedings under the Act 7th Victoria, Cap XXIX and for the Better Organization and Government of Common Schools in Canada West* (Cobourg, 1845), p. 30; *The Common School Acts of Upper Canada; and the Forms, Instructions and Regulations for*

Executing their Provisions; together with the Circulars Addressed to the Various Officers concerned in the Administration of the School Law by the Chief Superintendent of Schools (Toronto, 1853), pp. 70-71; "Original Communications for this Journal," JEUC, XIV (April, 1861), 57.

[29]*The School Book Question: Letters in Reply to the Brown-Campbell Crusade against the Education Department* (Montreal, 1866), p. 8. The favoured text, it should be noted, was by J. George Hodgins, Ryerson's protegé in the Education Office.

[30]*Report on a System of Public Elementary Instruction,* p. 32; Ryerson to Draper, 15 April 1844, DHE, V, 105; Ryerson, *The Clergy Reserves Question* (Toronto, 1839), p. 126.

[31]"Religious Instruction in the Common Schools, 1859," DHE, XIV, 267; "Programme of Public Instruction in Upper Canada," JEUC, VIII (February, 1855), 24.

[32]*Annual Report for 1866,* Part I, p. 9; "Educational Intelligence: Canada," JEUC, VIII (March, 1855), 45.

[33]"Religious Instruction in the Common Schools, 1859," DHE, XIV, 266. Ryerson wavered from this position for a brief period in 1862, when he for a while supported the idea of government financed charity schools for all denominations willing or able to instruct the poor. At that time, he implied that all religious instruction had to be sectarian in the sense that it was given by a member of some sect. See chapter 6; also DHE, XVII, 180.

[34]*Special Report on the Separate School Provisions of the School Law* (Toronto, 1858), p. 16; *Extracts from the Chief Superintendent's Report for 1857,* p. 27; *Copies of Correspondence between the Chief Superintendent of Schools, and other persons, on the Subject of Separate Schools* (Toronto, 1855), p. 233.

[35]*Annual Report for 1852,* Part I, p. 21.

[36]*Annual Report for 1857,* p. 28; see also *Annual Report for 1868,* Appendix A, p. 43 and "Industrial Day School for Vagrant Children," (1868), DHE, XX, 280.

[37]Sissons, ed., *Egerton Ryerson,* II, 500.

[38]"Doctor Ryerson on the Schools of the Continent of Europe in 1845," DHE, V, 238.

[39]*Annual Report for 1858,* Appendix A, p. 78; Charles Merrill to Ryerson, 24 October 1859, RG 2 C-6-C, PAO, is a complaint about the locking of school doors against children who had to walk between three and four miles to school.

[40]*Annual Report for 1866,* Appendix A, p. 23; "Difficulties of Young Teachers," JEUC, XVIII (October, 1865), 156.

[41]"Ontario Teachers' Association Convention in 1869," DHE, XXI, 288.

[42]*Extracts from the Chief Superintendent's Report for 1857,* p. 17.

[43]*Annual Report for 1863,* Appendix A, p. 112; *Copies of Documents Relating to the Common Schools of the City,* p. 9.

[44]William Frazer to Ryerson, 29 May 1849, RG 2 C-6-C, PAO.

[45]"System of Schools in Cities and Towns," JEUC, I (May, 1848), 151; Ryerson to the Provincial Secretary, 27 March 1847, DHE, VII,

193; "Free School-Agitation Crusade in Toronto, 1852," DHE, X, 278; *A Special Report on Systems of Popular Education* (Toronto, 1868), p. 139; "The Newly Revised Upper Canada Common School Bill of 1843," DHE, IV, 240; see also *Report of the Past History, and Present Condition of the Common or Public Schools of the City of Toronto* (Toronto, 1859), p. 24; *Annual Report for 1869*, Appendix D, p. 110.

[46]"Origin of the Principle of Free Schools in the Canadian System," JEUC, V (February, 1852), 24.

[47]*Special Report on the Separate School Provisions of the School Law*, p. 52; *Annual Report for 1848*, p. 38.

[48]*Elements of Political Economy*, pp. 151-52.

[49]Sissons, ed., *Egerton Ryerson*, II, 475.

[50]"Duty of Public Men of All Classes in Reference to Common Schools," JEUC, II (May, 1849), 72 ; *Annual Report for 1848*, p. 38.

[51]"The Importance of Education to a Manufacturing, and a Free People," JEUC, I (October, 1848), 289.

Chapter 6

Class and the Schools

And the erection of good school houses in cities or
towns is a necessary preliminary step to the classification of schools – to the removal of the objections as to
the improper and indiscriminate mixture of children at
public schools – the establishment of schools of different degrees, as well male as female, so that there will be
high or select schools for the more advanced pupils as
well as primary schools for the youngest children –
requiring as an indispensable condition of admission
(as always is the case in the American cities of free
schools in regard to schools of all grades) *good
clothing* and *personal neatness,* as well as good conduct.

Journal of Education,
January, 1852[1]

A fundamental proposition of mid-nineteenth century educational reform was that the schools, considered collectively, ought
to be for all classes of society. If they were made free, there was
no reason in theory why all children could not be schooled.
Ideally, rich and poor would be educated side by side, and
together acquire the values and disciplines required of successful
working people of whatever class, and the sense of community
that would prevent war between the classes.

Ideal and reality, however, parted company almost from the
beginning. The school system which emerged from the Ryerson
era reflected not only the twin goals of consolidation and univer-
sality, but also the contradictions involved in promoting at the
same time a class society. School reformers did not, perhaps,
intend to create respectable middle class schools for respectable
middle class children, and tough, nasty schools for poor children

who needed to be disciplined. Indeed, they wanted all children to be respectable and middle class as well as disciplined and orderly. But they clearly felt, nevertheless, that the school system ought to provide different kinds of education for different classes of people.

Free common schools were gradually adopted by communities across Upper Canada during Ryerson's superintendency. By the late 1850s, more than half were free and, in 1871 the public elementary schools into which the lower grades of the common schools had evolved were required to be free by law. The hope was expressed that the grammar schools and in 1871, the high schools and collegiate institutes created out of the old grammar schools and central common schools, would also become universally free and accessible to all classes. Reforms were introduced in the grammar schools during the period that were expressly designed to prevent them from remaining what many had apparently become, the elementary schools of the privileged. Finally, the compulsory attendance law of 1871 attempted to see that the largess offered to all was actually received by all. According to the law, all children between the ages of seven and twelve were to attend school for a minimum of four months a year. By all these measures, the schools were indeed transformed.

But the changes could not bring about genuine equality of educational opportunity, nor in the final analysis, were they really designed to do so. In their anxiety to promote educational improvement, school reformers tended to give financial rewards to those who were already most "improved," thereby adding to rather than diminishing existing inequalities. Equality was interpreted as getting everyone into the system, with all kinds of incentives and improvements provided for those who did well, and increasing pressure and even coercion for the rest. It is true that there was no simple pattern of development to this end: local communities at different times and places in Upper Canada displayed an immense variety of responses to the educational problem as local authorities saw it. One might add that it was to the credit of Upper Canadian school promoters that a variety of responses was for such a long time possible. Debate on the local level, as on the provincial one, was protracted and intense. But by the time the School Law of 1871 was passed, tax-supported schools, especially in urban centres, were well on the way to becoming the large, differentiated and complex institutions desired by the majority of educators, and instruction in them was, for those who could afford no alternative, compulsory in theory and in law. What is debatable is the social significance of these events.

139

Any discussion of education and class must deal with several basic questions. Who, we want to know, attended what schools and for how long? In what ways, secondly, may the schools themselves have fostered class distinctions among those who attended them? Although the evidence is often contradictory, the answers to these questions suggested by the sources confirm what has already been said so far, namely that schooling in Ryerson's Upper Canada was strongly influenced by considerations of class.

In 1859, Ryerson proclaimed the accessibility of the school system of Upper Canada. It was, he argued, an "agency of universal education" in which "the poor man" had "equal rights and privileges with the rich man." The ideal was echoed in the reports of local superintendents. According to John Fraser of Goderich, the common schools, at least, were the schools of the people and were open to "all classes and conditions," in 1858. S. D. Clark reported from Ernestown in 1860 that he could see a marked improvement in his native township. "I believe that no system has ever been produced so well calculated to place proper food for the mind within the reach of all, irrespective of wealth or station."[2]

To Robert McCrum of Leeds County, however, real equality was not a present fact so much as a future hope. Many subjects were neglected in the common schools of Leeds and Lansdowne Front in 1857. "I trust, however," said McCrum, "the time is not far distant when these important branches will be taught in every school throughout Canada, and that they will be equally accessible to the poor man's child as the rich man's, irrespective of classes or creeds or position in society."[3] McCrum had struck on what was to remain a central problem in the quest for equal educational opportunity: the fact that a school district where everyone was poor could not afford a good school. A second problem was that all schools were not really open to all children. The grammar schools were the most notoriously exclusive, but even entrance to common schools was restricted, in some cases by rates, in others by more subtle obstacles to attendance. William Ormiston, who was a grammar school inspector in the late 1850s, also placed his hopes in the future, anticipating a day "not far distant," when every school in the land would be opened to anyone wishing to enter it, "without distinction of class, or sex, or colour." Ormiston referred as well to another major problem facing mid-century educators, the apparent reluctance of some people to send their children to school, even when the common schools were made free. He looked for "wise and beneficent regulations" which would see to it that the boon of schooling – once "*provided* for all" – was actually "*secured* to all."[4]

At the heart of the matter was a basic ambiguity, not only about what the schools were supposed to do, but about who they were really for. There was a special ambiguity about the place of the common school, since different groups of people either flocked to them or rejected them for a great variety of reasons.

One view was that the common schools were basically for the poor, a view which alienated a good many people who did not like to think of themselves as recipients of charity. In the common schools, the *Toronto Patriot* wrote in 1850, "the lower classes" would learn "not only to read, but *to think.*" To the Reverend J. Benson Kellogg of Oxford County in 1864, the common schools were to give to "the great mass of our people" an education "befitting their station and circumstances in life." A speaker at the Ontario Teachers' Association Annual Meeting in 1869 described the clients of the common schools as "the children of the toilers," whose future was destined to be "the drudgery of material labour."[5]

Egerton Ryerson often displayed a similar attitude to the common schools. Free schools were necessary, he claimed in 1852, because it was essential not to exclude "the poor," the "very class of the population" whom it was most important to persuade to enter them. A decade later he still saw their essential purpose to be the education of the poor.[6] Nevertheless, Ryerson made a strong distinction between the national schools of Ireland which were meant *only* for the poor, and those of Upper Canada which he insisted were ideally for all classes. Thus to an audience assembled at the John Street School in 1855, he declared that the common schools were the colleges of "the Mass of the People," but added the important rider that the children ought to be sent to school neat and clean, so that rich and poor could not be distinguished there and the rich would have no excuse to withdraw their children.[7]

If there was confusion about who they were intended to serve, there was also disagreement about who was actually attending the common schools. In 1850, the Eastern District Teachers' Association maintained that the "gentry" held the local schools beneath them and tended to keep teachers in their families, or to send their children away to private or grammar schools. School reports from the 1850s reveal a similar situation in Toronto. The "more advanced, the more respectable and the older pupils have to a considerable extent withdrawn from the common schools," Toronto's Superintendent George Barber complained in 1851. A

Toronto alderman warned that the children of his constituents, who were mostly tradesmen (and not the "poorer classes") were virtually driven from the schools and that their parents would remain dissatisfied until Toronto added a "better class" of schools to the system – perhaps one or two central schools "to accommodate a better class of scholar and master and mistress." In 1857, George Barber attributed prejudice against the schools to the name "common" which suggested a low, vulgar meaning, and to the fact that the schools, because free, were associated with charity. James Porter, who was superintendent of the Toronto system in the 1860s and early 1870s expressed a similar point of view. He contrasted Ontario in 1872 with the United States, where, he said, public schools were attended by all classes. In Ontario, and especially in the cities and towns of the province, there were many parents who had not yet overcome their prejudice against the common schools and continued to prefer a private education for their children.[8]

But the evidence is not entirely consistent. The report of J. B. Boyle for Toronto in 1852 directly contradicts Barber's assessment of 1851. In Boyle's opinion, the respectable children were not withdrawing from the common schools of the city. In Ottawa, the local superintendent reported in 1861 that the prejudice previously noted among "the more respectable portion of our community" against sending their children to the common schools was rapidly declining. Not only were many of the well-to-do attending, but many of the best prepared grammar school candidates were now common school graduates. In Goderich in 1858, a new building had attracted the children of respectable families to the local common school, according to the superintendent.[9]

The alternatives to attending the common schools, then – and whether or not one chose an alternative – depended on the locality. As it turns out, the incidence of alternative schooling also depended on the decade. In the early years of the Ryerson era, quite young children could still go to colleges, to the preparatory schools that were sometimes associated with them, or to grammar schools. Many, no doubt, continued to be taught at home. There were also, throughout the period, numerous private schools and academies, especially in the urban centres. In Toronto, an interesting alternative to the city common school system existed in the model school attached to the provincial teaching training institution known as the Normal School. An examination of enrolment statistics for the province, furthermore, indicates that a sizable proportional increase in the very small numbers using private schools occurred in the 1850s. If one examines Toronto alone, the same pattern over time is discernable. The importance of locality is demonstrated, however, by comparing proportions of children attending common schools or using alternatives in Toronto and in the province as a whole. In 1859, only 62.8% of Toronto's children were in the common schools, compared to 79.7% recorded for the province. In the province, alternative schooling attracted only 3.2% of the school-age population, while in Toronto the proportion had reached 13.3% at the same date. A decade later, it is true, 80% of the city's school-age children were recorded as enrolled in the common schools, but alternative schooling remained relatively high in 1869 at 14.9%.[10]

We have the testimony of one Toronto parent on the reasons for choosing an alternative to the common school, in a letter dated 1868 from A. A. Riddell to a friend in Elora, Ontario. In it, Riddell reported that when he "became a professional" the common schools were "made uncomfortable" for his children. Since the family could not afford to send them to a private school, they went instead to "the Model." Somehow, the children of professionals didn't fit in, in at least one Toronto common school.[11]

An important alternative to the common school in more than one community was clearly the district or county grammar school. Very young children were frequently permitted to attend, the pupil-teacher ratio was usually lower than that of the common school and the teacher much better paid. It was certainly the belief of Ryerson and several of the early grammar school inspectors that some Upper Canadian families used the grammar schools for acquiring an ordinary English education, rather than for preparation for university or a profession. It was this belief, in part, that was behind the campaign to bring the grammar schools more closely under provincial control in the 1850s and, in the 1860s, to reduce or eliminate the enrolment of girls in these institutions. It was the contention of leading educators that attendance at the grammar schools, and the high schools and collegiate institutes that replaced them in 1871, ought to be tied to academic ambition and ability, rather than to social status or wealth.[12]

But great care must be taken not to exaggerate what has been called by at least one Canadian historian of education the "democratization" of the Ontario grammar school.[13] The grammar school students of the 1860s and the high school and collegiate pupils of the 1870s were to be no less an elite; their claim to status, however, was increasingly to be an "educational" one. Ryerson saw the grammar schools as providing a higher level of education for those who would become the future leaders of society. It was not the number of grammar school graduates that counted, his *Annual Report for 1857* emphasized; it was the "relation that such persons have always sustained, and must ever sustain, in administering the laws and institutions of every community, and in developing its highest material and general interest."[14]

All the evidence suggests in fact that it was considered very unusual for common school students to go on to grammar school even towards the end of the Ryerson period. In 1864, the school superintendent for Toronto argued that very few common school children proceeded to "higher" education; in 1869 there were only thirteen graduates of Toronto common schools in the grammar schools of the city. Even in London, where, apparently, nearly everyone went to the common schools, only a few "working class" children made it to the free grammar school there in 1864, according to the annual report for that year. Of eleven grammar schools which provided free schooling to some or all of their pupils in 1862, only Belleville reported a substantial number of common school graduates admitted free, with twenty-eight such scholars. Brampton had four, the remainder had none. It would appear that fees, the necessity of going to work, the expense of living away from home in some cases, perhaps the desire of parents to keep children at home, or even the old exclusive reputation of the grammar schools, prevented the vast majority of common school leavers from attending them.[15]

The grammar schools of the 1860s remained, therefore, almost as exclusive as they had been in the 1840s and 50s. A provincial inspector saw nothing wrong in 1869, for example, with the preparatory schools that had sprung up in connection with many of them. These were designed to prepare students for grammar school entrance and thus clearly provided another way to avoid attending the local common schools. Yet the inspector was able to suggest that such preparatory schools ought to be given formal recognition in the law.[16] Clearly, in spite of their desire to strengthen the common school, school men like this inspector sympathized also with the demand for something "above" a common school education for some privileged members of the community.

The English high schools and collegiate institutes of 1871 were also seen as providing not only a more advanced education than the public elementary schools, but an education that was somehow of a "better class." The prototype of the tax-supported English high school emerged to challenge the grammar school long before the School Act of 1871, in the form of the central common school in a number of the larger towns. This was a big, centrally located school made up of what had been, in theory, the higher classes in the various ward schools. Many communities took advantage of a provision in the law to create "union schools" which permitted the combination of grammar and common school funds, and the use of one building for both schools. The standards of the London Collegiate Institute, which was a school of this sort, were evidently so high that, by 1867, local "gentle-men" were giving up the practice of sending their sons to England and allowing them to obtain an education at the collegiate institute instead.[17] The extremely high use of alternative schooling in Toronto during the period may well have been related to the fact that the Toronto public system, unlike those of London, Hamilton or Brantford, did not have a central common school. And even though a great variety of alternatives were available in Toronto, the demand for such a school was nevertheless heard by the mid-1860s.[18] As Alexander Bartlett of Windsor put it, many parents were "averse to their children learning the classics," yet wanted them to enjoy "a much higher education than the Common School affords."[19]

High schools and classical collegiate institutes officially replaced the central common schools and the grammar schools of the 1850s and 60s in 1871. By 1879, Education Minister Adam Crooks was able to say that the proper functions of high schools and the former common schools were now completely understood as being for secondary and elementary education respectively. To show that the department was serious about restricting the high schools to their function of higher education, Crooks cited the entrance results for the two previous years. In 1877, only 3,828 out of 7,383 applicants were passed; in 1878, 4,814 out of 9,820.[20] But James Porter of Toronto argued in 1872 that the high schools would be restricted in more than just the academic sense. They were not, according to Porter, "strictly, as in the United States, a higher step or platform of that educational pyramid, of which the Public Schools are the base and the University is the apex." Rather, they constituted a "*distinct structure* of which a few choice materials may be supplied from the Public Schools, while the larger portion is obtained from other quarries." With a sort of gentle sarcasm, Porter poked fun at both the pretensions of those who scorned the public schools because they scorned what was "common" and those who supposed that human nature would be radically changed by changing the

145

names of institutions. The implication of his remarks was that the public schools and high schools or collegiate institutes of the early 1870s were little different, socially, from the old common and grammar schools of the past.[21]

During the Ryerson era then, the quest for something "higher" than the common school tended to frustrate the quest for equality of educational opportunity. In some localities, attempts to encourage greater participation by the poor in education may have driven wealthier families away from the common schools. In many places, and especially in the larger towns and cities, there were also ambitious or school-oriented parents who wanted more than the old local or ward common schools could provide, and who sought a better class of education for their children. Increasingly, superior schools were in fact provided within the system, in the form of central schools and it is this trend, presumably, that helps to account for the apparent levelling off of private school development in the 1860s. While the poor were not by definition excluded from the new high schools and collegiate institutes, the vast majority were in fact excluded from them both by the intention of their founders and by the twin barriers of examinations and fees.

The use of alternative schooling and the quest for something better than the elementary common school within the public system meant that at the top end of the social scale during the Ryerson era, inequality would continue to prevail in education. But even more significant, perhaps, was the gradually changing structure of the common school itself.

Several factors were at work. The simple expansion of pupil numbers often meant larger schools, which in turn put a premium on some kind of structuring and segregation. At the same time, reformers argued that the principle of division of labour dictated that schools be divided into classes and grades. Classification was thus associated with both growth and efficiency. The classification of scholars was also tied to that of their teachers. Children, it was thought, ought to be segregated according to age, achievement and sex, and appropriate teachers assigned to each group. The movement came full circle when reformers began to seek school consolidation as a means to these ends. Only in large schools, they began to realize, could the proper classification and segregation take place.

Social standing and wealth were also divisive factors within the common schools. For despite the concern to open them to the poor and the low in status, there continued to be ways in which the schools were discriminatory during the period. If, on the one hand, there were wealthy and even middle class parents who did not want their children in the common schools, there were at the other end of the scale poor and transient or minority parents who found it equally hard to make use of them. Because of this, schooling in predominantly poor urban neighbourhoods or very remote rural sections was unlikely to be genuinely equal to that which was offered in the long settled townships or the neighbourhoods of the well-to-do.

Sheer numbers were clearly a factor of vital importance. Schools grew not only because of increased demand for their services, it would appear, but also because of deliberate efforts to consolidate, to attract more students and create larger institutions, so that reorganization and restructuring could take place. The City of Kingston, for example, decided in 1850 to *"reduce* the number of ward schools and introduce one or two of a higher class" for two reasons. To begin with, this approach to reorganization was seen as a solution to overcrowding in the existing schools. Secondly, it was put forward as a way to deal with the problem of too many older children. In another locality, the school superintendent attributed a decision to divide a particular common school under his jurisdiction to overcrowding alone. What had been a "junior department" became, in this situation, two departments, a primary and a junior, and "a young female teacher" was engaged to teach the latter.[22]

But consolidation and its accompaniment, division into departments or grades, was at the same time held to be a means of actually attracting greater numbers of students. Charles Brooke, the Toronto trustee who was so anxious to promote a central school in the city during the 1860s, wrote to Ryerson in 1865 that "centralization and graduation of schools" was the natural accompaniment of the free school system, and would help to popularize the schools and increase attendance. He even felt that the proposed Toronto central school should charge fees in order to be able to offer "such additional and superior branches" as the trustees might deem advisable, and thus attract to the schools those families who wanted more for their children than was available in the ward schools of the city.[23]

Better teaching was also an important concern. Promoters of graded schools and school systems wished not only to introduce new subjects and to have the right number of students per teacher, per classroom or per school, whether or not they saw this as fewer or greater, but they were also anxious to promote what Ryerson called the "simultaneous mode" of teaching in Upper Canada. Increasingly, individual instruction of pupils in turn, while the others busied themselves or were taught by student monitors, was considered out of date and inefficient compared to any system whereby the teacher could instruct an entire "class," or even more ideally, a whole roomful of children at once. Graded text books and the grading of schools into primary, junior and senior divisions were thus intended to meet more effectively the needs of students grouped according to certain criteria. In 1850, Ryerson quoted from a Massachusetts school report reasons why school sections should be consolidated. The creation of single school boards to govern large areas, according to this statement, resulted in the trustees "having charge of all the Schools" in a municipality; they were thus able to "establish and classify them in such manner as to meet the wants of all ages and classes of youth." Even more important, perhaps, were the perceived needs of teachers. Graded textbooks and schools, it was argued, led to the most efficient use of the time of those in charge. Nothing could be achieved, it was increasingly thought, unless schools adhered in every way possible to the principle of division of labour.[24]

Closely related to educators' concepts of better teaching was the perception of the need for order. Dozens of pupils all doing something different in the same room seemed disorderly. The ideal situation, according to the thesis which Charles Clarkson submitted with his application for an inspectorship in 1871, was to have separate rooms for each class. But if this was impossible because of financial restrictions or the size of the school, Clarkson prescribed class groupings, lots of military drill and mechanical exercises, as well as rigid timetabling, so that no pupil would remain unoccupied or become restless. For others, large schoolhouses meant that the classification of students was easier; classification in turn made for better supervision by the teacher and the more orderly movement of pupils. The same urge was associated with the desire to do away with benches and replace them with individual seats and desks. Large numbers of children in a small space led not only to disorder but to disease. Space and separateness became the creed of progressive school authorities.[25]

A further reason for promoting graded schools was the need to encourage "emulation." Large, graded school systems, all agreed, permitted and stimulated competition among pupils, teachers and schools. Individuals competed for advancement, while teachers and schools competed to see who could produce the most successful pupils.[26]

The obvious way to classify and segregate children, of course, was according to achievement. Samuel Woods reported that by 1869 grading in Kingston was systematic and that no pupil was allowed to enter a higher grade unless he had first been examined by the local superintendent of schools.[27] But equally pervasive was the desire to classify children according to other criteria, and one of the most significant of these was age. Reminiscences of teachers and discussions among school promoters testify to the fact that in many of the common and grammar schools, as well as in many academies and colleges of the early part of the Ryerson period, age was a factor of secondary importance. In only two out of six institutions calling themselves colleges in 1855 were the majority of students over sixteen, while in the same period boys as young as seven attended grammar schools. As late as 1869, it was suggested that an appropriate age for English scholars entering grammar school might be thirteen, but that *bona fide* classical scholars should be admitted at the age of ten.[28]

The common schools ranged even wider. One teacher of the era later recalled that pupils' ages varied from five to thirty and that in several schools he had taught married pupils. He remembered one school in which there were five sisters in the same spelling book, another where whole families had attended the common school at the same time, and yet another in which seventeen out of the sixty-five pupils had been older than himself.[29]

Problems increasingly associated with such a wide age distribution were many and seemed to grow with numbers. The example of a Brantford common school teacher, who, with the assistance of a single sixteen year old boy, was attempting to cope in 1850 with 160 students in one room, may not have been typical, but large schools were more and more the order of the day.[30] Provincial statistics taken over the period from 1846 to 1866, and reproduced in Table 2, suggest furthermore that teacher numbers were not keeping up with pupil numbers.

TABLE 2
Teachers and Pupils in the Common Schools, 1846-1866

	1846	1856	1866
Common School Pupils	101,912	243,935	372,320
Common School Teachers	2,925	3,689	4,789
Pupil-teacher ratio: Pupils per Teacher	34.8	66.1	77.7

From Table S, *Annual Report of the Chief Superintendent of Schools for 1866*, pp. 139-40. The low pupil-teacher ratio for 1846 should probably be adjusted upward. In Ryerson's opinion, the fact that there were approximately 300 more teachers than schools indicated teacher turnover rather than 300 schools with more than one teacher.

Average numbers of pupils registered as attending school in a given year are not the same thing, of course, as average numbers in daily attendance. Official concern to promote regular attendance, moreover, suggests that many students on the registers in fact attended only irregularly.[31] Nevertheless, the campaign to educate more and more children more and more cheaply in the common schools was obviously resulting in a major qualitative change in the nature of such schooling. During the Ryerson era, the problem of overcrowding grew to major proportions.

One solution was to get rid of the youngest and oldest students, or, second best, to separate them. "School age" was variously defined as from five to sixteen or five to twenty-one, and some trustees of free schools began to demand fees from "over-age" scholars. Central schools were established not only to accommodate the most advanced, but also the older pupils, according to some commentators. Where they were not, it would appear that the older children often simply stopped attending the common school. This was the case at least in Simcoe County, where in 1864 William Harvey noted that they had "disappeared" to be replaced by young children who were "mere beginners."[32]

The very young were also increasingly perceived as a problem in the schools. As early as 1847, Ryerson argued that since one could not have small school sections and a good school system, the former ought to be sacrificed to the latter. And if larger sections meant schools too far from home for little children to attend, they should simply stay at home. It would be more efficient, he pointed out, to have a few small schools for little children exclusively, than to preclude the possibility of having large and efficient schools for the rest of the children. In the 1860s, reports from both Toronto and London indicate that authorities in the cities also found large schools and very young children incompatible. J.B. Boyle, who was principal of the London system in 1865, gave several reasons for his belief that five year olds should not be admitted to the common schools:

It may do very well in rural sections where the attendance of such children is only for a few months in the year, where the air is generally pure, out-door exercise unavoidable, and where the class-rooms in the summer time, but for these little ones, would be almost deserted. But in large cities, the case is widely different. In the summer months, children evidently under the legal age are sent to school not to learn, but to be out of the way of the family, and the teacher has no recourse but to accept the statement that the child is just "five." Now, unless the Board should open infant schools and procure the services of teachers properly trained for this department of the work, very little progress will be made with such subjects for the first year, the time of the teachers will be drawn away from others who would profit by it, and the children themselves injured by being kept confined in a classroom, when the nursery or play-ground would be the more fitting place for them.

James Porter also felt that large city schools were no place for very young children, and argued that more space, shorter hours, additional teachers and more suitable activities were essential if the youngest children were to be properly accommodated.[33]

Those in between the youngest and the oldest, it was felt, also ought to be classified by age. One of Ryerson's earliest descriptions of graded school systems divided the children neatly by age groups. Primary schools were for children from six to eight, intermediate schools for those from nine to eleven, and high schools for those twelve and over. He also thought it shocking that students as young as fourteen were admitted to University College in 1861 whereas in England university students had to be eighteen or twenty.[34] His view was that different institutions, or, at the very least, different departments in the same institution, should be set up to deal with students grouped according to age as well as according to scholastic achievement.

The interest of the Education Department in this question was demonstrated in 1871 when the first attempt was made to gather statistics on the ages of common school pupils. Table 3, con-

TABLE 3
Pupil Ages in Ontario Common Schools from 1871 to 1876

	Under 5	5 – 10	11 – 16	17 – 21	Totals
1871 number	2,291	197,293	198,168	22,491	420,243
percentage	.5	46.9	47.2	5.4	
1872 number	2,274	217,618	213,566	21,204	454,662
percentage	.3	47.9	46.9	4.7	
1873 number	1,570	222,712	215,427	21,275	460,984
percentage	.3	48.3	46.7	4.6	
1874 number	1,704	239,858	203,658	18,827	464,047
percentage	.4	51.7	43.9	4.1	
1875 number	1,737	246,689	205,492	20,323	474,241
percentage	.4	52.0	43.3	4.3	-
1876 number	1,321	253,994	212,499	22,723	490,537
percentage	.3	51.8	43.3	4.6	

From the *Annual Reports of the Chief Superintendent of Schools for the years 1871 through 1876.*

structed from data collected over a six year period from 1871 to 1876, illustrates the tendency of the common school to focus increasingly on the younger child.

Changes in the proportion of under-five-year-olds and those between seventeen and twenty-one are so slight that they cannot be said to reveal a shift. But if the numbers are accurate and the six year period represents a continuing trend, it would appear that there was a proportional decline in the number of eleven to sixteen-year-olds in the common schools and a corresponding increase in the proportion of children in the five to ten-year-old group. While there is little doubt that the increased availability of work for children over ten, in the form of factory jobs, was a crucial factor in this change,[35] it may also be the case that the campaign to restrict common or elementary school attendance to pre-adolescents was having an effect.

If one great divide of mid-nineteenth century educational reform was age, another was sex. It was an era when publications like the *Journal of Education* were advising parents that children should sleep in separate beds. Separation of the sexes, as we have seen, was also the ideal of most Upper Canadian educators. The degree to which sexual segregation was actually practised, however, seems to have been less a matter of ideology than of expediency. If numbers were small and only one teacher could be employed, but girls insisted on coming to school, then boys and girls would have to be schooled together. If, on the other hand, funds were adequate and an assistant teacher could be engaged, the assistant was often a woman and the school split into female and male departments, or separate male and female schools. The City of Toronto established its first exclusively female public school in 1851; by 1859 six out of eight of its common schools had separate male and female departments.[36]

In a letter to P. Jaffray of Galt, Ryerson speculated about the possibilities for a village school with a reasonable number of pupils in 1847:

In such a case there should be two branches – male and female – and at least three departments in the male branch, including substantially a Primary and Intermediate and an English High School; each department under a separate Teacher – the pupils advanced from one department to the other according to their attainments, but the whole establishment under one control. But considerable difficulty attends the selection of proper officers in the different departments and the harmonious working of so extensive an establishment – especially were *(sic)* both sexes are included – unless it be a more settled management than that of a rural common school. I am inclined to think you will succeed better by having two schools – male and female – with a good playground attached to the former.[37]

Clearly Ryerson was only thinking at this stage in terms of higher education for boys. Somehow, girls – especially older ones – didn't fit into the scheme. In his uncertainty, he finally advised the safer plan, two completely separate schools. But solutions were left to local authorities and in 1849 an anonymous critic of Upper Canadian education writing under the pseudonym of "L" took Ryerson to task for his failure to provide by law for separate schools for girls.[38]

The concern felt by educators when faced with typical common schools where the sexes were mixed was expressed by W.H. Landon, who was Superintendent of the Brock District in 1848. He noted that most common schools were in exposed and public places and that, in addition, few had privies. The result was that no "delicacy of feeling" could ever be cultivated among school children and that they would grow up brutalized. The Brock District report for the following year predicted the serious degradation of the whole community if these conditions were not remedied, and urged the segregation of the sexes in education.[39]

E. C. Guillet, in his study of the Ontario Teachers' Association, suggests that sexual segregation in the common school system was almost a *fait accompli* by 1864 and cites areas of discrimination ranging from the types of rewards given in the common schools (grammar school scholarships for boys, prizes for girls) to the separation of school libraries into shelves marked "male" and "female." At the Normal School in Toronto, male and female students were not permitted to address each other in the school, let alone meet outside. In the village of Elora it was discovered that the creation of junior and senior common schools out of what had been the boys' and girls' schools, did not give "universal satisfaction," the girls having retreated, for the most part, into private schools. In 1865, Elora decided to build a new school, with two departments, for junior and senior boys respectively. The old schools, it was decided, would be used as junior and senior schools for the girls and sexual segregation once again firmly institutionalized in the public system.[40]

If segregation by sex, age and achievement were the most widespread ways of dividing children, they were of course not the only ones. Separate schools reflecting racial and religious differences were also a product of the period. Perhaps because educational opinion was generally against them, and because in the case of the Roman Catholic separate schools they had important

153

political repercussions, they have received more attention from historians.[41] But people who had no racial or religious differences to divide them found other reasons. Quarrels over school section boundaries and schoolhouse locations were endemic to the period, especially in rural areas where distances were great. The question of rates versus free schools created dissension from one year to the next in the countryside where rate-payers themselves continued to have the choice. In the case of Carlisle, the "poor in the village" who had "4 or 5 children for school" could not afford the 25¢ rate that "the farmers in order to make the school cheap to themselves" had imposed on each child, and wanted their own separate village school.[42]

The segregation of children into groups, classes and separate schools was accompanied by and related to the feeling that children themselves formed a class that should be, as much as possible, segregated from society as a whole. The longer the time in which children stayed in school during the year, and the greater the numbers that attended proportionally, the more this segregation did in fact take place. There is also evidence of a desire to remove the schools, both physically and psychologically, from the wider world. As early as 1819 a citizen complained of the proximity of the public school in Kingston to the blockhouses where troops were quartered, and the consequent indecent scenes and language witnessed by children of both sexes. Later on, scattered protests came to Ryerson about the location of schools near taverns or too close to public roads, and were echoed in the reports of superintendents and in the *Journal of Education*. In 1857, the *Journal* provided, along with printed plans for school buildings, the advice that schools should be sited "apart from railways, factories etc." and in "agreeable and cheerful neighbourhoods." In the meantime, in response to complaints from correspondents and local superintendents about the frequent disruption by rowdies of school proceedings, the government passed a law permitting fines of up to £5 or thirty days in jail for any person who should "wilfully disturb, interrupt or disquiet any Common or other Public School, by rude or indecent behaviour, or by making a noise either within the place . . . or so near as to disturb the order or exercises of such school."[43]

The provincial Normal and Model Schools in Toronto are good examples of the concern to protect scholars from the outside world. When the "annoying conduct of strangers" bothered the "grown-up girls" at the Model School in 1859, Principal Robertson suggested a better fence to solve the problem. Education Office correspondence shows that the whole question of access to the enclosed Normal and Model School grounds (grounds that had originally belonged to the city and been used more or less as a park) was occasionally a stormy one, as school employees did their best to protect not only the students but the gardens from the "depredations" of the public.[44] The same feeling was behind the campaign, one strongly supported by provincial authorities, to do away with rented premises for schools. School buildings and grounds that were owned outright by boards of trustees could be controlled. Rented rooms in buildings used for other purposes, and even the private residences of schoolmasters – commonplace locations for schools up to the middle of the century – began to be thought unsuitable.[45] The correspondence of the Education Office also reveals that local school authorities were beginning to find irksome the claims of religious and other groups to the use of the school house after hours.[46] The school had become property and its use by the public at large too often meant not just moral contamination, but financial loss. The desire to segregate children in various ways cannot be understood apart from this more general urge to separate schools and children from the larger society. At least the children would, in theory, be protected from the adult world and from each other.

The tendency to fragmentation and separation was also intimately associated with the countervailing tendency, especially in urban areas, to consolidate – to create larger and larger schools, as well as school systems composed of more and more schools. The latter clearly must have increased the problems of disorder and social mixing that some educators felt were so dangerous. But on the other hand, it was only in large schools or school systems that the kinds of segregation that school promoters desired could actually be carried out. Robert Campbell of Galt saw the paradox in 1865, and decided that in the final analysis, small ward schools were to be preferred to centralization. Not only were the large schools and school systems plagued with moral and social problems, he argued; they also failed to live up to the claims of cheapness and efficiency which had been made for them:

> Apart from the objection – which is a very strong one – that the morals of children suffer by their all being brought into contact with each other, an evil seen in its fullest fruits amongst the young men of towns and cities, an old adage seems illustrated, "one black sheep infects a flock." When the children are massed together almost everything is sacrificed to government; at least much time and energy are necessarily spent in organi-

zation. It cannot be doubted that, upon the principles of political economy and the better distribution of labour which a Central School might be expected to afford, both greater cheapness and higher results in education ought to be looked for; but in this, as in many other things, plausibility in theory seems to be corrected by experience.[47]

But opposition to school consolidation produced little but scorn in educational reformers like Ryerson. The alternative was little "independent paltry school sections," the weakness and uselessness of which could only be deplored.[48] Ryerson and his fellow school promoters wanted large, graded schools because it was only in such institutions that distinctions of age, sex and achievement could be made. These in turn were necessary because segregation was necessary. They required it first of all on moral grounds, secondly because segregation meant order and efficiency. Finally they required it because they wanted to create educational environments in which competition would flourish and which would attract those who were looking for a "higher" kind of schooling in the public educational system.

The drive for larger schools and school systems was also related, however, to the goal of bringing into the schools the children of the labouring classes and the poor. And it is perhaps in this area that conflict between the ideal and the reality in mid-nineteenth century education was most apparent. Over and over again educators protested that the common schools, and especially free schools, were intended to provide for the education of children whose parents could not afford to finance it themselves. And over and over again they pronounced their disillusionment. The children of the poor, it seemed, did not come regularly to school, even when the schools were free.

The Reverend John Campbell reported from Nottawasaga in 1860 that his major regret was that those for whose benefit the wealthy were "so heavily taxed" too often failed "to avail themselves of the offered boon." Equally disillusioned was George Barber of Toronto, who reported at length on the subject in 1857. It had been his understanding that the creation of free schools, financed by a general assessment on property, had been intended as the way the rich educated the poor. He saw this not as a charity but as an economy, it being "better to *educate* than to *punish* at the *public* expense." The experiment, however, had not worked. It was Barber's opinion that far from attracting those children for whose "training and reformation" the free school principal was justified, the Toronto common schools had "*failed altogether to bring that particular class of children, in any way at*

156

all, within the restraining influence of our Schools." The problem of "unschooled vagrant children" in fact, was to remain virtually unsolved throughout the Ryerson era.[49]

Free education was not the only way to get the children of the poor into the schools. As early as the mid-forties, Ryerson raised the possibility of compulsory schooling. In 1848 he pointed out, in a circular addressed to Upper Canadian mayors, that communities had the power to withdraw their assistance from indigent parents whose children did not attend school regularly, or from pauper children who failed to go to school. Legislation was proposed but not passed in 1854 that would have enabled municipalities to pass by-laws penalizing parents who neglected the schooling of their children.[50] Despite this check, Ryerson kept the discussion going in county conventions, department circulars to local school authorities, draft legislation, the *Journal of Education* and in correspondence with local authorities throughout the 1850s and '60s. Solutions were proposed by the Education Department and local communities and individuals were requested to bring forward ideas of their own. In 1862, Ryerson went so far as to draft a bill providing that the work of independent benevolent and religious societies devoted to the education of the poor be subsidized by the government, an astonishing proposal in view of his usual concern about the fragmentation of the national system by denominational schooling. This bill, however, was never brought before the legislature.[51]

In Toronto, a survey of non-attenders was carried out by the school board in an attempt to discover the true nature and extent of the problem. The results, which appeared in Toronto's annual report to the chief superintendent in 1863, showed that a variety of causes prevented children from going to school. Probably because Roman Catholics had been accused of particularly lax attitudes towards school attendance, the school board's survey provided for a religious breakdown of the population. The results may be seen in Table 4.

If the figures are correct, it would appear that slightly less than one in five Roman Catholic school-age children did not attend school, while among Protestants the number was one in six. But the chief conclusion drawn by the writer of the report was that the whole problem of non-attenders had been exaggerated. "It must afford great relief to every benevolent mind," he wrote, "to learn that the evil of unmitigated juvenile ignorance does not prevail so widely in Toronto as was feared."

157

TABLE 4
The Toronto School Board Census of 1863

	Protestants		Roman Catholics		Totals	
	No.	%	No.	%	No.	%
Numbers of school age children	7,053		2,455		9,508	
Numbers and percentages of the above not at school	1,165	16.5	464	19.0	1,632	17.2
Reasons given for non-attendance:						
Employed	340	29.9	113	24.2	453	27.7
Wanted at home	203	17.4	60	12.8	263	16.1
Sick	91	7.8	37	7.9	128	7.8
Too young or too far from school	149	12.8	68	14.6	217	13.3
Lately come to city	38	3.3	1	0.2	39	2.4
Want of clothes	127	10.9	89	19.0	216	13.2
No return	217	18.6	99	21.2	316	19.4

From the *Annual Report of the Chief Superintendent of Schools for 1863,* Appendix A, p. 150.

The census, he argued, showed that the vast majority of those staying away from school had very good reasons for their non-attendance.[52]

But despite the evidence presented by the Toronto board, many school promoters remained unconvinced. The Education Office continued throughout the sixties to request information on the subject of non-attendance from local authorities, who in turn attempted to get the answer from school trustees. A wide assortment of opinions came back to Ryerson and were recorded in the published annual reports, or filed away in departmental correspondence. An all too common cause of non-attendance, according to these opinions, was "the indifference of parents" – so common that the phrase had become a stereotype, in the view of one superintendent.[53] Parental "apathy" was, in fact, such a widely held cause that one suspects educational authorities of putting words into the mouths of respondents by way of their questions. But there were some superintendents and trustees who attempted to find out more, and their answers are eloquent testimony to the deeper reasons for parental reluctance or inability to send children to school.

Simple poverty headed the list. An extreme case was the community of Coldwater in 1859, impoverished by a falling-off in the shipbuilding business that had lasted for two years, and virtually destroyed by a "whirlwind" which had wrecked both schools and homes. There simply wasn't enough money in the community to pay a teacher. In more normal communities, where schools were running and the teacher could be paid, the usual reasons for non-attendance were lack of clothing for the children, inability to buy the necessary books and paper, distance from the school and bad roads. Illness and epidemic were frequent obstacles. "Want of ability rather than want of will" was the simple answer from Napanee in 1865.[54]

Then there were the children who were otherwise occupied. In many regions, not only did the children prefer to work when they were able to, but their labour was often desperately needed to support the family. In the back townships and where people were poor, farmers were not able to "hire strangers" and depended entirely on the assistance of their children, it was reported. Older children were sometimes needed at home to care for younger ones. In Streetsville, many children were employed in the wool and flax mills of the village. Superintendents occasionally noticed that the children of particular classes of people tended to be irregular or non-attenders at school. The children of recent immigrants were singled out, as were the children of transients, of Roman Catholics, and of French Canadians. In all such cases, poverty, even if not specified, was clearly a related factor in the children's failure to attend.[55]

It was difficult to discuss the non-attendance of the poor without discussing the schools themselves. Superintendents mentioned inadequate or unpopular teachers and schools that did not appeal for one reason or another. The poor of Kingston, Samuel Woods concluded in 1869, were simply uncomfortable in school. "Not but they *can* go, if they desire it, but they *will not*; for in such an atmosphere and with such surroundings, they feel they are *not at home*."[56] Indeed one wonders that any children could feel comfortable in many mid-nineteenth century schools. For the most part small and ill-ventilated, increasingly overcrowded and understaffed, it is perhaps a wonder that the common schools attracted as many children as they did. In Kingston it was reported in 1850 that children of all ages were "packed in their seats as close as one's fingers," and were equally in danger of suffocating as of freezing to death. According to the chairman of the Toronto Board of Trustees in 1851, the schools were so destructive to the health that teachers were dying as a result of working in them. As the superintendent from Kingston pointed out, the bodily health which was essential to a vigorous mind could not long be retained in "an atmosphere reeking with the

159

impurities of sixty or seventy bodies." Efforts to improve school buildings were thus founded in real necessity, but they went slowly. In 1865, "prison-like" schools were still commonplace, and in 1866 A. Dingwall Fordyce of Wellington County reported a particularly noxious school under his jurisdiction. "The schoolhouse lowest in height of all, being only 6 feet inside, was only 24 by 10 feet; and yet in that confined space, the teacher told me he had ninety-seven scholars present on the 21st of June. Surely," Fordyce argued, "there is a crying need for some improvement here."[57]

Unfortunate teaching methods often combined with such poor conditions to make the schools even more unattractive. Once again, R. S. Henderson's descriptions of the schools of Kingston are especially graphic. In 1850, he ventured the opinion that "shouting at the children like a fury, beating them about the head, pulling their ears, or cutting them with cow-hide," was hardly the best way to help them learn. In 1852 he was concerned about the negative effects of almost total idleness on the children. Twice a day the pupil might be called upon to recite his ABC – the rest of the time pupils were forced to spend in "listless inactivity and stupor."[58]

Worsening pupil-teacher ratios over the years must have accounted for much reluctance to send children to school. James Porter set the number of pupils per class in Toronto at a maximum of seventy-five in 1869, but admitted that most teachers had from ninety to one hundred pupils on their registers and that he was thinking of introducing a half-day scheme in order to accommodate everyone.[59] Clearly overcrowding was as serious a problem at the end of the Ryerson era as it had been at the beginning. Attempts to provide improved accommodation through school building campaigns failed in many cases to keep up with expanding numbers.

To all the reasons for the failure of many parents to send their children regularly to school must be added the tendency of some schools to actively discourage the attendance of certain children. The Education Office correspondence is witness to the fact that children were sometimes prevented from going to the school of their parent's choice. One Roman Catholic father complained to Ryerson in 1859 of numerous harassments perpetrated upon himself by the local Protestant common school teacher, who, furthermore, was known to have unjustly expelled at least one Roman Catholic pupil. This parent did not "dare" to send his children to the school; the local superintendent had only advised him to try the next section. In the same year, another correspondent wrote from Kent County demanding to know what could be done for coloured children sent to school by a resident tax-payer, when the teacher simply ignored and refused to teach them. Refusal to teach black children in predominantly white schools gradually became the norm in many communities.[60]

Then there were a few children who for one reason or another were refused entry to the school building. Complaints reaching Ryerson's office told of children excluded from school because it was thought that they had the "itch"; of children barred because the teacher and "others" apparently wished to turn the school into a private school; or simply because of overcrowding.[61] Gradually, teachers also began to use their power to lock out latecomers and to expel or suspend pupils for reasons having to do with discipline or differing notions of proper school behaviour.[62]

The way provincial funds were distributed to the schools also had an adverse effect on the attendance of the poor. The School Law of 1850 provided that funds should be apportioned locally according to average attendance, rather than according to the number of children in the school section. Ryerson argued that it had been the experience of Massachusetts that poor rural areas had as high if not higher attendance rates than others, and that this means of distribution would reward ambitious schools that paid their teachers well and attracted large numbers of children to attend regularly.[63] The method did, no doubt, have the effect of increasing the number of free schools and average attendance rates over the province; but there is no evidence that it encouraged the schooling of the poor, and considerable testimony to the contrary. As contemporary critics did not fail to point out, apportionment according to attendance could easily have the effect of "making the strong stronger and entirely breaking down the weak," as comparatively rich and thickly settled communities increased their attendance averages more rapidly than did others.[64] Poor, thinly settled areas suffered doubly. Poor average attendance figures led to a relative decline in grants, as others' grants got larger. Poverty was likely to mean a continuing cycle of poor teachers, poor attendance and poor schools.

If the policies governing the distribution of school funds were factors in the inequality of educational opportunity, it may also be that provincial policies with respect to teachers were another. The campaign for educational improvement directed at teachers was no less pervasive than that directed at other classes of society, and in this area the provincial Education Department gradually acquired the power to regulate and control. The stated goals of the reformers were to improve the financial and social status

161

of common school teachers, as well as their efforts in the schools; the result of the campaign was the creation of hierarchies within the occupation, based partly on a provincially designed system of teacher training, classification and certification, and partly on sex.[65]

The provincial Normal School in Toronto, founded by the School Law of 1846 and opened to students in 1847, was at the heart of the campaign to create a "better class" of teachers. The course of instruction included training in respectablility, as well as training in school subjects and how to teach them. The ultimate hope was that the first class graduates of the "Normal" would not only become the educational leaders of their generation, but living examples of the status and financial rewards that could and should ideally accrue to the properly qualified teacher. Larger schools and school systems also contributed to hierarchy in teaching, as female teachers or teachers with inferior certificates were relegated to the lower grades or to all-female schools and classes within the larger systems, while male, first class teachers sought jobs as principals and superintendents, or after 1871, in the professional inspectorate that by provincial law replaced the lay superintendency that had existed since the 1840s. The certification and classification of teachers helped to define the class structure of schools and school systems, and those with the lowest status were assigned to the "inferior" grades, classes or schools; those deemed superior were placed at the top. It was often the hiring of lower status and lower paid female teachers, in fact, that made possible the division of schools into primary and junior sections and similar patterns of school reorganization and consolidation. The very expansion of schooling itself must have depended in large part on the savings that could be made by hiring large numbers of "cheap" teachers.[66]

Some teachers may have resented the gradual creation of social and financial hierarchies within the occupation. This did not prevent large numbers of Upper Canadians, however, from flocking into it. The same thing, it has to be said, applies to the school children of the mid-nineteenth century, who clearly were also flocking into schools. If school promoters occasionally sounded a note of optimism, therefore, it was because, in spite of everything to prevent them, more and more children proportionally were enrolled every year in the common schools during the Ryerson era. But even this brief survey reveals that there were serious obstacles to the fulfillment of the goals of class harmony and equality of opportunity through education. The rich, the poor and sometimes even those in the middle found themselves uncomfortable or even unwanted in the common schools. Especially in the larger towns and cities, there were ambitious and school-oriented people who sought a "better class" of education for their children. In the meantime, poverty, the need to work, lack of clothing and many other factors associated with poverty frequently prevented the attendance of the children of the poor. Some attended irregularly; others failed to attend at all.

To the extent that the classes did mingle in the same schools or school systems, the introduction of competitive grading and of segregation by age and sex were clearly designed to perpetuate concepts of class. The old hierarchies of ranks and orders may have gradually been abandoned, but graded common school systems would do their best to sift and sort the population according to other measures. In some cases the sorting was by religion or colour, although these criteria were not often greeted with enthusiasm by leading educators. Their stated preference, rather, was to sort children according to sex and the ability to achieve success (at the right age) in a school system which every year seemed to grow larger and more complex.

The distribution of educational funds according to average attendance tended to favour the already favoured classes, since the wealth and age of communities exercised considerable influence over the ability of families to send children to school regularly. With the growth of wealth, older, closely settled school sections and city suburbs occupied by the well-to-do would have the advantage. In addition, it should be noted in passing, the grammar schools were always far more generously supported by provincial funds than were the common schools. Nor were the union, central or high schools and collegiate institutes that eventually replaced the grammar schools ever reduced to sharing the money equally on a per pupil basis with the elementary schools of the province.[67]

Contemporary observers differed not only in their sense of what was going on in the schools, but also in their estimates of the significance of what they saw around them. Egerton Ryerson and the promoters of compulsory schooling professed to be appalled at continuing child vagrancy and crime and were increasingly upset by the failure of free schools to solve the problem. But other observers argued that the children of Toronto, for example, were not nearly as bad as some would have them.[68] Nor were school attendance statistics for the province necessarily as appalling as Education Office sources continually implied. Some critics, at least, felt that errors in statistics and the transience of the population accounted for most of the so-called non-attenders by the 1860s. As a perceptive school superintendent pointed out in 1860, moreover, it was perhaps wrong to assume that "all those registered as not attending any school during the year" were "strictly barbarians." Many of them had attended school in previous years of their lives, and, it could be argued, were not completely uneducated.[69]

Also, different things were clearly going on at different places. Certainly, Toronto did not present the same picture as London and Hamilton, or Kingston and Ottawa. There were no "beggar children" in the streets of London in 1863, according to one contemporary account, and according to another, the schools of Hamilton were "equally attended by rich and poor." Toronto, on the other hand, had proportionally far fewer children in the common schools for many years, compared to the other cities of the province.[70] Small villages, rural school sections and remote settlements must have offered entirely different prospects again, depending on their wealth, the condition of the roads, and the religious, social and political orientations of their inhabitants.

But if there were local variations on the theme, the theme itself emerges clearly from what leading educators said they wanted and what they appear to have been doing during this formative period in Canadian schooling. The professed goals of bringing all classes into the common schools, on the one hand, and of encouraging educational opportunity for the labouring classes and the poor on the other, were seriously compromised by the way in which the two goals conflicted with each other, as well as by countless practical and psychological obstacles to the fulfillment of these ideals. School consolidation, moreover, went hand in hand with fragmentation and separation, and the emphasis on educational improvement led to segregation and hierarchy for both pupils and teachers. From the complex interaction of motives and means, there was beginning to develop in mid-nineteenth century Upper Canada an educational class system no less pervasive than the ranks and orders of the dying past.

NOTES

[1]Unsigned editorial, JEUC, V (January, 1852), 9.

[2]*Dr. Ryerson's Letters in Reply to the Attacks of the Hon. George Brown* (Toronto, 1859), p. iii; *Annual Report for 1858,* Appendix A, p. 89; *Annual Report for 1860,* Appendix A, p. 165.

[3]*Annual Report for 1857,* Appendix A, p. 156.

[4]*Annual Report for 1859,* Appendix A, p. 160.

[5]"The Normal and Model School," JEUC, III (March, 1850), 36; *Annual Report for 1864,* Appendix A, p. 40; "Ontario Teachers' Association Convention in 1869," DHE, XXI, 298. See also the *Annual Report for 1851,* Appendix A, pp. 118 and 121, in which the clients of the common schools are described as "the humbler portion of our people" and "the industrial classes."

[6]*Report on a System of Public Elementary Instruction* (Montreal, 1847), p. 146; *Annual Report for 1852,* Part I, p. 16; "Memorandum on the Draft of Bill for the Promotion of Education in Cities and Towns ..." (1862), DHE, XVII, 177.

[7]*Annual Report for 1855,* Part I, p. 21; JEUC, VIII (April, 1855), 58-59.

[8]Resolutions adopted by the School Association of the Eastern District, in D. P. McDonald to Ryerson, July 1850, RG 2 C-6-C, PAO; *Annual Report for 1851,* Appendix A, pp. 117-18; *Report. . . of the Public or Common Schools of the City* (Toronto, 1859), p. 31 and 37; *Documents relating to the Common Schools of the City* (Toronto, 1858), p. 14; Rev. James Porter, "The Public Schools of Ontario," *The Canadian Monthly and National Review,* I (June, 1872), 484-85.

[9]*Annual Report for 1852,* Appendix A, p. 124; *Annual Report for 1861,* Appendix A, p. 200; *Annual Report for 1858,* Appendix A, p. 79.

[10]Prentice, "The School Promoters," pp. 222-25.

[11]Edith Wagner, "Education as Revealed in Family Papers, Ontario 1800-1900," (M. A. Thesis, University of Toronto, 1954), pp. 69-70.

[12]"The School Promoters," pp. 228-31.

[13]Phillips, *The Development of Education in Canada,* p. 198. Sylvia Carleton has erred in the same direction. She misleadingly refers, for example, to the high school of the 1870's as a "people's school." Carleton, "Egerton Ryerson and Education in Ontario, 1844-1877," (Ph.D. Diss., University of Pennsylvania, 1950), p. 354.

[14]*Annual Report for 1857,* Part I, p. 8.

[15]*Annual Report for 1864,* Appendix A, pp. 59-60; *Annual Report for 1869,* Appendix D, pp. 112-13; *Annual Report for 1858,* Appendix A, p. 82; *Annual Report for 1862,* Part II, Table F, p. 43.

[16]*Annual Report for 1869,* Appendix A, pp. 12-13.

[17]Excerpt form the *Free Press,* February 1867, JEUC, XX (March, 1867), 50.

[18]Excerpt from the *Leader,* JEUC, XVII (October, 1865), 160.

[19]*Annual Report for 1869,* Appendix D, p. 115.

[20]Adam Crooks, *Speeches, 1879,* p. 31. The change to a ministry of education occurred after Ryerson's retirement from the Chief Superintendency in 1876.

[21]Porter, "The Public Schools of Ontario," p. 484.

[22]"City of Kingston," (Report of the Special Committee,) *Annual Report for 1850,* p. 187; George Bell to Ryerson, 18 January 1869, RG 2 C-6-C, PAO.

[23]Chas. R. Brooke to Ryerson, 6 December 1865, RG 2 C-6-C, PAO.

[24]*Annual Report for 1849,* Part I, pp. 7-9; *Annual Report for 1850,* Part I, p. 19.

[25]School Organization and Discipline, 8 March 1871, RG 2 C-6-C, PAO. See for example, W. H. Landon, *Report of the Superintendent of Schools for the Brock District, presented to the District Council, November 7th, 1848* (Woodstock, 1848), pp. 15-16; *Annual Report for 1859,* Appendix A, p. 162.

[26]In Massachusetts during this period, a debate developed between the promoters of "emulation" and those who were agitating for graded schools, the argument being that grading would reduce competition among the children. Ryerson and his supporters appear not to have perceived any conflict between the two concepts and promoted both, although the Education Office campaign to increase prize giving was certainly of later origin, not emerging as a major effort until the 1860s. For the American debate see Michael B. Katz, *The Irony of Early School Reform* (Cambridge, Mass., 1968) pp. 55-57. Upper Canadian comments on the relationship between grading and competition may be found in the "Annual Report of the Assistant Superintendent of Education on the Common Schools of Upper Canada, 1842," DHE, IV, 264; *Annual Report for 1865,* Part I, p. 9; and *Annual Report for 1869,* Appendix D, p. 107.

[27]*Annual Report for 1869,* Appendix D, p. 107.

[28]Student ages in colleges in 1855 were as follows:

	Under Sixteen	Over Sixteen		Under Sixteen	Over Sixteen
Victoria	65	157	Bytown	78	58
Queen's	7	87	St. Michael's	52	30
Regiopolis	50	20	Upper Canada College	128	44

"Returns of Colleges in Upper Canada receiving aid from the Government in 1855," DHE, XII, 242; "Reorganization of the Model Grammar School for Upper Canada, 1861," DHE, XVIII, 10; George Cox to Ryerson, 3 January 1859, RG 2 C-6-C, PAO; *Annual Report for 1869,* Appendix A, pp. 8-9.

[29]"Reminiscences of Superannuated Common School Teachers, 1842-1847, DHE, VI, 305.

[30]Master of the Brantford Common School to Ryerson, 12 April 1850, RG 2 C-6-C, PAO.

[31]For a detailed analysis of school enrolment and attendance, see Ian E. Davey, "Educational Reform and the Working Class: School Attendance in Hamilton, Ontario, 1851-1891," (Ph.D. diss., University of Toronto, 1975). A discussion based on Toronto is Haley P. Bamman, "Patterns of School Attendance in Toronto, 1844-1878: Some Spatial Considerations" in Katz and Mattingly, eds., *Education and Social Change,* pp. 217-245. See, in addition, the articles by Katz and Davey, cited in footnote 9 of the introduction.

[32]Archibald Frank to Ryerson, 5 February 1859, RG 2 C-6-C, PAO; *Annual Report for 1867,* Part I, p. 62; *Annual Report for 1863,* Appendix A, p. 121.

[33]Ryerson to Jonathan Woolverton, M.D., 31 May 1847, RG 2 Cl, Letterbook C, p. 387, PAO; *Annual Report for 1865,* Appendix A, p. 63; *Annual Report for 1868,* Appendix A, p. 42.

[34]Ryerson to Daly, 27 March 1847, RG 2 Cl, Letterbook C, p. 223, PAO; "The University Question in a Series of Letters, 1861," DHE, VII, 283.

[35]Davey, "Educational Reform and the Working Class," esp. chapter 4.

[36]JEUC, V (January, 1852), 11; *Report . . . of the Common or Public Schools of the City,* pp. 25, 58 - 59.

[37]Ryerson to P. Jaffray, Esq., 27 January 1847, RG 2 Cl, Letterbook C, pp. 223, PAO.

[38]*Remarks on the State of Education in the Province of Canada, by "L",* (Montreal, 1849), p. 21.

[39]W. H. Landon, *Report of the Superintendent of Schools for the Brock District,* (Woodstock, 1848), p. 5.

[40]Edwin C. Guillet, *In the Cause of Education: Centennial History of the Ontario Education Association, 1861-1960* (Toronto, 1960), pp. 12, 32; "Reminiscences of Superannuated School Teachers, 1848-1851," DHE, VIII, 303; *Annual Report for 1865,* Appendix A, p. 69.

[41]On separate schools for black children see Robin W. Winks, "Negro School Segregation in Ontario and Nova Scotia," *Canadian Historical Review,* L (June, 1969), 164-91.

[42]George Beranson to Ryerson, 4 January 1859, RG 2 C-6-C, PAO.

[43]Letter to the Editor of the *Kingston Gazette,* 20 June 1814, DHE, I, 83; Landon, *Report of the Superintendent of Schools for the Brock District,* p. 5; *Annual Report for 1858,* Appendix A, p. 41; "Plans for Grammar, Union or Superior Common School," JEUC, X (February, 1857), 17; Christopher McAlpin to Ryerson, 23 January 1850, RG 2 C-6-C, PAO; "An Act Supplementary to the Common School Act for Upper Canada . . .," JEUC, VI (June, 1853), 84.

[44]Robertson to Ryerson, 26 March 1859, RG 2 C-6-C, PAO. Members of the public were ejected from the grounds by Normal School janitors on occasion. Complaints about this may be found in the letters of Alfred W. Otter to Hodgins, 12 July 1859, and to Ryerson, 25 July, 1859, RG 2 C-6-C, PAO.

[45]W. F. Checkly, for instance, remarks on the necessity of suitable accommodation for grammar schools in the "Report on the Grammar Schools of Upper Canada, 1863," DHE, XVIII, 95.

[46]Edmund Dyer to Ryerson, 9 March 1859 and Henry Stevens to Ryerson, 8 February 1859, RG 2 C-6-C, PAO; Ryerson to R. J. Bouchier, 28 February 1848, RG 2 Cl, Letterbook D, p. 175; *Annual Report for 1866,* Appendix A, p. 4.

[47]*Annual Report for 1864,* Appendix A, p. 66.

[48]Ryerson felt that such fragmentation would be the inevitable outcome of the Cameron Act. "The Abortive School Legislation of 1849," DHE, VIII, 247.

[49]*Annual Report for 1860,* Appendix A, p. 170; *Documents relating to the Common Schools of the City,* p. 9; "Additional Reasons given by the Chief Superintendent for the Bill relating to Vagrant and Neglected Children . . . " DHE, XVII, 191.

[50]"Circular to the Mayors of Cities and Towns in Upper Canada, 15 January 1848," DHE, VII, 221; DHE, XVII, 175.

[51]"Draft of Bill, relating to Vagrant and Neglected Children in Cities and Towns, 1862," DHE, XVII, 175-176. The non-introduction of the bill and subsequent failure of the Anglicans to press for legislation in this area was discussed in the Anglican synod of 1862: DHE, XVII, 184. It also led to further requests from the Education Office to local authorities for ideas on the subject of vagrant children. See Circular to the Board of School Trustees in the Cities and Towns of Upper Canada, 22 November 1862, RG 2 Q, PAO.

[52]*Annual Report for 1863,* Appendix A, p. 150.

[53]*Annual Report for 1865,* Appendix A, p. 22.

[54]Henry Clifford to Ryerson, 14 November 1859, RG 2 C-6-C, PAO; *Annual Report for 1863,* Appendix A, pp. 102 and 114-15; *Annual Report for 1861;* Appendix A, p. 167; *Annual Report for 1860,* Appendix A, pp. 170 and 178; *Annual Report for 1865,* Appendix A, p. 66.

[55]William Hutton to Ryerson, 3 June 1850, RG 2 C-6-C, PAO; *Annual Report for 1865,* Appendix A, p. 72; *Annual Report for 1868,* Appendix A, p. 5; *Annual Report for 1866,* Appendix A, p. 12; *Annual Report for 1869,* Appendix A, p. 189 & Appendix D, p. 116; *Annual Report for 1864,* Appendix A, p. 3; *Annual Report for 1862,* Appendix A, p. 114; *Annual Report for 1869,* Appendix A, p. 189; *Annual Report for 1858,* Appendix A, p. 23.

[56]*Annual Report for 1861,* Appendix A, p. 173; *Annual Report for 1857,* Appendix A, p. 158; *Annual Report for 1866,* Appendix A, p. 65; *Annual Report for 1864,* Appendix A, p. 35; *Annual Report for 1862,* Appendix A, p. 107; *Annual Report for 1869,* Appendix D, p. 107.

[57]*Annual Report for 1850,* Appendix A, p. 188; A. F. Corson to Ryerson, 1 October 1850, RG 2 C-6-C, PAO; *Report . . . of the Common or Public Schools of the City,* p. 34; *Annual Report for 1851,* Appendix A, p. 121; *Annual Report for 1865,* Appendix A, p. 13; *Annual Report for 1866,* Appendix A, p. 42.

[58]*Annual Report for 1850,* Appendix A, p. 188; *Annual Report for 1852,* Appendix A, p. 127.

[59]*Annual Report for 1869,* Appendix D, p. 112.

[60]James Feagan to Ryerson, 5 March 1859, RG 2 C-6-C, PAO; Lewis L. Arnold to Ryerson, 10 February 1859, RG 2 C-6-C, PAO.

[61]Noble Waterson to Ryerson, 14 November 1859; Superintendent of Schools in the Townships of Westmeath, Pembroke and Stafford to Ryerson, 30 January 1851; J. B. Killerne to Ryerson, 20 January 1869, RG 2, C-6-C, PAO. Killerne suggests that students were excluded because of overcrowding, because they were too old, or because they were not the children of the people with whom they were living.

[62]For example see John Agnew to Ryerson, 20 January 1869, RG 2 C-6-C, PAO.

[63]"Report to the Government on the School Laws of 1846 and 1847, with Draft School Bill of October 14, 1848," DHE, VIII, 92.

[64]Dexter D'Everardo to Ryerson, 30 April 1850; W. Hutton to Bella Flint, 21 May 1850; Trustees of S.S. 3 Nr. Plantagenet to Ryerson, 5 April 1850; V. Waugh to Ryerson, 12 February 1850; J. D. Hageman to

Ryerson, 11 February 1865; RG 2 C-6-C, PAO.

[65]"The School Promoters," chapter 8.

[66]*Ibid.,* p. 310.

[67]In 1868, Grammar School apportionments amounted to more than twenty times the apportionment for common schools, according to a Circular to the Members of the Legislature of Ontario, respecting the Common and Grammar School Law, Oct. 10, 1868, RG 2 Q, PAO.

[68]"Proceedings of the Anglican Synod of the Diocese of Toronto on the Bill relating to Vagrant and Neglected Children, 1862," DHE, XVII, 187. See also the optimistic commentary on the Toronto Board Census, cited above.

[69]*Annual Report for 1861,* Appendix A, p. 165. For optimistic opinions on parental efforts to educate their children, see also *Annual Report for 1864,* Appendix A, p. 46 and *Annual Report for 1869,* Appendix D, p. 97. James Porter, local superintendent in Toronto, was among those who had doubts about the accuracy of child population estimates. See Porter to Ryerson, 14 May 1859, RG 2 C-6-C, PAO.

[70]*Annual Report for 1863,* Appendix A, p. 154; *Annual Report for 1856,* Appendix A, p. 279; JEUC, VI (October, 1853), 157.

Chapter 7

Nature, Order and National Education: The Government as Parent

If Government exists for the prosperity of the public family, then everything relating to educational instruction demands its practical care, as well as legislative interference . . . To be a State system of Public Instruction, there must be a State controul (sic) as well as a State Law . . .

Egerton Ryerson, 1846

The State, therefore, so far from having nothing to do with the children, constitutes their collective parent, and is bound to protect them against any unnatural neglect or cruel treatment, on the part of the individual parent, and to secure them all that will qualify them to become useful citizens to the state.

Egerton Ryerson, 1858[1]

Running through all of the arguments the school promoters made for the improvement of Upper Canadian children and their teachers was their expanding conception of the role of the state in education. Thus they pushed the constant extension of government control over schooling. Tied to this was an ultimate vision, the perfecting of a Canadian nation whose status in the scale of nations would be second to none.

Underlying this general view, as we have seen, was a view of human nature as susceptible and weak. Upper Canadians, particularly, seemed ignorant, apathetic and desperately in need of improvement, especially when compared to the energetic citizens of the neighbouring United States. Exactly what was meant by improvement, who would be improved, and how, was however a subject of considerable complexity. School promoters had several aims in mind. The promotion of an intelligent and respectable class was one aspect of their programme; another the general elevation and improvement of the labouring poor. They were concerned about those Upper Canadians whose occupational status was threatened by industrial change, change which nevertheless they strongly supported. The only hope for these displaced people seemed to be an education designed to prepare them for the new order.

Their overall intention was to rescue the entire society from the threat of an "underfoot" position as against the rest of the world. If Upper Canadians didn't advance quickly, they felt, they were doomed to remain "hewers of wood and drawers of water" for their richer and stronger neighbours. The same logic applied to the country as applied to individuals, classes and communities; if Upper Canada did not move ahead, it would fall behind. In the final analysis, it is clear that concern for the social and economic status of the province as a whole, and for those classes most likely to benefit from education and to produce "improvement" came first in the opinion of school promoters. Education, therefore, could no longer be strictly a family or a church affair. The public itself was a "family" and the education of future citizens therefore required the parental interference of the state.

To understand this belief, one has to return to the ambivalent stance with which many nineteenth century educators faced the world around them. A society in a state of flux, the disintegration of existing class structures, the potential for class warfare in existing social disorder – these they believed to be the threats they faced. The answer, school promoters felt sure, was to be found in the institutionalized state and a new educational order under the general direction and control of the state.

The search for a better society in mid-nineteenth century Upper Canada was rooted in an essentially dualistic view of the world. And nowhere was this dualism better illustrated than in the attitudes of school promoters to nature. Nature was portrayed alternatively as "chaos" and "order." As chaos, nature was to be feared; as order, she was to be imitated and loved.

School promoters were religious men and characteristic of their religious outlook was a strong belief in natural law, which they generally equated with divine law. They cited the "laws of nature" or "divine providence" as justification for much that they wished to promote, from acceptance of social inequality on the one hand, to acceptance of particular approaches to school management on the other. Above all, they used natural and divine law to justify their quest for order. What was true of the macrocosm ought to be true of the microcosm. Harmony, law and order, Ryerson argued, were the outstanding characteristics of all earthbound creatures striving to "imitate" nature and especially of human beings, whose need for moral and social law was paramount.[2]

Teachers were advised to teach according to "nature's laws," and to relate the work of the school to the "natural development" of the human mind. Educational systems, it was also claimed, ought to imitate the harmony of nature. This at least was the argument of J.G.D. Mackenzie, who, as inspector of grammar schools in 1869, was anxious to prevent conflict between the common and grammar schools of the province. "We must see to it," Mackenzie warned his readers, "that each member of the (school) system is in a healthy condition and performing its proper functions." A primary notion of natural law was the idea that in any given whole, the various parts ought to perform their assigned roles in harmony. What was true of the school system ought also to be true of society as a whole, the various social classes and institutions ideally performing their roles as Providence ordained, while Providence meted out the appropriate rewards.[3]

If nature was basically harmonious, or at least in constant search of equilibrium, disharmony and disorder were the more to be feared and despised. To encourage conflict within society, according to Ryerson, was "to reverse the order of nature." In 1839, when still editor of the *Christian Guardian* and much preoccupied with raising funds for the Upper Canada Academy, he challenged Church of England educational monopolies on just these grounds. The wealthy denominations were pensioned by the state, he argued, while the poorer ones were cast off with nothing; an "unnatural" battle between the two sides under such circumstances was inevitable. Rich and poor were meant to perform their parts without conflict and in this case the rich would have to make some sacrifices. Ryerson's attack on the rich did not mean, however, that he favoured the elimination of the fundamental differences between rich and poor. Many years later, in his textbook *Elements of Political Economy,* Ryerson explained how the divinely-appointed laws of nature affected the relations between classes and orders of men. "Why [was] political economy called a science?" common school readers were asked. It was called a science, the text explained, because it taught "that systematic arrangement of the laws which God has established, for the accumulation of the blessings of this life." God had ordained that the animals should be subject to man's authority and that, as a result of industry, men and societies could grow rich. The laws of nature were thus responsible for individual and collective differences in wealth, which were "as really a part of the order of Providence, as differences in sex, complexion or strength." Most important, man could not change the divine order.[4]

Natural law ideally meant health and beauty, harmony and progress, but the intensity with which these ideals were sought reveals nineteenth century men's fear of nature as they encountered it in reality. The yearning for order clearly signalled, more than anything else, profound disquiet in the face of existing disorder. For, as often as not, the natural world was apprehended by Upper Canadians as alien and chaotic, and its basic attribute held to be not law, but really a dangerous kind of freedom from law.[5]

Thus the mid-century author of Upper Canada's first legal manual for schools and families was able to base some of his claims about the legal and moral responsibilities of wives, children and servants on the argument that in the "state of nature," no one was in subjection to another.[6] The social subordination presumed by Ryerson and many of his contemporaries to be a law of nature was here discarded, if only to make people accept a measure of individual responsibility for their actions. Whatever the theoretical basis of the legal relations of individuals, however, very few actually espoused such notions of equality for economic and social relations. When Ryerson was promoting compulsory taxation for the support of schools, the threat of just such social chaos was in fact the crux of his argument. In a society where each individual's will was sovereign, he argued, there could be no government. There was "a state of nature." A return to the voluntary principle in education would be to abandon rising generations to "the freedom of nature," clearly a freedom to be deplored.[7]

In Ryerson's case the preferred approach to the world seems to have depended on who the audience was. For the readers of a common school catechism like the *Elements of Political Economy,* the laws governing the accumulation of wealth and the structure of society had to be shown as natural, God-given, and above all unchanging. This world was static. The members of the Legislative Assembly and readers of the superintendent's annual reports, however, were another kettle of fish. They controlled the provincial education funds and the future of the school system. It was essential to demonstrate to these men the threat of social disintegration inherent in educational voluntarism. Order in nature may have been the ideal, but the reality was always the possibility of chaos, the chaos of nature unleashed.

To counteract the awful vision of nature on the rampage, a vision particularly threatening to pioneer societies like that of Upper Canada, nineteenth century reformers looked to technology. School promoters shared this fundamental vision. The enlarging of man's "empire over nature," the planting of civilization in the "savage haunted wastes" of Upper Canada, were goals that school promoters believed could or should be shared by everyone. The order in society which Ryerson and his contemporaries proposed and yearned for was, as the chief superintendent of schools pointed out, the universal practice not of savages, but of "civilized" mankind.[8] Promoting the latest technology in all fields of human endeavour, as a result, became a continuing preoccupation of the Education Office. Ryerson's search for inventions to exhibit in the museum that he attached to the Normal School ranged far beyond equipment and artifacts of interest to school teachers alone, and the pages of the *Journal of Education* were full of illustrations and descriptions of all kinds of new machinery. Labour-saving devices and their inventors were promoted and praised, and the future held out for Upper Canada was one which involved "the creation of villages, the extension of towns and cities, the subjugation of forests, the multiplication of settlements, the increase of population, the growth of wealth," in short, a vision of civilization and industry replacing the engulfing wilderness.[9]

Promoters of technology like Ryerson clearly felt some need to reassure both themselves and their critics about the relationship of technique to the natural environment. When talking about the inanimate agents employed to do men's work the chief superintendent felt called upon to characterize them as "natural." "Inanimate natural agents cost less," he pointed out to his common school readers; they "work with more force, more speed, more certainty, uniformity and precision, and are more under control." Control was the thing. All the other characteristics that he listed led to it; together they helped men to predict and to act in the face of nature's vagaries. Nature was deficient, as Ryerson asserted elsewhere, but "art and industry add to the bounties of nature, and marvellously supply its deficiencies."[10]

To achieve control over the resources of the nation, over nature and the future, and to ensure that all classes worked harmoniously to this end, it gradually appeared to school promoters that elementary schooling had not only to be made free, but finally, to some degree at least, compulsory. The structure and "content" of education, moreover, had to be brought under the authority of the state.

It is interesting to trace the development of Egerton Ryerson's thought in this area, from the voluntarism of the 1820s to his espousal of state compulsion several decades later. In 1826, Ryerson feared the interference of the state in education, arguing that as a field of endeavour, it belonged essentially to all of the churches, not just one. Above all, the state had no right to compel in this area. Ryerson spoke of the people's *"natural* aversion" to what came to them "clothed with *compulsory* power," and prayed that the Methodists would "never have it in their power to lord it over the conscience of a fellow creature, with the rod of *civil authority."* In the 1840s Ryerson still claimed to believe that coercion was wrong in education. "To compel the education of children by the terror of legal pains and penalties, is at variance with my idea of the true method of promoting universal education," he explained in 1848. The school system, he declared in the following year, was designed to be the embodiment of voluntarism: "The education of the people through themselves is the vital principle ... Coercion is alien to the spirit of the system."[11]

What Ryerson had in mind was a kind of municipal voluntarism, with each community free to make whatever provisions it wished for the schooling of its children. A certain loss of freedom occurred, of course, with the acceptance of provincial funds, as these were increasingly tied to provincial objectives. But communities were theoretically free to take or leave the largess offered to them by the central government. In addition, individual parents who disliked whatever local arrangements were made were always free to resort to private schools, although Ryerson admitted at least once that these were in fact too expensive for "a large class of the inhabitants of cities and towns."[12]

The principle of legally compelling school attendance was put forward, nevertheless, in the *Report on a System of Public Elementary Instruction* which was written in 1846. In this work, Ryerson cited the school attendance laws of Prussia and other European states, which were based on the belief that if the parent could not provide his child with an education, the state was bound to do so. If the parent refused to allow his child to be educated, in countries with compulsory school laws, it was considered the duty of the state to protect the child against such a parent's "cupidity and inhumanity." The subject continued to be discussed. The *Journal of Education* began in the early 1850s to print articles from American journals on the subject of compulsory school attendance, and by 1855, Ryerson seriously proposed the idea for Upper Canada in his annual report.[13]

In 1857, the *Journal* announced that it was the duty of the municipalities to make education compulsory, and expressed the hope that legislation to provide for this would soon be forthcoming. The annual report for that year once again placed the responsibility on local authorities. They were "worthy of praise or blame" and were "benefactors or enemies of their country and posterity," as they did or did not use every legal channel open to them to get children into the schools. In the early 1860s Ryerson was still proposing that municipalities be empowered by the legislature to pass compulsory attendance bylaws. If his 1862 bill providing for public assistance to denominational charity schools was, as he claimed, intended to be an alternative to "resorting to the measure of coercion," it was either a deviation from his usual approach to the subject, or a way to avoid what he had frequently implied that he was trying to avoid, namely a provincial compulsory attendance law. Certainly in that year Hodgins told the members of the Anglican synod, as they deliberated on the problem of vagrant children, that only "a very small minority" favoured a truancy law for the province as a whole. By the midsixties, however, Ryerson seems to have been convinced that he had a provincial majority for the cause, and in 1871, the chief superintendent officially abandoned his concern for municipal voluntarism in the areas of common school attendance and rates. The provincial government assumed the role of "collective parent" when it made some years of elementary schooling, as well as the provision of free common schools by communities, compulsory by law. Most school promoters agreed that the two things went together. Taxpayers who paid for the schools to be free had a right to insist that all children attend them.[14]

Throughout the Ryerson period there was opposition to the principle of mass schooling under the auspices of the state. Did the state really have the right to interfere in what had once been a family matter? Was universal schooling a good idea in fact? Could the rapidly expanding schools and school system really fulfill the social goals put forward by the promoters of universal education?

Much of the criticism focused on the condition of the schools, although what aspect was criticized depended on one's point of view. One polemicist singled out for attack the "stately edifices" and "gigantic mansions" that were the common schools of Toronto, paid for by "Catholic as well as Protestant money," but from which all genuine religion was in fact banished. Rural common school superintendents, on the other hand, tended to dwell on the wretchedness of school accommodation, with its evil effects on the health of Upper Canadian children. Concern was also expressed about the physical and psychological damage resulting from the prolonged confinement of young children in school, and complaints were heard that the schools hurt children by concentrating too exclusively on their mental development.[15]

Critics were especially apprehensive or skeptical, when it came to the effect of schooling on the working classes and the poor. Would the common schools succeed in breaking down social barriers? Some were afraid of precisely such an outcome, expressing concern that lower class children might develop "a distaste for the humble and useful occupations of their parents," and become dissatisfied with their lot in life as a result. Such theorists deplored the mixing of the classes in the schools. Others may have approved of the idea, but argued that it was wishful thinking to suppose that such mixing would actually take place. It was highly unlikely, in their view, that social distinctions would be swept away and all ranks persuaded to enter the common schools.[16]

An enormous amount of the criticism, however, focused on the Education Department and the administrative machinery which seemed such an integral part of educational reform. The school system was "cumbrous" and "expensive." Too much money went to pay the salaries of Ryerson, local superintendents and the employees of the provincial office. The District Council of Gore thought in 1847 that money paid out to administrators would be "more profitably applied in the payment of common school teachers," while the very necessity of any kind of centralized system of education was seriously questioned by the *Huron Signal* in 1850. "Wherefore, then, all this anxiety and zeal for maintaining a provincial uniformity in class books?" the *Signal* wanted to know. Roman Catholics maintained that the Education Department stocked school libraries with anti-Catholic books and book sellers were incensed by the department's interference with free trade. Complaints were also lodged against the Normal School, whose graduates were either immoral, inadequate or capable only of "parrot education." One critic claimed that few Normal School graduates remained in teaching. Whether this was because they were too incompetent to get jobs, or basically uninterested in teaching did not matter; in either case, their training constituted a waste of public funds.[17]

In 1871, in a lengthy criticism of the school legislation of that year, the leader of the Reform Party, Edward Blake, reiterated many of the standard complaints and added a few of his own. Blake claimed to be not so much opposed to the centralization of power in the Education Department, as to the unrepresentative nature of the Council of Public Instruction. He deplored the many regulatory powers enjoyed by Ryerson and the council, accusing the chief superintendent of having almost usurped the legislative function. To such opponents, Ryerson and the superintendency represented the inflated powers of the state. They saw themselves, on the other hand, as defenders of the people at large and of their liberty and intelligence, as individuals, and as members of local communities. Blake, for example, denounced the school law of 1871 as precipitate, on the grounds that there had been insufficient demand for it, and that the government badly underrated the intelligence of the people. Two decades earlier, a memorial to the legislature from the counties of Stormont, Dundas and Glengarry had taken the same tack, arguing that control over educational institutions, as well as over all provincial and county funds for school purposes, ought to be vested in the individual counties, rather than with the provincial government. In the 1860s, resolutions deploring the government's past or potential interference in educational matters were still being put at county school conventions, although they did not always pass. In Cayuga, one irate taxpayer objected that since the laws and Parliament did not prescribe what the people should eat, drink or wear, they should hardly require that children attend school. The matter, it was argued, ought to be left "to the good sense and progressive civilization of the people."[18]

But perhaps the bitterest objections that were heard concerned the rights of families. In 1847, the Hon. Robert Spence was certain that the granting of free schools would undermine parental responsibility in educational matters. Once the parent ceased to pay for the schooling of his children, the crucial link between himself and the teachers was severed, and a gradual decline in family interest in the schools would take place. To John Strachan in 1851, the situation was less clear cut. There were "two extremes in public education," he argued: one was where every child was considered "the child of the state"; the other was where the state paid no attention to children and left all to the parent. Strachan believed that Upper Canada's system of education, while very "complicated," represented neither extreme. The Normal School did much good work, and even the chief superintendent of schools was more to be praised than blamed. In the Bishop's opinion, it was nevertheless true that the common schools took away from parents their "natural" privilege and power to "judge and direct" the education of their children, with respect to that most crucial of all educational matters, religion. In this way, the state stepped unjustly between the parent and his child.[19] Strachan's argument was to be repeated by countless supporters of separate schools and later on by the opponents of compulsory attendance laws as well as of free schools.

Promoters of universal state schooling countered these criticisms by expounding their own theories of the true relationship of parents and children to the state. To David Mills of Camden and Chatham in 1856, the right of the parent to direct any action of his children was *not* "a natural one." Every person living in a civilized society enjoyed certain benefits as a social being and, in return, the society had the right to demand reciprocal benefits. No one recognized a right in the parent to force his children to steal, and in this way injure the state; "then why recognize a right to keep them in ignorance?" Mills demanded. The Toronto *Patriot* believed that destitute children, and especially "the uncared for children of the idle and the profligate," had to be regarded as the children of the state. A report by John Sangster of the Hamilton Central School on the educational system of Boston, written in 1855, focused on the rights of the child. The parent did not own the child, Sangster argued. As a member of society, the child had both rights and duties; so far as these related to the public, the government had the same right to control the child as it had to control the parent. "It has an equal right, therefore, to command the *child* to attend the school, and to compel the *parent* to permit him."[20]

Throughout his career, Ryerson insisted that the public school system did not interfere with parental or class rights. The government did not feed or clothe children, nor did it, in his view, interfere with their religious education, since sectarian teaching was left to the parent and pastor. When it came to compulsory attendance, he took the view that enforcing "the father's duties" did not constitute an invasion of his parental rights. In the *Annual Report for 1857* he explained why he thought the state had not only the right, but the duty to act:

It is clearly within the province of the State to provide for its own safety, and to do much for the well-being of man in his temporal and social relations; and as education is essential to the security of government, the supremacy of public law, and the enjoyment of public liberty, as well as to the individual interests of the members of the community, it becomes the duty of the State, or of the people in their civil capacity, to provide for it.

179

Ryerson was able to tolerate some criticism of the schools – after all, he criticized them himself. But he had little use for those who criticized the statist approach to educational reform. They were mistaken or ignorant, partisan, selfish or just mean. But then, in the chief superintendent's view, it was just because of such ignorance and selfishness that the whole campaign had been necessary in the first place. As he finally admitted in response to Blake's criticisms of the School Law in 1871, the educational improvement of the people had not necessarily been a result of their own desires; it was "not the redressing of a felt grievance, but the remedy of a defect, the supply of a deficiency."[21] The deficiency was in the people themselves – it had been the mission of the schools to change them.

The ideology of public or state education, as preached by Egerton Ryerson and his fellow school reformers, grew out of their experience of economic and social change in mid-nineteenth century Upper Canada. Change came later to the province than to Western Europe or to the northeastern United States, and as a result, educators drew heavily on the ideas and experience of these more industrially advanced countries. Like those of many Americans and Europeans of the period, the reactions of many Upper Canadian educators to their times were extremely ambivalent. In the end, most chose to idealize technological change, while deploring its more distressing social consequences, and generally to ignore the causal connection between the two.

The ignorance and apathy of the laboring classes and the poor were attributed to the fact that the rich had abandoned them, rather than to their poverty or to industrial dislocations brought about by mid-century economic change. Yet even this limited observation of the growing gulf between the classes reflected a major transformation in society and attitudes. In Canada, as in other western nations, pre-industrial village communities, perceived as hierarchies of interdependent ranks or grades, closely associated in living space and, ideally, bound together by attitudes of deference, were disappearing. They were to be replaced by an industrial and urban society, composed of two broadly defined economic groups, perceived as potentially or actually hostile to one another. It was this change that preoccupied the school promoters. Not only were the rich no longer concerned with the education of the poor, the poor seemed increasingly composed of brutes and criminals, of men, women and children who were essentially in a "state of nature" and were in desperate need of civilization and instruction. Educators like Egerton

Ryerson believed that it was the job of the schools to bridge the gap between these two warring, or potentially warring, classes, and by the co-option or control of the uncivilized poor, to make them one.

School promoters' protestations about the energy and talent of Upper Canadians, contradicting complaints that they were selfish, listless and uninvolved, reflected, therefore, unstated attitudes to class. It was the traditional governing classes, the idle rich, or even some irresponsible members of the business and professional classes who were selfish and uninvolved; it was the poor who were apathetic and lacking in energy. When Ryerson and his contemporaries talked about the energy and commitment of Canadians, they meant those educated middle class members of society who were enterprising, and at the same time gentlemen. The trouble was that there were too few of them. To the possibility of social disintegration through class conflict, therefore, was added the prospect of social degeneration, of the whole society being dragged down to the lowest level, a threat continually reinforced by the condition and numbers of the immigrants who made their way to Upper Canada. There were other causes for concern: the interference in Upper Canadian affairs of "foreign ecclesiastics" like the Roman Catholic Bishop Charbonnel, or the threat inherent in the superior initiative, know-how, or actual penetration into the province of Americans. Such external threats were used to help reduce internal tensions. The solution to society's problems which educators proposed was a "national" or state school system which would exclude or control outsiders. Their metaphor was taken from nature. Listless Canadians would be aroused and brought to life by government, which, like the sun, was the source of all energy and warmth.

The rift between rich and poor would be healed by bringing the lower classes closer to the intellectual and moral level of the higher, and this was to be done by gathering all children, rich and poor, into the province's common or public schools. But the reality of the public school movement scarcely matched its heady rhetoric. It is difficult to know exactly who went to the common schools between 1841 and 1871, when minimal attendance became compulsory by law. What is sufficiently clear is that many school promoters saw the common schools mainly as institutions for working class children and the children of "common labourers." Their chief function was a social one. The poor would be elevated by means of the discipline considered essential for urban industrial living. Punctuality, cleanliness, obedience, and above all, order, would be taught to lower class children in the common schools. So would self-reliance, in the hope that poor families would learn to take care of themselves, and also that some of their children could be recruited to middle class professions and offices, in a country which seemed to be desperately short of qualified people. These were the values that Upper Canadian middle class children would also be taught, but further goals would be sought for them as well, sometimes in private schools, academies, or colleges, but increasingly in the growing grammar schools, central common schools, high schools or collegiate institutes, and even in the model and normal schools of the province. Within the common schools, moreover, grading and classification of both pupils and teachers would gradually create new class hierarchies to replace the old.

There is no simple explanation for the changing organization and structure of education in mid-nineteenth century Ontario. Attitudes towards class were clearly vital factors in what occurred, but were of course not the only ones. Certainly, the very complexity of educational change during this period precludes any interpretation that would brand Ryerson and his supporters as a monolithic group of enthusiasts determined to press at all costs and at all times a single conception of education upon the people of Upper Canada. Partly because of the length of his career, and the extent of his public and private writings, the thought of Egerton Ryerson does not form a consistent whole. He started out attacking one establishment, and ended up defending, if not virtually creating, another one. What he said about education and schools changed, not only with the passage of time, but also according to the audience of the moment. His addresses to college students must therefore be compared with his Mechanics' Institute lectures or the superintendent's annual reports, and these again with the contradictory and ubiquitous propaganda of his sermons and political pamphlets, not to mention the massive *Journal of Education for Upper Canada* published by the Education Office during the period of his ascendancy. The Toronto *Globe* may be forgiven, in fact, for complaining that a more inconsistent man than Dr. Ryerson never walked the face of the earth.[22]

Yet the contradictions are in many ways the keys to the man, as they are to an understanding of the era. The school promoters were essentially divided men, individuals who were at once fascinated and repelled by their rapidly changing environment. Their dominant feeling about the world around them seems, in the end to have been one of profound distrust. They claimed to believe in progress; indeed they promoted it. They hailed educational change as a great reformation in society. Yet one cannot ignore their even greater pessimism. The world, as they saw it, verged on chaos; the question uppermost in their minds often seems to have been how to tame rampant nature and the devil in man, and their real quest a quest for control. There was accordingly the desire, on the part of those who saw themselves as the reasonable, civilized and respectable elements of society, to exert control over the unreasonable, savage and disreputable at all social levels, but especially among the poor. This control, they hoped, would be exercised through the schools. Then, as more and more children were brought into the schools, there arose the urgent need to classify and define, separate and organize, in order to control these more and more unmanageable institutions. The final result was a complex and ever expanding educational system, which seemed increasingly to be run by and for the state, as much as for the children who were to be educated within it.

Looking back over the educational developments of the Ryerson period it is difficult to distinguish the various threads as exclusively cause or result. Each thread necessarily became entangled with all of the others. If all of one's neighbours were marching into schools for more and more formal education, surely those who did not would be left behind. Families competed for the best and the most education as a guarantee of future status for their children; teachers competed for the best schools or positions in the growing educational bureaucracies as a means of getting ahead in the world; and municipalities, like nations, competed for the biggest slice of the educational and economic cake. All looked to the schools to solve their problems. In this way, an essentially conservative people became future-oriented, as each stage of schooling became a preparation for the next, and education held out as the key to future bliss, provided that Upper Canadians were willing to subscribe to new and improved systems of schooling.

This is not to deny the more altruistic motives of Upper Canadian school promoters, whose concern for social improvement was obviously genuine. Yet, as observers on the outside, and even some of the innovators themselves began to notice, the school systems created to solve a generation's problems in some ways exacerbated those problems, actually reflecting and even contributing to the very processes of alienation and stagnation that they were designed to cure. Critics of government schooling attempted to slow down the growth of bureaucracy in education or the progression towards mass schooling. Many of these pressed for alternatives in the form of separate, private or parochial schools; others worked inside the system as it developed to provide better schooling within it. On the other hand, the opposition sometimes seems to have forced nineteenth century school promoters into taking more rigid stands than they otherwise might have. As they fought to preserve their creations, original motives were often lost sight of, to be replaced by mere loyalty to institutions. Occasionally, the survival of the new schools and school systems themselves seemed to take precedence over all other considerations.

But then the original motives were also perhaps questionable. This was a generation, which like other more recent ones, tended to look to future generations to solve some of their more pressing social problems, problems which they might have tackled more directly themselves, had their basic search been other than the search for control. The response of school reformers in Upper Canada to the social dislocations of their times was, in sum, to promote an essentially inegalitarian view of society and an equally inegalitarian approach to schooling. Control of the uncivilized poor, on the one hand, and the promotion of middle class respectability and achievement on the other, were clearly their fundamental aims. Their approach to educational reform, moreover, was governed by a view of the middle class state as genuinely representative of society in its competitive quest for advancement. The schools could not help but reflect these social and political biases.

NOTES

[1] *Report on a System of Public Elementary Instruction* (Montreal, 1847), p. 205; *Special Report on the Separate School Provisions of the School Law* (Toronto, 1858), pp. 14-15.

[2] "Lecture on the Social Advancement of Canada," JEUC, II (December, 1849), 179.

[3] Annual Report for 1869, Appendix A, p. 7.

[4] *Report on a System of Public Elementary Instruction, pp. 22-23 and 137;* Ryerson, *The Clergy Reserves Question* (Toronto, 1839), pp. 98; *Elements of Political Economy* (Toronto, 1877), pp. 10, 22-23, 35, 73-74.

[5] See for example, Rev. David Rintoul, *Two Lectures on Rhetoric* (Toronto, 1844) II, 26; *Annual Report for 1864,* Appendix A, p. 15.

[6] Israel Lewis, *The Youth's Guard Against Crime* (Kingston, 1844), pp. 28-29.

[7] "Original Prospectus of the *Journal of Education for Upper Canada,"* December 1847, Appendix No. 12 of "Returns Relating to the Receipts and Expenditure of Upper Canada," Appendix L.L.L., *Jour-*

nals of the Legislative Assembly of the Province of Canada, 1852-53, Appendix No. 7 of the Eleventh Volume; also, *Annual Report for 1858,* p. xiii.

[8]Rev. H. Esson, *Strictures on the Present Method of Teaching the English Language* (Toronto, 1852), p. 5; "Dr. Wilson's Address to the Upper Canadian Teachers' Association," JEUC, XVIII (October, 1865), 146; *Annual Report for 1863,* pp. 17-18. Ryerson was defending the giving of prizes in schools on the grounds that competition for rewards reflected the real world as Providence had ordered it.

[9]JEUC, VI (December, 1853), 182.

[10]*Elements of Political Economy,* p. 44; *Inaugural Address at Victoria College* (Toronto, 1842), p. 15.

[11]*Letters from Ryerson to Strachan,* (Kingston, 1828), p. 17; "Address to the Inhabitants of Upper Canada," *Annual Report for 1848,* p. 36; JEUC, II (September, 1849), 136.

[12]*Special Report on the Separate School Provisions of the School Law,* pp. 50-51.

[13]*Report on a System of Public Elementary Instruction,* pp. 180-81; JEUC, III (May, 1850), 74; *Annual Report for 1854,* p.3.

[14]JEUC, X (January, 1857), 9; *Annual Report for 1857,* p. 17; *Annual Report for 1858,* p. xxxi; "Draft of Bill, relating to Vagrant and Neglected Children in Cities and Towns, 1862," DHE, XVII, 182, 176; "Proceedings of the Anglican Synod of the Diocese of Toronto on the Bill relating to Vagrant and Neglected Children, 1862," DHE, XVII, 185; *Annual Report for 1865,* p. 99. "Of FORTY County Conventions, THIRTY-SEVEN affirmed the principle of the duty of the state to render penal the neglect of parents to avail themselves of the opportunities afforded for the education of their children."

[15]*Controversy between Dr. Ryerson, Chief Superintendent of Education in Upper Canada and Rev. J. M. Bruyère, Rector of St. Michael's Cathedral, Toronto . . .* (Toronto, 1857), p. 15; *Annual Report for 1856,* Appendix A, p. 151; *Annual Report for 1857,* Appendix A, p. 153; "Proceedings of the Annual Convention of the Ontario Teacher's Association," DHE, XXI, 295; *Annual Report for 1860,* Appendix A, p. 191.

[16]Adam Townley, *Seven Letters on the Non-Religious Common School System of Canada and the United States* (Toronto, 1853), p. 49; *Report of the Common or Public Schools of the City* (Toronto, 1859), p. 30.

[17]Memorial of the Gore District Municipal Council, November 1847, RG 2 C-6-C, PAO; *Huron Signal,* 17 January 1850, and *Dundas Warder,* 11 January 1850, miscellaneous records, RG 2 T, Box 3, PAO; "Petition of the Municipal Council, United Counties of Stormont, Dundas and Glengarry, 29 January 1852," DHE, X, 101; *Controversy between Dr. Ryerson . . . and Rev. J. M. Bruyère,* p. 18; Sissons, ed., *Egerton Ryerson,* II, 510-11; Angus Dallas, *Statistics of the Common Schools: Being a Digest and Comparison of the Evidence furnished by the Local Superintendents and the Chief Superintendent of Schools in their Reports for 1855, by a Protestant* (Toronto, 1857), pp. 25-27.

[18]Edward Blake, *Remarks on the School Bill* (n.p., 1871), pp. 4-5,

16-18; DHE, X, 101; "County School Conventions in Upper Canada, 1860," DHE, XVI, 89.

[19]DHE, VIII, 61-62; "Church of England Separate Schools Advocated by Bishop Strachan, 1851," DHE, X, 91.

[20]*Annual Report for 1856,* Appendix A, p. 196; JEUC, III (May, 1850), 74; "Report on the Public Schools of Boston," JEUC, VIII (April, 1855), 51.

[21]*Copies of Correspondence . . . on the Subject of Separate Schools* (Toronto, 1855), p. 28; Ryerson, *A Special Report on the System and State of Popular Education on the Continent of Europe, in the British Isles, and the United States of America . . .* (Toronto, 1868), p. 150; *Annual Report for 1857,* p. 18; *Annual Report for 1847,* p. 21; *Annual Report for 1850,* p. 370; JEUC, XIV (February, 1861), 25; Sissons, ed., *Egerton Ryerson,* II, 170, 587.

[22]*Ibid.,* I, 474.

Index

Addington County, 79
adolescence, 29, 37-40
adolescents: discipline of, 38-39; and grammar schools, 40,112
adults: as distinguished from children, 36, 39
agriculture, 96, 105
Alexander, James L., 66
alternative schooling, 139, 143, 146, 184
American: accent, 81; books, 77; Civil War, 46, 130; competition, 52-55, 182; educators, 53-54; schools, 53-54, 142, 145
Americans, 53-54, 170, 182
Anglicans, 60, 71-72, 176
apprenticeship, 15, 88-89, 96
Ariès, Philippe, 32, 36
artisans, (or tradesmen), 61, 77, 91, 95, 142. (See also mechanics)
attendance, 19, 54, 150, 157-58, 160-61, 163-64

Baldwin, Robert, 105
Barber, George, 124, 141-42, 156
Barnard, Henry, 53
Bartlett, Alexander, 145
Belleville, 144
benevolent societies: and education, 157
Bible reading in the schools, 75, 128-29
black children and the schools, 161
Blake, Edward, 177-78, 180
Blair, George, 78, 131
Board of Education (provincial), 18, 124
boarding halls and colleges, 47, 57, 60
books, 53, 69, 78, 82, 94, 128, 148, 178
Boyle, J. B., 142, 150
boys: and boarding halls, 47; education of, 153; in common schools, 112;
in grammar schools, 40, 111, 112, 113
Brampton, 144
Brantford, 79, 145; grammar school controversy, 38-39; schools of, 149
Brock District, 153
Brooke, Charles, 147
Brown, George, 92
businessmen, 102, 103, 104

Carlisle, 154
Cameron School Act, 121
Camden, 180
Campbell, John, 156
Campbell, Robert, 155
capitalists, 96, 123
Cayuga, 179
central schools, 146, 147, 164
centralization in education, 17, 18, 143, 155-56, 162-63, 177, 178-79
Charbonnel, Armand de, 72, 115, 122, 182
charity, 123
charity schools, 177
Chatham, 180
child nature, 31-37, 40
children: animalism of, 32; employment of, 152; innocence or guilt of, 31-32; malleability of, 21; moral responsibility of, 36-37, 174; natural development of, 14, 33, 34, 35; reasoning powers of, 32-33; sexuality of, 32; subordinate status of, 108, 110, 174; and the community, 20, 40-41, 45; and the law, 36-37; and cities, 58-59; restraint of, 33-35, 132
Christian: civilization, 26; education, 29-31, 120, 128-29
Christian Guardian, 20, 107
Christianity, 70, 71, 129
Church of England, 72
churches and education, 29, 59-61
cities: evils of, 38, 57-58; education in, 126; importance of, 59; and educational reform, 58; and children, 58-59
city: boards of education, 19; schools, 150; workers, 96
Clark, S. D., 150
Clarkson, Charles, 28, 33, 34
class: attitudes, 182-83, and note 22, 116; attitudes to childhood, 36; conflict, 67, 83, 119-22, 124, 130-31, 138, 172-73, 182; definitions of, 22, 91; distinctions, 97, 178; improvement, 67; relations, 98, 123-24, 134, 181-82; and the schools, 163-64
classification: of children, 146-48, 153-54; of schools, 138, 146-47

cleanliness, 70, 141
Clinton, 112
Clinton, De Witt, 57
Cobourg, 57
Cockburn, G. R., 33, 37
co-education, 40, 111-113
Colburne, District of, 26, 31, 54
Coldwater, 158
college education, 93
College of Regiopolis, 72
colleges: 149; denominational, 29, 38, 130; for ladies, 119-20; for gentlemen, 119; graduates of, 115
collegiate institutes, 139, 143-46, 149, 164
Collingwood, 131
commerce, 59, 94
common schools, 15, 80, 96, 128, 139, 140-42, 144, 146, 149-52, 154, 156, 164
common school visitors, 124-25
communication: written replacing oral, 78-79, 80-81
communism, 133
competition: 60, 62, 172, 184; among children, 35, 75, 148 and note 37, p. 167; among teachers, 148; economic, 123
compulsory attendance, 16-17, 37, 139, 157, 176-77, 180
Confederation, 45, 55
Connecticut, 57
consolidation of schools and school sections, 148, 155-56
consumerism, 82-83
Council of Public Instruction, 18, 138, 179
crime: 26, 36, 37; increase of, 47, 51; class conflict and, 130; ignorance and, 51-52; prevention through increased education, 50-52, 132
Crooks, Adam, 145
Cunningham, E. William, 79

Dalhousie District, 110
denominational conflict, 46, 60, 71, 73, 161
D'Everardo, Dexter, 126
discipline in schools, 35, 36, 38, 131-32, 155-56; of the poor, 131-33, 182
disease: of immigrants, 56; and school architecture, 148
division of labour, 110, 146, 148
District: Brock, 153; Colborne, 26, 31, 54; Dalhousie, 110; Eastern, 126, 132; Gore, 49, 77, 79, 178; Home, 49; Niagara, 49, 126

Duncombe, Charles, 109-110
Dundas County, 179
Durham County, 78, 131

Eales, Walter, 61, 89, 95
Eastern District, 126, 132
Eastern District Teachers Association, 141
economic change and education, 55-56, 59
economic growth, 59
Education Department: 178-79; sale of books, 94; authorization of books, 81, 128, 178; and co-education, 112; and the grammar schools, 111-112; and religious instruction, 127-28; and centralization, 175-79; and equality of educational opportunity, 162-63; and the schooling of the poor, 157, 158
educational apparatus, 50
educational opportunity: equality or inequality of, 140, 163, 165
educators: Canadian, 20-21; American, 53; British and European, 54
efficiency, 146, 155-56
elementary education, 145, 152
Elgin, Lord, 48, 82, 105
Elora, 143, 153
Emerson, George, 53
English grammar, 78-81
enrolment, 19-20, 142-43, 149-50, 163
entrance examinations: high school, 145; grammar school, 79
Ernestown, 140
Esson, Henry, 31, 33, 34
exclusion of children from schools, 161-62

factory operatives, 59, 95
family, the: and consumption of goods, 82; and education, 61, 172, 179-80; and religion, 72
farmers: 91, 96, 105, 110, 114; and education, 83; and language, 77
fathers, 108
Fenianism, 130-31
Fordyce, A. Dingwall, 161
Fraser, James, 62
Fraser, John, 140
Frazer, William, 126
free school debate, 125, 144, 179
free schools, 13, 16, 50, 52, 120, 125-26, 133, 139, 140, 141, 156, 175, 179-80
French-English conflict, 46
Frontenac County, 13

Galt, 152, 155

gentlemen, 91-92, 114
Geography: study of, 15, 80, 128
girls: aptitude of, 40; and grammar schools, 111-113; and common schools, 152-53
Glengarry County, 179
Goderich, 140, 142
Gore, District of, 49, 77, 79, 178
grading, 147, 148, 149, 164
grammar schools: 15, 27, 129, 139, 140, 149, 164; age of pupils, 142-43; examinations for entrance to, 79; admission of girls to, 40, 143
Guillet, E. C., 153

habits: of industry, 131, 133-34; of order, 132
Haliburton, Thomas Chandler, 58
Hamilton: 58, 145; grammar school, 69, 80;
separate schools, 80
handwriting, 70, 81
Haney, M. F., 77-78
Harvey, William, 150
Hastings County, 52, 96
Henderson, R. S., 124, 161
high schools, 139, 143, 144, 145, 146, 169
Hind, H. Y., 105
history: of Canada, 138; of education, 13-14
Hodgins, John George, 47, 51, 128, 177 and note 3, p. 23
Home District, 49
human nature, 25-31, 44, 171
husbands, 108

ignorance: in Upper Canada, 47, 49-50; of Roman Catholics, 74; of the poor, 124; in Toronto, 157
immigrants: 56-57; necessity of educating, 56; upper class, 90; and social degradation, 182
Indians, 29
individual instruction, 147-48
infant schools, 151
intelligence: of Upper Canadians, 49
inspectors, 18
Irish: accent, 78, 81; immigrants, 46, 56, 72; national readers, 77; national schools, 141

Jaffray, P., 152
John Street School, 29, 141
Johnston, John, 52
Journal of Education, 128, 183
juvenile delinquency, 47, 51-52, 58-59

Kellogg, J. Benson, 141
Kent County, 82, 162
King's College, 71
Kingston: 124, 147; schools of, 149, 154, 161
Knox College, 31

labour: agricultural, 106; educated and uneducated, 89-90; manual, 89-90, 107
labourers: 84, 91, 106-07, 114-15
labouring classes, 29, 95, 106-07, 119, 122, 133-34, 156, 172, 181
ladies, 91-92, 109-10, 113-14
Lanark County, 48, 75
Landon, W. H., 153
language, 76-81
Leeds County, 80, 140
Lennox County, 48
Lewis, Israel, 36-37
literacy, 16, 49, 50, 51, 84
Lively, Henry, 79
London: 150, 175; collegiate institute, 144, 145; trustees of, 49; school board, 127

Macdonell, Alexander, 72
Macdonell, Angus, 72
manliness, 108-09
Mann, Horace, 53, 54
manners, 39, 66, 68-70, 72, 84
married pupils, 149
masculinity, 115
Massachusetts, 78, 133, 148, 162
masters, 108
material prosperity: the quest for, 46, 59, 62
materialism, 47-48
McCrum, Robert, 140
mechanics: 69, 91, 95-96, 114-115, 137; and language, 75, 81
merchants, 94
Methodists, 30, 60, 68, 71-72
middle class: 115, 182, 183; consciousness, 119; schools, 138-139; respectability, 185; state, 185
middle classes, 92, 123
military drill, 148
Mills, David, 82, 180
Model Grammar School, Toronto, 70
Model School, Toronto, 142, 143, 154-55
model schools, 70
monitorial schools, 15
mothers, 108, 109, 110
Murdock, John A., 75
music: 69; and the working classes, 90

natural law, 182, 184
nature: attitudes to, 182-85; and education, 34; conquest of, 26, 134, 185
neatness, 76, 138, 141
Nelles, Samuel, 22, 33, 52, 132
new world: impact of, 26, 36
newspapers, 121
Niagara, District, 49, 126
Normal School, 18, 26, 78, 79, 80, 96, 105, 142, 153, 154, 155, 163, 175, 179
Northumberland County, 132
Nottawasaga, 156

occupations, 88-96, 105-115
operatives, 95
opposition to educational reform, 14, 20, 50, 177-81, 185
order: need for, 25, 33, 148; search for, 173
Ormiston, William, 140
Ottawa, 142
Oxford County, 141

parents, 15, 16, 18, 35, 36, 37, 38, 39, 61, 80, 112, 125, 132, 144, 157-58, 161
parliament buildings, burning of 1849, 121
patriotism, 47, 52
pauperism, 124-25
pedagogy, 33, 147
penal institutions, 37
Perkin, Harold, 67, 114
Phillips, Charles, 39
political economy, 173
political parties, 122, 127
politics, 127-28
poor, the: 119-34; and the schools, 74, 156-58, 162; children of cities, 59
poor relief, 123
Port Hope, 107
Porter, James, 76, 142, 145, 151
Potter, Alonzo, 53
poverty: 132, 164; and attitudes to children, 37; and education, 146-47, 162; of immigrants, 56; of Roman Catholics, 74; cause of, 122
power: of the educated, 83, 114-15; of language, 76; man over nature, 134, 175; of the civilized over the uncivilized, 184, 185
Presbyterians, 71
private: and public eduation, early lack of distinction between, 16; venture schools, 15, 19; alternatives to the common schools, 143, 146; schools and the segregation of the sexes, 113
professions, 92-93
pronunciation, 78, 81
progress: belief in, 60, 183; promotion of, 45, 59, 61-62
property: and education, 83; concept of, 81-82; respect for, 120, 133; safety of, 120, 133; school as, 155; taxes and education, 125-26, 156
protective role of the school, 20, 154-55
Protestantism in the schools, 75, 129; and note 23, p. 86
Protestants: and local school disputes, 60, 73-74; and school attendance, Toronto, 158
provincial school funds: allocation of, 74, 162, 164
public: education, 16, 17, 18, 61; schools, 142, 145, 146, 152; servants, 93-94, 108
punctuality, 131
punishment, 35
pupil: age, 38, 142, 143, 147, 149, 150, 151, 152, 164; and note 48, p. 44 numbers in individual schools, 19, 146-47; teacher ratio, 19, 149, 161

ratepayers, 125
reason versus passion, 28-30
rebellions of 1837-38, 45
religious instruction, 75, 128-29, note 33, p. 136
respectability, 68-70, 72, 74, 106, 107, 108, 115, 163, 185
restraint: in education, 33, 34, 35; of men and children, 36; exercised by schools, 132, 156-57
rewards, 35, 153
Ridell, A. A., 143
Rintoul, 96
Robertson, Thomas, 79, 154
Robinson, John Beverley, 81
Rolph, Thomas, 77
Roman Catholics: and class, 71-72; and crime, 130; and Fenianism, 131; and local school disputes, 73-74; and religious instruction, 75; and school attendance, 157-58; and separate schools, 73-75, 129-31, 157; their interference in Upper Canadian affairs, 182
Ryerson, Charles, 92
Ryerson, Egerton: career of, 20-22; inconsistency of, 183; on agriculture, 96, 105; on boarding halls, 47; on charity, 123, 126; on cities, 58; on

class, 89-91, 114-15, 140-41; on compulsory schooling, 176-77, 180; on discipline, 35, 37; on the education of the poor, 125, 133; on the family, 61; on gentlemanliness, 92; on grammar schools, 143-44; and the history of education, 13-15; on human nature, 27-31; on labour, 89-90; on labourers, 106-07; on language, 76-77, 78, 79, 81; on mechanics, 95-96; on merchants, 94; on moral education, 30; on natural law, 173-74; on the professions, 93; on private property, 81; on public controversy, 120-22, 123; on pupil age, 150-51; on religion, 70, 75; on religious education, 129; on respectability, 68-69, 70; on school consolidation, 156; on servants, 107-08; on separate schools, 73-74, 75, 129, 130, 131; on sexual segregation in schools, 152-53; on the state, 171, 180; on textbooks, 128; on women and girls, 108, 110-112, 113-114
Ryerson, Sophie, 92, 113

Sangster, John, 180
Scarlett, Edward, 132
science: 30; of education, 27-28; as a common school and normal school subject, 95-96
School Act: of 1841, 17, 18; of 1843, 17; of 1846, 18, 50, 124, 163; of 1847, 125; of 1850, 125, 162; of 1871, 16, 17, 18, 80, 139, 145, 179, 181
school bill of 1862 (draft), 157, 177
School Book Depository, 94
school: boundaries, 154; buildings and grounds, 47, 73, 155, 161, 177-78; furniture, 148; houses, 154; laws, 15, 16; systems, 17, 19
Schoolmasters' Social Science Association, 1861, 28
schools: appearance of, 47, as private property, 155; and the community, 154-55
Scovil, Seabury, 80
Sears, Barnas, 78
secondary education, 145
secular education, versus religious and moral education, 30
sensuality, 29, 40
separate schools, 18, 73, 74, 75; 129-30, 153
servants: 107-08; moral responsibility of, 174; public, 93-94, 108
service, ideology of, 108

sexual: differences, 40, 174; segregation in the schools, 40, 113, 146, 152-53, 164
sexuality, 40
Sifton, H. F., 90
Simcoe County, 150
social: disorder, 46, 56, 60, 172; harmony, 120, 127-28, 134, 163; order, 88-89, 91-92, 126-27, 173-74
social structure, 67-68, 83, 126-27, 134, 172, 181
socialism, 133
spelling, 79-80, 81
state, the: 19, 22, 50, 122-23; and education, 171-172, 177-79, 180-81, 182, 185
status: and education, 36-37, 75, 83-84; and occupations, 89-96, 105-109, 113-14
Stormont County, 179
Strachan, John: and conflict with Egerton Ryerson, 20-21, 120-21; on Americans, 53; on appropriate knowledge for children, 39; on child nature, 36; on the employment of children, 37; on human nature, 29; on the Methodists, 68, 71; on poor relief, 122-23; on the prevention of crime through schooling, 50; on professional education, 93; on the science of education, 27; on social hierarchy, 91; on the state and the family in education, 179-80
Stratford, 45-55
strikes, 89
Sullivan, R. B., 39, 55, 56, 95
superintendency: creation of, 17, 124; and politics, 127-28; and information on local school attendance, 155; as representative of the wealthy classes, 125

teachers: and English grammar, 80; and grading, 152; and problems with unmannerly pupils, 132; and segregation of the sexes, 152; certification of, 18, 77, 79, 163; classification of, 162-63; competition among, 148, 184; female, 108-10, 163; grammar school, 112; hiring of, 17, 80; importance of respectability of, 69; male, 163; numbers of, 19, 149; powers of 31-32, 132; regulation of, 162-63; rights of, 38; status of, 108; training of, 26, 163
teaching methods, 148, 161
technology, 134, 175

Thornton, Patrick, 77, 79
three Rs, 16, 80
Tidey, John S. 70, 81
Toronto: 150, 152, 164-65; and educational reform, 58; common schools of, 51, 73, 76; influence of, 58; moral dangers of, 38, 57, 58; poor people of, 82; Roman Catholics of, 73; respectable behaviour of ladies in, 113; schools of, 141-43, 145, 147, 156-158
trade schools, 96
trustees: establishment of, 17; ignorance of, 49; illiteracy of, 79-80; powers of, 125, and information on school attendance, 158

uniformity in education: 16, 128; criticism of, 178
union schools, 145, 164
United States: comparisons with, 53-55; competition with, 46, 53-55
University Bill (Draper), 1845, 105
University College, 150
university preparation, 111
Upper Canada Academy, 57, 58, 70, 111
urbanization, 57-59

vagrancy, 58, 157
Victoria College 21, 57; Ryerson's inaugural lecture at, 76, 89, 90, 93; co-education at, 93
voluntarism in education, 16, 176

wealth and education, 83-84
wealthy classes, the: 124-25, 133, 153
Wellington County, 161
Wilson, Daniel: 22; on the senses and learning, 30; on the teacher's power, 31; on child nature, 32; on the nature of education, 34; on materialism, 48; on child vagrancy in Ontario, 58; and conflict with Ryerson, 108
wives: as subordinant to husbands, 108; girls' future as, 109; moral responsibility of, 174
women: and professional training, 111; and school board elections, 111; as heads of households, 111; education of, 109-110, 153; occupations of, 88, 91, 108, 113-14; status of, 108, 109, 110
Woods, Samuel, 149

Young, George Paxton: 22; on coeducation, 40, 54, 112-13; on Horace Mann, 54
Young, William, 58

THE CANADIAN SOCIAL HISTORY SERIES

Terry Copp,
The Anatomy of Poverty:
The Condition of the Working Class in Montreal, 1897-1929, 1974.

Gregory S. Kealey and Peter Warrian, Editors,
Essays in Canadian Working Class History, 1976.

Alison Prentice,
The School Promoters: Education and Social Class in Mid-Nineteenth Century Upper Canada, 1977.

Susan Mann Trofimenkoff and Alison Prentice, Editors,
The Neglected Majority: Essays in Canadian Women's History, 1977.

John Herd Thompson,
The Harvests of War: The Prairie West, 1914-1918, 1978.

Donald Avery,
"Dangerous Foreigners": European Immigrant Workers and Radicalism in Canada, 1896-1932, 1979.

Joy Parr, Editor,
Childhood and Family in Canadian History, 1982.

Howard Palmer,
Patterns of Prejudice: A History of Nativism in Alberta, 1982.

Tom Traves, Editor,
Essays in Canadian Business History, 1984.

Alison Prentice and Susan Mann Trofimenkoff, Editors,
The Neglected Majority: Essays in Canadian Women's History, Volume 2, 1985.

Ruth Roach Pierson,
"They're Still Women After All": The Second World War and Canadian Womanhood, 1986.

Bryan D. Palmer, Editor,
The Character of Class Struggle; Essays in Canadian Working-Class History, 1850-1985, 1986.

Angus McLaren and Arlene Tigar McLaren
The Bedroom and the State: The Changing Practices and Politics of Contraception and Abortion in Canada,
1880-1980, 1986.

Alan Metcalfe,
Canada Learns to Play: The Emergence of Organized Sport, 1807-1914, 1987.

Marta Danylewycz,
Taking the Veil: An Alternative to Marriage, Motherhood, and Spinsterhood in Quebec, 1840-1920, 1987.

Craig Heron,
Working in Steel: The Early Years in Canada, 1883-1935, 1988.

Wendy Mitchinson and Janice Dickin McGinnis, Editors,
Essays in the History of Canadian Medicine. 1988.

Joan Sangster,
Dreams of Equality: Women on the Canadian Left, 1920-1950, 1989.

Angus McLaren,
Our Own Master Race: Eugenics in Canada, 1885-1945, 1990.

Bruno Ramirez,
On the Move: French-Canadian and Italian Migrants in the North Atlantic Economy, 1860-1914, 1990.

Mariana Valverde,
The Age of Light, Soap and Water: Moral Reform in English Canada, 1885-1925, 1991.